To Lhasa and Beyond

To Lhasa and Beyond

Diary of the Expedition to Tibet in the Year 1948

Giuseppe Tucci

With an appendix on Tibetan medicine and hygiene by R. Moise

Foreword by
His Holiness the Dalai Lama

Snow Lion Publications
Ithaca, New York USA

Snow Lion Publications
P.O. Box 6483
Ithaca, New York 14851
USA

Original title: *A Lhasa E Oltre*. Translated by Mario Carelli
First published 1956. Reprint 1985. This edition published
by arrangement with Oxford & IBH Publishing Co., New
Delhi, 1987.

Printed in USA

Library of Congress Catalog Number

ISBN 0-937938-57-2

Library of Congress Cataloging-in-Publication Data

Tucci, Guiseppe, 1894–
    To Lhasa and beyond

    Translation of: A Lhasa e oltre.
    "Translated by Mario Garelli"—T.p. verso.
    1. Tibet (China)—Description and travel.
2. Tucci, Guiseppe, 1894–   —Journeys—China—
Tibet.   I. Title.
DS785.T813   1987   915.1'504   87-16441
ISBN 0-937938-57-2

Contents

3

4   *To Lhasa and Beyond*

Foreword

THE DALAI LAMA

THEKCHEN CHOELING
McLEOD GANJ 176219
KANGRA DISTRICT
HIMACHAL PRADESH

Prof. Giuseppe Tucci is one of those few in the West who has an intimate understanding of the Tibetan civilization. I am happy to know that his book, TO LHASA AND BEYOND, is being reprinted at a time when there is renewed interest in Tibet the world over.

TO LHASA AND BEYOND is a light, entertaining but no less informative travelogue in the classic tradition. The journey to Tibet which this book deals with took place in 1949 when Tibet was a free country and its civilization intact. In the course of his journey Prof. Tucci visited all the important cities and towns in central Tibet including Lhasa, Shigatse, Samye, Gyantse and Phari. Prof. Tucci's description of the timeless civilization of the Tibetan people is as perceptive and relevant today as it was when he wrote the book thirty years ago. It is hoped that the reproduction of this book will contribute towards a better understanding of the Tibetan people and their values.

June 26, 1982

5

Preface

To the knowledge of Tibet the Italians have given a remarkable contribution. Oderic of Pordenone and Marco Polo, though they never crossed her frontiers, gave the first accounts of Tibet. Subsequently the Capuchins and the Jesuits could stay in that country for several decades in the 18th century. They left a lasting record in their journey reports, especially in the book the Jesuit Ippolito Desideri wrote on his Tibetan experiences and on the religion of that country. He then translated for the first time the theological summary of a great Tibetan thinker and confuted it in an extensive polemical work he wrote himself in Tibetan, thus bringing about a remarkable encounter between Buddhist dogmatics and St Thomas Aquinas on the Roof of the World. Roman Catholic missionaries, perhaps Orazio della Penna himself, drew up the first Tibetan dictionary ever known. The manuscript got later into the hands of Major Latter, who handed it over to Schröter, a missionary in Bengal. This replaced Italian with English and published it at Serampore in 1826. But another Italian scholar, Giorgi, had exploited the materials sent by the missionaries to Rome and published an account of the Tibetan language already before that time.

Even after Tibet's doors were finally closed to missionaries in 1745 she still fascinated our explorers. As these were stubbornly denied access, they had to confine their researches to the neighbouring areas. From Roero di Cortanze to the Duke of Abruzzi, De Filippi and Dainelli, Italians led expedition on expedition to Karakorum and Ladakh, a Buddhist, Tibetan-language district politically dependent on Kashmir. For various reasons I have been luckier. I succeeded in crossing repeatedly the forbidden frontier, and was gradually so gripped by a scientific interest in Tibet and bewitched by her lost horizons, that I visited several of her provinces in the course of eight expeditions. I began with Western Tibet where many a temple, having survived the ravages of time and war, supplied me with remarkable evidence of Tibet's spiritual dependence on India. Together with the pilgrims streaming on from the whole of Asia I made the round of Mount Kailāsa in whose forbidding peaks Buddhist, Hindus and Shamans see the gates of heaven, and of the Manasarovar Lake (13,000 ft), whose banks are studed with shrines built by the faithful as landmarks of their pilgrimages. Those places deserve to be sacred, if for nothing else, for the natural beauty God lavished on them in the luckiest days of His creation. My further journeys took me farther east, to Sakya, Tashilhumpo and beyond. Sakya was Tibet's capital in Kubilai Khan's and Marco Polo's days. In 1939 I explored its temples and above all its libraries enclosing several works of Buddhist thought, written in Sanskrit on palm leaves and carried into Tibet by the Buddhist missionaries when the Muslim invasions destroyed India's universities and made the lives of the Buddhist masters unsafe.

The results of such journeys were summarized in two diaries: the *Cronaca della Missione Scientifica Tucci nel Tibet occidentale*, published by the Accademia d'Italia, 1934; (English translation: *Secrets of Tibet*, Blackie, London, 1935; American translation: *Shrines of a Thousand Buddhas*, McBride, New York, 1936. It was translated into Hunga-

rian as well) and *Santi e Briganti nel Tibet ignoto*, published
by Hoepli, Milan, 1937. Those were followed by seven
volumes of *Indo-Tibetica*, published by the Royal Italian
Academy, which sponsored some of my journeys, while
most of the money came from private sources. At the end of
the war, the Italian Academy was shut down owing to the
political plots contrived by some book-worms claiming to
have the last word in cultural matters and clinging to out-
dated notions on the subject of academies. Some scholars
who had a finger in many a political pie, and still nursed a
private grudge against the Academy as membership had
been refused to them in spite of all their influence and
pressures, gladly lent a hand. So I had the results of my
further researches published by the Poligrafico dello Stalo
(Italian State Library) in 1949 under the title *Tibetan
Painted Scrolls*.

Such researches had raised some new problems, and I
had to lead another expedition to have a further look in the
matter on the spot. I started laying the ground for it in
1946, had to overcome some official incomprehension, but
managed in the end to have the Italian Foreign Office file an
application for me with the British Foreign Office which,
before India's independence, still was the only link of Tibet
with foreign countries.

Count Carandini, then Italian Ambassador in London,
rose to the occasion and forwarded my request to the British
Government, which referred me directly to Lhasa. The way
was paved by Sir Basil Gould, former Political Officer in
Sikkim and head of a mission in Lhasa. I applied to the
Tibetan Government for permission to visit Lhasa, Samye,
Yarlung and other celebrated spots of Central and South-
Eastern Tibet in the company of two or three assistants. In
June, 1947, the Italian Foreign Office forwarded to me,
through London, the Tibetan Government's favourable
answer: "Our Embassy in London has asked us kindly to
inform you that, according to a message from the British
Foreign Office, the Tibetan authorities have authorized

your planned journey". However, as the season was advanced already, I decided to postpone my expedition and
informed Lhasa accordingly, adding that I would leave in
the first months of 1948, with three assistants. Then I went
to work promptly at the short-range preparations. I got the
Italian Geographical Society, a body which during a century
of life efficiently contributed to the exploration and the
study of little-known countries, to set up a sponsoring
Committee. Among its members were General Toraldo D.
Francia, the President of the Society itself, H.E. Edward
Keeling, Admiral Luigi Valli, Dr. Alberto Giuganino and
Dr. Nicola De Pirro. The Committee bravely weathered all
my ceaseless requests and carried out its delicate program-
me. In the meanwhile I was gathering the personnel of my
expedition and approaching both the Italian Army and the
Navy, which had detailed an officer to join my 1933 and
1935 expeditions. Admiral Emil Ferreri, who had been
Secretary General at that time and was Chief of the General
Staff now, granted my request by detailing Lt. Col. Regolo
Moise, of the Navy Medical Corps, to assist me as a
surgeon, and gave orders to the Navy's Commissariat and
Medical Departments to supply an expedition with canned
food and medical stores whose plentifulness stood us in
good stead later in Tibet. As a photographer I chose Mr. P.
Mele, whom I entrusted with the photographing of the
landscape and of the works of art. At a later date Mr. F.
Maraini joined the party as a cameraman in Mele's pay.

Lloyd Triestino granted us reduced fares on our outward
journey, the Firm Moretti replaced my two old tents, worn
out by previous expeditions, with new ones; Ducati's handed me a microfilm camera and a wireless set to offer to the
Tibetan authorities, the Italian Industrial Union (Confin-
dustria) placed at our disposal some Sangiorgio and Galileo
field-glasses, and felt hats, which proved to be the gifts
most coveted by Tibetan high officials; and the Olive Grow-
ers' Association gave us a liberal supply of olive oil to
guarantee our daily intake of vitamines.

The scientific results of the expedition were considerable. Inscriptions were copied, chronicles, liturgical and theological treatises collected, temples and places of historical interest visited. Such material was destined to be detailedly worked out in a scientific series started by the Italian Middle and Far East Institute. This book, on the other hand, tells the story of the journey, hints at the routes and deals with the most important localities in detail, but without imposing on the reader of a travel book the unnecessary burden of technical erudition. It is as if I were taking the reader along the roads I followed and opened his eyes to the landscape, the customs, the art and the religion of a country he was crossing the first time and the meaning of which was likely to be lost on him most of the time. The number of photographs published was kept low in order to reduce expenses. Those without any caption were made by Moise, and the Lhasa views by the Sikkimese photographer I hired at Yatung, whereas the pictures taken by Mele, who was in charge of the photographic side of the expedition, bear his name.

The book was written on the blue print of notes I took during the travel. A few chapters I wrote in full on the spot, in our short rests between marches. As soon as I reached home again, I added those explanations I held indispensable for the educated layman, that he may get a better insight into foreign forms of art and religions, and rearranged the subjects. I have not changed anything, even after the events following upon my return seemed to suggest slight reappraisals. On Tibetan politics, after all, I have not dwelt at length, as, if there is anything I intensely dislike, it is just politics, anywhere and at any time. To the vanity, inconsistency and double-dealing of politicians I have opposed the saints and the heroes, the poets and the scientists, in a word those few whose wisdom and industry, imagination and hard work conjure up or create the things which the course of events and the fury of fools never quite succeed in destroying. By birth I am rather predisposed to take an interest in past rather than in present events and people, in order to look at them with detachment and picture them to me as it pleases my fancy.

As a conclusion, I want to thank not only the Tibetan authorities, who lavished their help on me, but all Tibetans I met in the seven months I spent in their country. They vied with one another in friendliness and so overwhelmed me with their kindness that I was filled with regret and sorrow when, as autumn was setting in, I had to retrace my steps towards a world which, by a screwy slant of our languages, we call civilized.

1 From Rome to the Gateway of Tibet

While I was making the last arrangements for my expedition, an event took place in Rome which made a great stir. The head of a sect named Bodha, who posed as a Living Buddha and the chief abbot of the Bodhamandala of Tashilhumpo — a town where I was twice without detecting the least trace of such an institution — and claimed to be an official representative of Tibet, said many abusive things against me and asserted that, if I had ever set foot in Tibet again, I would not come back to tell it.

Everybody remembers how I unmasked that fellow, whose real citizenship, not the one displayed on his passport, is certainly known to the international police and has very little in common with Tibet. I addressed him in Tibetan and he could not answer. I asked him some technical questions on Buddhist subjects which left him equally speechless. Compelled to leave Italy, a country where the people are not so gullible as to be taken in by such improvised Messiahs, he sent from Switzerland to the Rome newspapers a letter where he gave me an appointment at Darjeeling, stating that in that town, in his own surroundings, he would give me full satisfaction and answer at last those questions which had embarrassed him so much in

13

Rome. However he failed to appear at Darjeeling on the
appointed time, and proved to be totally unknown there.
He had also boasted of being related to the Nepalese ambassador in London who, informed by me about this claim,
rightly branded it as "a brazen piece of false impersona-
tion". The rightness of this debunking was confirmed
beyond the shadow of a doubt by a subsequent statement of
the Tibetan Government dated the 10th January, 1949 and
reading as follows:

"We have received your letter and a copy of the report of
the Italian police on Cherenzi Lind. We have referred the
matter to the Kashag (Cabinet) and been instructed to
inform you that the supposed, self-styled Cherenzi Lind has
nothing to do with Tibet. As the report goes, he neither
mentions his place of birth nor of origin and he misleads
many people with his teachings. We should be thankful to
you if you could send detailed reports about him to other
countries that he may be unmasked there as well. We
should be very glad to hear from you on any other activities
which may be harmful to Tibet.

Years Earth-Mouse, 11th Month (= January 10, 1949)".

So, here I am, hale and hearty, and glad to thank the
Government and people of Tibet for the kind hospitality
with which they have received me and favoured my researches.

At Darjeeling, if I was not lucky enough to wind up the
fight begun in Rome, I could at least make the first arrangements for my caravan.

After Kalimpong, Darjeeling was the biggest market in
the borderland between India and Tibet. In 1835, when it
was ceded to the Government of India by the Maharaj of
Sikkim, it became Bengal's summer capital, a rank which,
at least for the time being, it has lost now, as the Government of Bengal, as a measure of economy, has given up the
expensive yearly move. The town has suffered from this
and looks now subdued and forlorn. Also the business
centre has finally moved to Kalimpong, where caravans

coming down from the Jelapla[1] and Natula passes flood the bazaar with their loads of Tibetan wool destined to the factories. Tibet's wealth is gauged on this market and rises and falls with the price of wool. However, Darjeeling is still a cheerful, motley town. Built on hills befringed with the spruce foliage of tea plantations, entrenched by the steaming undergrowth of the jungle where the earth seems to push her wild fury of creation to its ultimate climax, Darjeeling enjoys the superb sight of the Kanchenjunga, the world's third highest peak after Mt. Everest, which watchfully towers in the north. The Kanchenjunga has something chaste and discreet about its beauty, as if it feared that too much familiarity with the eager looks of its admirers may mar the ever fresh wonder of its shape. But when the icy gleam of its summit soars free from the wrathful turmoil of clouds below, it looks like an Isle of the Blest floating in the heavens. It is as unattainable as a dream and as inexorable as divine justice.

Kalimpong instead owes its life to the expedition led by the British against Tibet in 1904, when the caravan road to Lhasa was opened. The then obscure village became a large town and grew into the largest emporium of Northern Bengal. The outlook from Kalimpong is not as majestic as the one from Darjeeling. The Kanchenjunga can also be seen from there, but not so towering and steep, as it rises from a saddle between two wooded hills, an earthly seat which somehow lowers its heavenly majesty.

A walk through the streets of either town will not provide one with the expected supply of local colour. There are no special features giving those towns an unmistakable imprint. There is no style even in the houses: they are the dull kind of buildings you could find in any other big Indian bazaar. The several races meeting and melting here seem to have agreed on an impersonal pattern which all have accepted without objections. The Bengalis, who should outnumber the others as this is Bengal, are scarce. One will meet them especially among the policemen, the small merchants and the office clerks. The whole economic life is in the hands of the Marwaris, who are everywhere, possess the most profitable industries and trades, get hold of the most thriving firms, lend money to the societies and to private people and control the imports from and the exports to India. They hail from an area not too distant from Bombay, but there is no village in India where they have not set foot. Even the Himalaya is no barrier to them. When it still was possible, some of them went to Tibet and some to Turkestan in search of their luck. Wrapped in lengths of snow-white muslin, a small turban perched precariously on their head, they squat from dawn to dusk in their shops where only the safe and a few chattels can be seen as their staple goods lie stored in their godowns.

As if they disdained their own dependence on the cunning Indian businessmen, the Tibetan merchants have built at Darjeeling, and on an even large scale at Kalimpong, a town of their own, where they have transplanted and fenced in, as it were, a bit of their homeland. There one can meet itinerant lamas, beggars who turn their prayer wheels while waiting for alms, and even the Kham nomads, with their grim faces and their long daggers in sheaths of wrought silver. The Tibetans look dreamy and giddy when they reach those towns. They submit to the tyranny of trade, but behave like resentful captives, wistfully yearning back for the boundless expanses and the lonely tracks of their deserts. They only stay a few weeks, then others take their place. India, a country in whose huge extension we Europeans nearly feel lost, is for the Tibetans oppressively narrow.

Beyond the Tibetan quarter the Chinese town unfolds along the main road, with its cobblers, its faience, china and silk vendors, another landmark on the way of the Chinese conquest of the Tibetan trade. From Shanghai the goods used to come to Calcutta through Singapore, and were then despatched up the Himalayan slopes and stored up at Kalimpong and Darjeeling. From these two markets they were subsequently spread out fanwise to all the bazaars and the fairs in Tibet, thus reaching this country by a huge detour weighing heavily on her meagre resources. But no shorter way could be found as long as the inroads of highwaymen and the borderland troubles made the overland route unsafe between China and Lhasa.

Kalimpong and Darjeeling are towns thrown like a bridge between two cultures. But these come in touch with each other only outwardly. There is no real welding of the souls or the customs. The people meet and look at each other with suspicion, they are thrown together but keep innerly apart.

It looks as if India wanted to become Tibet here and Tibet India, only to repent of it soon after and to decide to stay what they were. Customs, dress and languages brush shoulders but do not mix, as if they were engaged in a mutual resistance test. There isn't even the smallest hint at a bridging over which could precede a merging of both cultures. The borderland area is hence an unusual, contradictory, motley show, like a large fair, and finds therefore just in the bazaars its most natural expression, in their mixture of scents, smells, tunes and songs. The shops, as anywhere else in India, stay open till the small hours. The people show a total unconcern in business: they talk, wave their arms, read sacred books and doze off. Their voices get mingled with the tunes of records played on old-fashiioned horn gramophones which look as if they had just been bought off a dawdler's shop and squirt waves of shrill, jarring, deafening notes. Yet, in these patches and shreds of music and in the songs bandied in different languages from shop to shop a note of profound sadness can be detected. Images and scents of distant countries crop up with their nostalgic appeal, hopes and memories withered and buried in the course of time are revived for a fleeting instant by the magic of music. Unaware, the people stand by, as silent and collected as if they were watching a ritual.

The Europeans are only represented by the two missions,

the Protestant and the Roman Catholic ones, and by the businessmen, the last European owners of the tea plantations, which are also gradually falling into the hands of the Indians.

Though Kalimpong is steadily gaining ground in the sphere of trade, Darjeeling is still the best place where to organize a caravan for Tibet. All the major expeditions which attempted the conquest of the Everest and the Kanchenjunga started from Darjeeling, a town teeming with mountain guides and specialized servants. A Tibetan who had been living there since his childhood held sway on that humble crowd, who faithfully followed the Europeans on their daring undertakings and often risked their own life with childish naiveness. His name was Karma Pal. He dressed in the European way, wore the colonial sun helmet, spoke good English and, when blowing his nose, he first used his hands then his handkerchief and always managed well. He promptly supplied me with the cook, Van Tendsin, and with the *sirdar* Tenzing. The *sirdar* is the head of the caravan on the leader's behalf, the link between this latter and the bearers, the caravan personnel and the manifold retinue following in the wake of the expedition. He is supposed to find the conveyances, to bargain and haggle, and is responsible for the services. Both the cook and the sirdar had been with the best known climbers and taken part in many attempts at the peaks of the Himalaya. They were both recommended by the Himalaya Club.

It was a harder job to find a lama who could accompany and help me in my researches; but a good lama was needed to open severals doors which would have stayed shut otherwise. Karma Pal came to my help this time too and produced one Rev. L. Sangpo, a Geshe or, as we would say, a Doctor of Divinity of the Drepung monastary, one of the largest yellow sect lamaseries a few miles off Lhasa. He was an Urga Mongolian who had been educated in Tibet, had written a few grammatical and rhetorical works and boasted of many connections in Lhasa. He was forty-five, short and spotless, wore the hint of a moustache on the upper lip, which developed into threadlike, pointed whiskers, like a cat's, on both sides of the mouth. I thought he would suit me quite well: he was a cultured, sociable and honest man. He would get six hundred rupees a month and assist me in my work. He had a working knowledge of Hindi, a smattering of Sanskrit and was just beginning to learn English in his own peculiar way, which was like a memorizing exercise. He snatched patches and shreds of conversation as they reached his ear, and it was the funniest thing in the world to see how he suddenly slunk away from our group and made for a corner, where he set about reciting the words and idioms he had got hold of, like litanies. When we were about to start, he made his appearance all dressed up in khaki with a sola topee covered by a waterproof sheath, looking like a Chinese police sergeant. His monkish robes were stowed up in a suitcase, but not the rosary, whose beads he let slip through his fingers while muttering long prayers and changing the tone of his voice as he addressed peaceful or terrific deities.

The framework of my caravan thus formed, there was nothing left for me but making a move from Gangtok. Moise, Mele, the Lama and I rode two small cars down the winding, unsafe roads along the Tista valley. We rapidly sank from the cool, humid heights of Darjeeling into a sticky tropical heat shattered by sudden thunderstorms. At Jelle Kola on the Tista we picked up Maraini, worn out by the heat and the endless struggle with the baggage, the railway personnel and the porters, and headed up again toward Gangtok in the sullen, soggy slush. A storm was gathering again, and on our leaving the Tista valley the first drops fell. Then the floodgates of heaven collapsed. Angry streams were lashing down the boulder-strewn gullies, swelling into threatening floods as they tumbled into the valley, washing away whole chunks of the road. As night had set, we thought it better to head back for the Martam guest house. Our head lights awakened the slumbering

village, as we went hunting for some rice and eggs, which
Karma Pal cooked for us as best as he could. An ominous
beginning, undertoned by the lama's untiring propitiatory
prayers.

On April 4th we reached Gangtok (6140 ft. on the sea
level) after negotiating the gaps carved by the storm in the
road.

Sikkim, called Drenjong (*qBras ljoṅs* = the land of
wheat) by the Tibetans, is a square-shaped enclave between
Tibet in the north, Bhutan in the east, Nepal in the west
and Bengal in the south. It has all kinds of weather and all
altitudes, from Kanchenjunga's peaks supporting the
canopy of the heavens to the scorched, malaria-ridden valleys. The white leopard lives on the borders of its glaciers
and its deadly lowlands teem with mosquitoes. The thermo-
meter jumps from boiling to freezing point within a few
miles. On the rocks which, as they climb towards Tibet,
stand barren and gaunt, pines and firs bear lonely and
stubborn the brunt of the storms; whereas giant red and
white rhododendrons wave and creep in the dark, treacherous tangle of the jungle where, as if the ground were not
enough, plants grow on top of each other in the brewing,
pregnant moisture. Rice, cinnamon and spices are grown in
the valleys It often rains in this paradise of leeches, and
water gushes, trickles and sputters at every corner, as if an
underground ocean were swelling and surging towards an
outlet. A shroud of grey fog weighs heavily upon the country for many months, like leaden remorse: but winter is a
glory of light and a dazzle of sparkling snows. Spring and
summer are the worse seasons. When we were there, what
the Indians call the small monsoon had already begun, and
heaven and earth were daily dulled by a glum dripping of
rain. However Gangtok (= the mountain spearhead) is a
delightful little town, strewn like a wreath around the royal
palace and the temple, with broad, clean, park-like alleys,
spick and span like a summer resort. The small state of
which Gangtok is the capital, Sikkim, counts hardly more

than a hundred thousand inhabitants. The original population, the Lepchas, have taken refuge into the Lachen valley and a steady trickle of Nepalese has been flowing into Sikkim in the latest decades. As these are good, hardworking and prolific farmers, they have got the upper hand. The small trade is also in their hands, whereas the big one has stayed the monopoly of Indian merchants. The ruling class belongs to the local aristocracy, related to Tibets' leading families. In Sikkim the most widespread languages are Tibetan and Nepalese, but the Lepchas have a language of their own, their books and their own rituals. The present ruler, Maharaja Tashi Namgyal, boasts descent from a famous Tibetan family. His is a fatherly and wise rule courageously wrestling with the present hardships and the lack of resources. Rice, the staple food of the local population, has not yet been rationed, but there is no lack of grumblers even here, and of late a local congress was set up at Gangtok to demand a larger say in the matter of public administration for the people. If the roads were repaired and the ban on the free entry of foreigners lifted, Sikkim would become one of the best mountain resorts of the whole of India, as only Kashmir can vie with it for wealth of game, surface of snow field and height of peaks to be climbed.

Horses for Yatung, the first village beyond the Tibetan border, could be hired at Gangtok. To speed up our journey and avoid useless suspicions by the Tibetan authorities we reduced our luggage to the least and left the rest in the trust of an Indian merchant who was in constant business relations with Tibet. However, we left with forty-one horses, as the caravan leaders always do everything in their power to spare their poor pack animals and keep the load well under the normal weight of one hundred and fifty pounds. The bickering and wrangling of the first day had left us breathless, but at last we set out under a streaming rain. The European sense of seasons gets neary lost here, and while spring is heading towards its climax, one would believe that autumn comes and winter can not be far behind.

Two roads lead into Tibet from Gangtok: the former reaches Kampadsong (*sKam pardsoṅ*) through Lachen and the Donkhya-la, and the latter, further east, crosses the Natu-la (14,295 ft) and joins the road leading into Tibet from Kalimpong through the Jelap-la (14,398 ft). I had already crossed the Natu-la several times and, accustomed as I was to the vast landscapes of Western Tibet, I had found it rather dull and a sense of weariness and boredom went with it in my memory, as it usually happens with the places one does not care for. This time the season was less far progressed and I grew somewhat reconciled with that road. At Changu, the second stop after Gangtok, we found snow already, and we could reach that place in one day only, as Prince Dondub Namgyal (*Don grub rnam rgyal*) had given us a lift in his jeep for the first ten miles. The car had boldly conquered the hairpin bends, cleared the muddy flood of crumbling scree rushed by the rain from the over-flowing ravines on to the mule track we were following, had floundered dizzily on the edge of precipices, but had had to stop eventually in front of a collapsed bridge. Ten more miles were left till Changu, which we did on foot and on horseback. Some years ago a Baby Austin reached the sum-mit of the Jelap-la, which goes to show that, with a slightly increased budget on road maintenance, cars could easily climb up to the threshold of the forbidden country. Changu is a mountain rest house, a *bungalow* built in a snowy dell at whose bottom a small lake rests under the watch of basalt-like black rocks crested with blossoming rhododendrons.

It snowed every day, and Maharaj Kumar seized the opportunity to improve his skiing proficiency under Maraini's and Mele's guidance. Snow was deep on the Natu-la, but we climbed it on foot in order to feast our eyes at leisure on the beauty of our surroundings and to grow slowly accustomed again to the height, which was making itself felt already, As custom will have it, those crossing the pass must pick up a stone and lay it on the abode of the god (in Tib. *Lha rtse*), a bare rock where the invisible, dreaded spirit ruling the mountain lives. While doing so, one must shout at the top of one's voice in Tibetan: "Hail, o god! Blessed be the god!" Small banners imprinted with prayers and fringed with motley ribbons, offered by pilgrims on this road, hoisted on slender sticks and lashed by the high wind, flutter rustling and quivering among the boulders. The Tibet-bound traveller crosses into the area of Tibetan Buddhism while still in Sikkim, and it behooves him to respect its beliefs and rites, to bow his head before the aura of religion radiating everywhere and filling every place with mysterious presences. I always thought, with Ramakrishna, that one should "kneel where others kneeled, as there is the presence of God".

2 Beyond the Frontiers — First Hardships — Propitiatory Rites

One day after crossing the frontier we arrived at Yatung, a long, narrow strip of a village squeezed between two barriers of wooded mountains on the banks of the river Chumbi. Its houses were all of wood with stone roofs, but one and a half miles before entering the village we had met the first towering Tibetan houses, as stout as fortresses, with broad windows encased in richly carved wood framings — an advanced wave of Chinese architectural patterns lapping at the shores of India. As long as the Chinese Empire ruled over Tibet, Yatung was the headquarters of a Chinese governor and changed therefore its original Tibetan name, Sharsing-ma[2] for a Chinese one. When we were there, the only trace of China left were a few red-paper bills with good luck inscriptions at the inn doors. We paid the first visit to the Tibetan trade commissioner or rather his deputy (Tib. *sku ts'ab* = representative) as the commissioner himself was on a mission to China and the United States. He was a stout, tall fellow like a warrior, his speech was solemn, his manner kind. Kindness, a carefree amiability and a ready smile kindling their sedate faces are some of the outstanding

24

qualities of the Tibetans. Their hospitality is ruled by a strict etiquette. First, a linen or silken scarf — according to the guest's rank or wealth — is exchanged as a token of good luck. Questions on the journey and one's state of health follow, leading up to a conversation during which tea is liberally served. Books on Tibet are so full of details on this kind of tea that it is hardly worth one more description. Should any of my readers want to taste it, here is the recipe: the tea, after boiling for a long while, must be poured into a wooden mixer together with some butter, salt and occasionally a pinch of soda and shaken well till all ingredients have thoroughly mixed. Then it is heated again and poured from a copper or silver pot into copper, silver or jade demi-tasses.

The headman of the village then came to see me; his native designation was "genpo" (*rgan po*), which means the elder one, and larger villages could have two or three at the same time. His task was to supply the holders of regular passes with victuals, fuel and horses. Moreover, he was the district commissioner's representative and was expected to report to him on all events. No foreigner was supposed to journey beyond Yatung without the permit of Lhasa, *lam-yig*, failing which he had to turn back. I was myself in no trouble, but trouble, it seemed, was unexpectedly brewing for my friends. Since 1947, when my permit to visit Tibet was issued, things had been happening. On the Dalai Lama's death in 1933 the power had passed into the hands of the abbot (*Rwa sgreńs*), north-east of Lhasa, a young man with modern ideas, who was not loath to submit Tibetan policy to far-reaching changes, by favouring relations with foreign countries and — subject to certain restrictions — the entry of foreigners. Whereas the late Dalai Lama had leant more and more heavily on Great Britain, the Reting abbot inclined towards on agreement with China, an attitude which failed to please many.

Realizing that he could not carry out the proposed reforms and fearing that the consequences of his failure could recoil on himself, he abdicated in favour of the Takta (*Brag k'ra*) abbot. But his followers did not approve of this step and in 1947 plotted against the Takta abbot and tried to get rid of him by means of a time bomb, which went off too early, resulting into the capture of the abbot of Reting, the confinement of his relatives and the seizure of his property. He died in jail himself after a few weeks, and the Takta abbot came to the power. But the end of his rival, who had many supporters, hurt a large section of the people, especially the monks of Sera, a great lamasery in the neighbourhood of Lhasa, well-known for its military traditions and its soldier monks. These rebelled and threatened to overthrow the Government. For two days Lhasa was in great danger of being sacked both by the Sera monks and by the troops the regent had mustered to face the revolt. Eventually the regent managed to get the upper hand and the Sera warriors had to surrender before the artillery which was pointed at the convent.

These events, the wish to hush them up and the mistrust of foreigners led against the new Tibetan government to a policy of more guarded seclusion. Request upon request of entry permits were turned down. Two U.S. citizens whose application had been warmly supported by the Chinese Government, an Indian Buddhist monk of German origin and a Briton who had been at Shigatse in 1947 were all in for a negative answer.

That was why Lhasa answered my cable of the 13th April, which informed the Tibetan authorities of my arrival and applied for a *lam-yig* for me and my companions, as follows: "Please cable us whether your three companions are Indian, Tibetan, Sikkimese, Bhutanese or foreigners: if so, of what nationality, and also the duration of your stay in Tibet. We shall cable an answer". Only Tibetans, Sikkimese, Bhutanese and Nepalese could enter Tibet without a passport. On my cabling back the required information, the Lhasa Foreign Office, however, answered on the 24th April: "As you are a Buddhist, you may stay in Tibet three months. Please cable the number of horses and beasts of burden required for yourself. We shall send your *lam-yig* to Yatung as soon as your cable is at hand. As to your three companions, we are sorry to confirm that, as several applications by foreigners to visit Tibet have been turned down, our Government can hardly grant them a permit. Please inform them. Tibetan Foreign Bureau".

This cable left little ground for hope; however I left no stone unturned in order to persuade the Lhasa Government that at least the physician, without whom I would not venture on the long and risky journey, and one of my disciples, who could draw a great spiritual advantage from the sight of the holy land, had to follow me. Thus, waiting for an answer, we had to stop longer than expected at Yatung. But that time was not altogether wasted, as our bodies grew accustomed to the height and our minds to the new world unfolding itself before us. Living among foreigners is always somewhat uncomfortable if one does not conform to their customs, and what I mean here is not so much their clothes or exterior habits, as rather their way of thinking.

I have always regarded human beliefs — the ones that flowed down to us together with the blood from our forefathers and that we find congealed, as it were, in the common opinions until new ideas break into their circle and upset them — as an invisible, undemonstrable yet present reality, endowed with more life than things you can lay your hands on; a mysterious fluid surrounding, carrying us and leaving us breathless whenever we try to resist it, as when running against the wind. Wherever I am, I always try to attune myself to that spiritual atmosphere, which I feel at the beginning as something new and different, and which always ends by carrying me off. Now too, I had to forget I was a European, accustomed to split logical hairs and to distil ideas through the intellectual alembic, and had nearly to dissolve my own personality into the collective subconscious of the people in whose country I was, as into a still

sea not yet ruffled by the breeze of new and rebellious
opinions. Before setting out on my journey I would do what
the Tibetans do on such occasions when sensing from
mysterious clues the presence of hostile forces and have
recourse to a ceremony meant to appease and scare away
those forces, styled *barche selwa* (*bar c'ad bsel ba*) or "re-
moval of the obstacle".[3] To be honest, I felt I needed it.
The difficulties to overcome had been so many till now,
while new ones were cropping up, that I had begun wonder-
ing whether I had not better do something to purge the air
around me, where I often had sensed an inexorable enmity.
Shortly before leaving Europe I had read, in the Italian
"Revista di metapsichica" lovingly edited by my friend Mr.
Schepis, the review of a book on the evil eye, written by the
President of the Athens Society of Psychic Research.[4] The
author of the book had gone to work with an open mind on
a number of such facts in the light of modern science and
found out their indisputable reality, as if malignant
thoughts were concrete forces acting at a distance. Dazed
by science's limpid brightness and the clarity of its tenets,
we have grown accustomed to sneer at beliefs that escape
scientific proof and, deluded by our one-track mind, we
have forgotten our own superstitions. Our haughtiness has
blinded us to the fact that science is the most arrogant of
superstitions. Our modern extrovert habits have cut us off
from everything that takes place within us, in a world
connecting our unconscious present with man's hoary past,
harbouring a turmoil of fears and hopes, forebodings and
premonitions, on which only our dreams shed sometimes an
ambiguous twilight. Fear of the unknown lets our intellect
drive back that uncomfortable mystery. But the further
down it is thrust, the more peevishly it will shoot back to
the surface again and again with deceitful, sudden upwell-
ings which shake up, churn and darken the serene mirror of
consciousness. At Yatung there was a renowned exorcist,
one Gyese Lama (*rGyal sras bla ma*), or "the prince lama",
born of a noble family in Kham (*K'ams*) on the border of

China. He had been wandering long in Tibet, had a wife and five children. There is nothing astonishing in that. Yoga is an exercise, and as such it cannot last eternally. It admits of breaks now and then, which are subsequently bridged over again by spells of confinement and concentration. The lamas will withdraw into their hermitages at times and chastise their bodies with the hard penance of yoga for several months at a stretch, thus reawakening the slumbering supersensible faculties in their souls and bodies and storing up reserves of spiritual bliss. Then they will plunge into this world again. Not all Tibetan ascetics live walled in mountain caves. An outstanding example is the one of Marpa, the translator, who was the master of Tibet's greatest mystic and poet, Milaraspa. Marpa was throughly broken in, as no one else has been since, to the mysteries of yoga, and was married to a good lady, Damemā, who nursed with motherly tenderness restless, unhappy Milaraspa and even protected him against her husband's short temper.

Gyese Lama looked some fifty years old, had flowing hair knotted on the top of his head, wore the traditional robe of red wool and silver ear rings shaped like Mercury's wands of the kind worn by terrific deities, and white pendants made either of sea shells or of splinters of human bones. We made friends at once. I was impressed by his open heart and his watchful mind, and asked him to perform the *barche selwa* rite for me. It would not be worth while describing it here, as such a rite ought to be seen. And there is something else too. By nature I am much more inclined to believe what I cannot see than what science would have me believe this way today and that way tomorrow. Mystery and the unforeseen make all the difference between real living and a humdrum existence.

My Geshe, the Rev. Sangpo, was, like all theologians, rather skeptical. He was chiefly interested in doctrine and speculation: logic was his strong point. Besides, there was a difference of school between the two, as he belonged to the

Yellow sect and Gyese to the Red one.

Two main sects share the sway of the souls in Tibet: the Red and the Yellow or, as we should say, the ancient and the reformed church. They are also the two main schools of thought into which Tibetan Buddhism split, which many, still following Waddel's tracks, style Lamaism. This word ought no more to be used for Tibetan Buddhism. Lamaism comes from the Tibetan word *bLama* which means spiritual master, and therefore even fails to refer to the monastic organization, as not all monks are necessarily spiritual masters. A monk becomes a Lama only when he imparts some religious instruction to the others, otherwise he will be a mere friar (trapa, *grwa pa*). Strictly speaking, Lama is a title to which only the great religious figures, the heads of monasteries, the so-called "incarnates" (tul ku, *sprul sku*) have a right. That is why Tibet's religion ought rather to be called Tibetan Buddhism than Lamaism. But even this term requires an explanation. When speaking of Tibetan Buddhism, we should not believe that the Buddhism of the Land of Snows is a peculiar interpretation of that religion. As a matter of fact there is quite a difference between the present-day religion of Tibet and the doctrine of primitive Buddhism, but the rift is much narrower, if any, between the former and esoteric Buddhism as it was known in medieval India. In a certain sense, Tibetan is much nearer to the latter than is Japanese Buddhism; this is also easy to explain, as the Japanese people, when it took up Buddhism, had reached a remarkable ripeness in artistic, social and political life. This could not but influence the imported religion which, owing to its very fundamental tenets, was wide open to all influence from the new spiritual surroundings where it was introduced. The Tibetans, on the contrary, had nearly no cultured traditions when Buddhism set foot in their country through the work of the first Indian missionaries. Art, thought and even some social habits therefore migrated together with Buddhism from India into Tibet. Once there, Buddhism undoubtedly also absorbed some local beliefs and cults; as a matter of fact its beginnings were marked by a harsh struggle against the indigenous religion known as Bon po. But Buddhism, true to its traditions, ended by adopting and including the local gods and genii into its Olympus. That is why Tibetan Buddhism, especially in its popular and less orthodox form, contains quite a few aboriginal elements, if in Buddhist disguise, just as many heathen deities have landed, with a different name and some formal alterations, in the Roman Catholic calendar. But this is still a far cry from what has been stated by some. i.e. that the religion of Tibet is hardly more than gross Shamanism. On any tourist who could not stay long in Tibet or could not interpret what he saw because he did not know Tibetan, that religion must of course make the impression of an idolatrous jumble. The sight of so many rites performed mechanically, of so many priests who read the scriptures without understanding them, of the jungle of idols heaped up on the altars in attitudes which are not always pleasant or chaste, of the crowd of greedy and suspicious monks, may lead one to think that religion is in a state of decay. But here it should be remembered that this kind of Buddhism is, as it were, the grafting into Tibet of one of the last shoots of Mahāyānic Buddhism, namely of the school called Mantrayāna or Vajrayāna, initiatory or esoteric sects whose membership is subordinated to a particular kind of baptism, one of the eleven forms of baptism the liturgic handbooks of such schools are enlarging upon. This baptism is regarded as indispensable, as it not only works like a sacrament by wiping out the spiritual ignorance inborn in every human being and thus making us capable of receiving the redeeming light, but also paves the Way to the revelation of such secret doctrines as explain the symbolism of each act of worship, and gives the key enabling us to see and realize a truth leading to release in the figures of deities and diagrams, where that truth is perceptibly, if still symbolically, expressed. Failure to understand the iconography and liturgy of Tantric Buddhism — the

one introduced into Tibet — concealing such a wealth of
meaning, would prevent us to grasp the innermost core of
this religion: a religion which, on the other hand, ran a
great risk of being misunderstood just because of its secret
and esoteric character when it was grafted upon a huge
monastic structure and spread among a crowd of the laymen. It was essentially the religion of an elite, who would
be able to see through the surface of symbols and rituals the
trials and ordeals reserved to the initiate's soul, the inner
drama of his revulsion on leaving the world of appearances
for the one of spiritual truth. Once it had come in touch
with the masses, this school of Buddhism could hardly
preserve the purity of its conceptions. The symbols were
taken at their face value. The rituals, once deprived of what
they meant for the soul's life, ran the risk of decaying into a
magic ceremony, that is, into something which, if carried
out exactly according to the book, fatally sends out a particular force acting on the others at a distance; and thus
losing its worth as a way to the individual's release. This,
however, should not lead us to look down upon the whole of
Tibetan Buddhism. People who have fathomed the deep,
essential core of Vajrayāna have lived and live still today.
Even today one can meet in the convents, and more often in
the solitary mountain cells, the "perfect men", Trutob
(*sGrub t'ob*), uninterrupted "dynasties" of mystics, in
which the secret doctrine has been handed over from master
to disciple and lived up to.

Nor can one very well claim that the huge monastic
structures have dimmed the light of the ancient Buddhist
doctrine. For a long time a great number of masters and
doctors were educated in the convents, who delved deep
into the lore received from India, shed light on it with notes
and commentaries and stayed as faithful to the systems of
interpretation followed in the great Indian universities as no
Chinese or Japanese school ever did. For example, the
works of Buston, who lived in the 14th century and the ones
of Tsongkhapa, of the 15th, do not only help us to under-

stand Tibetan Buddhism, but constitute an indispensable help to the right interpretation of Buddhist doctrines and Buddhist mysticism, not only the dogmas but the innermost meaning of the experiences as well.

In the long run, however, the overgrowth of convent institutions has ended by troubling the purity of the monks' strict training. Hardening of the arteries set in with the double threat of formulas replacing the mind's independent striving after truth, and a withered theology taking the place of the yearning for spiritual rebirth. A tendency to formalism and worship of the letter gained ground on spiritual research.

Two great attempts at reformation were made: the one of Buston, which I have mentioned above, and the one of Tsongkhapa. The former should not be regarded as a true reform. Buston's purpose was rather to draw up a critical summary of the whole of Buddhism by accurately sifting and trying its ritual, iconography and tradition, lopping anything which had not its roots in unimpeachable authorities and building up the rest into a monumental work bearing on the essentials of faith, the monastic discipline and esoteric liturgy. His was the first all-embracing and well-planned digest of Tibetan Buddhism, which dealt a deadly blow to arbitrary fancy and personal vagaries in the interpretation of doctrine. Buston, however, never meant to found a school. He lived in the convent of Shalu near Tashilhumpo[5] and all he aimed at was to show the way to the wise, devout people who should have followed him.

But decay had set in and gained ground around him. In the convents, discipline was relaxing and the doctrine drifted further away from its source. This further crisis gave birth to the reform of Tsongkhapa, thus styled after his birthplace in Amdo, but originally called bLo bzañ grags pa. He was not satisfied with a re-arrangement of liturgy or a fresh formulation of dogmas. He went so far as to found a new sect boasting a greater severity of customs. Whereas other schools did not rigorously respect celibacy and some of them even openly admitted of the monk's marriage, Tsongkhapa was a stickler for observance of the rules and barred both meat and alcohol from the monks' diet. Tibetan Buddhism was split in two through his reform: on one side the sect he built, on the other the several schools which had previously arisen and which frowned upon the newcomer and closed ranks against it. Tsongkhapa's followers wanted to look outwardly different from their opponents too. They kept on the monks' traditional red woollen robe, but donned a yellow cap, thus bringing about the generally accepted division of Tibetan monkhood in two groups, the Yellow and the Red sect, from the colour of the caps they wear.

The former, however, though sometimes styling themselves *ser po* (yellow ones) are usually known as the Gelukpa (*dGe lugs pa*) i.e. "the ones of the virtuous school". Their red-cap opponents do not belong to one and the same sect. All those who do not belong to Tsongkhapa's reformed movement wear a red cap. Foremost among these latter are the Nyingmapa (*rNin ma pa*), namely the ancient, the followers of the oldest school. As the founder of their school they hail Padmasambhava, a famous wonder-worker who came into Tibet from the Swat valley in the 8th century and was the first to introduce into Tibet Tantric Buddhism, many liturgical works of which he translated into Tibetan. Though this sect has lost some of its former power and size, it still carries weight especially in the Kham district; it looks upon Padmasambhava as the highest embodiment of the Buddha, as the eternal truth which took human shape in order to reveal to men the mysteries of release. Their sect greatly stresses the importance of magic, and has gone out of its way to borrow several beliefs and rituals from the Bon po aboriginal religion. But their branch known as Dsokchen (*rDogs ch'en*), which keeps a firm foothold in Eastern Tibet, has instead developed into a quietistic school bent on discovering in the innermost core of our being the mysterious presence of the unalloyed, dazzling, colourless world consciousness, the source of all things, the Absolute, the embryo of the Buddhas. This sect bears some resemblance to the Chinese Ch'an and the Japanese Zen schools, which are chips from the same old block. Then there are the Kagyupa (*bKa' rgyud pa*), who continue in Tibet the traditions of Indian Hathayoga and engage on those hard exercises which open subtle channels of correspondence between the body and the soul. They are particularly adept in producing at will some extrasensorial and supersensible feats which prove in their eyes their achieved perfection and escape from the physical laws hampering human actions. The Kagyupas are themselves split into several currents, the main ones being the Drigunpa (*ɑBri guṅ pa*), from the name of a convent east of Lhasa; the Grugpa (*ɑBrug pa*), from the Tibetan name of Bhutan, where this sect has its widest spreading; and lastly the Karmapas (*Kar ma pa*) whosc headquarters is Tsurpu (*mTs'ur p'u*), west of Lhasa.

Astride between the Reds and the Yellows are the Sakyapa (*Sa skya pa*), thus named from the Sakya monastery south-west of Tashilhumpo. Nowadays the Sakyapa are no more so powerful as they used to be when, at the time of the Mongol dynasty ruling over China, they won over those emperors to their cause and were invested with power over the whole of Tibet. This led to a revival in the hands of the religious leaders of the political power the successors of Srongtsen gampo (*Sroṅ btsan sgam po*), the famous king who had unified the country, had long lost. Faithfully interpreting the doctrine of the Buddha, these leaders did not prove intolerant and refrained from exploiting their political power to impose their dogmas, thus letting the other sects live and thrive as they would. Tsongkhapa himself had a motley religious background as he had studied with the Sakyapa and the Kagyupas at the same time. When later on his followers formed into a church and, in the struggle for political predominance, the district of Central Tibet (Lhasa and Yatung) clashed with the district of gTsaṅ (Sakya, Gyantse and Shigatse), the conflicting political interests led to sect rivalries and violent theological squabbles. Now all this is past and done with. The people has been long accustomed to respect and fear all the endless aspects of God and to worship likewise all those who, in whatever way, are supposed to be in touch with the Powers ruling this Universe. Tradition had given first rank to Padmasambhava and his miracles and the yellow sect was therefore compelled to accept him into their heaven, though changing the story of his life to suit their interests, so that nowadays there is hardly any temple in Tibet where Tsongkhapa's image is not to be seen near the one of Padmasambhava. Such sectarian quarrels do not affect the people, who with equal devotion set out on pilgrimages to the red and the yellow temples and treat the monks of both sects with the same awed respect.

But to return. The *barche selwa* ritual takes two days and is placed on the first day under the protection of Padmasambhava — whom I mentioned above — and on the second of Jampeyang (*aǰam dpal dbyaṅs*), the god of wisdom, usually depicted as holding in his left hand the book of sacred knowledge and in his right the sword meant to rend the veil of ignorance. The ceremony took place in an old friend's private chapel. At nine o'clock on the morning of the first day I found Gyese lama near a huge copper boiler, kneading flour and butter to make a Torma (*gtor ma*). Then, with his long, slender fingers he lovingly modelled the figures to be placed on the altar: shapes of gods to be invoked, of demons to be scared away, and of the propitiatory offers too. The biggest Torma depicted the chief God himself or rather the world of which he was the essence. It had a square basis where a tapering spire rested — which is the way the Buddhists represent the universe rising gradually from coarse matter up to its spiritual peak and, at the same time, the state of subtle existence the ascetic reaches through meditation. Beyond this, time and space cease on the plane of ecstasy and Nirvana. All Tormas, except those representing the evil beings, were painted red with the juice of a root which, when boiled in butter, oozes a blood-like fluid. On each of the biggest Tormas the lama laid five butter rings, one in the middle and four at the sides, in a flower-like arrangement. These meant the offerings corresponding to the five senses, and therefore to the objects they perceive, or, in other words, the whole of life in its essential elements. When all *tormas* were ready, the lama placed them in order on the altars with seven metal cups before them containing water, rice, flowers, butter and sandalwood to be burned, all things that Mother Earth herself, as it were, bore as an offer to the Supreme Essence. Then the ceremony proper began. Everything in it was shrouded in symbols. Lacking the keys to them was like listening to a speech in an unknown language. The arrangement of the offers on the altar had been like building up the world itself in its true image. Now the Lama held sway over it. He did not lapse into a gentle, trance-like state of grace, as a vessel to receive Divine light and love which would efface all earthly stains. He was not a mystic, but a magician: he acted. Through his magic operation he rose to a sphere transcending all, even the divine, forms; and dissolved his personality into the world of the Mothers whence, through endless channels and gradual changes, everything has arisen; as if from an originally quiet, smooth ocean, unruffled by any outward wind, ripples started, driven by an inward impulse, row after row of them, lapping and relieving each other in turn, range on range of foamy, short-lived waves on the background of infinite time and space.

The Tormas are the symbols of the images conceived by Divine consciousness when It shifts from unruffled stillness to the first dawning of creative thought, and the pattern of the rising Universe — demons and gods, Good and Evil — flashes into sight. Creation means power — power over life and death. The exorcist, by force of his magic, drives himself back to the moment when the world is born. Then he destroys and blots out all traces of evil in the world thus re-created, which, in terms of ritual, is meant by the scattering and destroying of those Tormas, which represent the devils. Thus world disharmony is effaced, balance is restored, evil is conquered. There is no trace of prayers. The interplay of mental forces embodying the divine ideas in terms of the concrete world is created afresh, bidden again into being within the magic circle of symbols. The spells of the lama claim each as his slave, evoke, scatter, couple and re-group them even as an orchestra conductor moves and sways an invisible choir.

It is a solemn, complicated liturgy, where the offers, the hymns and the gestures fall into a sharply outlined pattern. The least neglected motion of the hands, the slightest lapse in speaking a word may make the whole structure collapse. Magic is like high calculus: it does not admit of "near misses". The ritual acts were fulfilled in an atmosphere of tense expectation. The formulas, spoken from the depth of the throat, sank at times into a hollow, threatening rumble, and at time glided smoothly like a rivulet on a meadow. At regular intervals the lama stressed his chant by smartly rapping a bent stick on a large drum tottering on one shaky stake. This clearly pointed to a survival from Shamanism[6] and it sounded like the rhythmical hammering from a dark forge, or the haunting recurrence of an obsessive thought. The lama's hands in the meanwhile wriggled and joined as in a nimble dance, making up the "seals" (*Skr. mudrā*, Tib. *p'yag rgya*), ceremonial postures of the fingers which are supposed to guide the formulas towards their aim and to load the ritual words with an effective charge without which they would be aimless utterances of sound. His hands suddenly rose like flames of an invisible fire, then shrunk like the petals of a lotus flower shunning the blazing sun, then seemed to clasp and embrace, and again to ward off. It was, in itself, like a mute dialogue between the priest and the mysterious presences. The forces of evil renewed assault on assault, like the refrain of a hellish dirge. The lama's litanies hardened and stiffened against the onrush in a threatening, quickening rattle of the drum, in a hastier throwing of handfuls of rice right, left and forward, meant to get the upper hand over the foes. The everlasting fight between the two principles is the constant undercurrent of any spiritual drama when stripped down to its essentials, like a clash of disembodied wills wandering in the empty space, but ever ready to take possession of a human heart and to make it into the battlefield where their respective strengths can measure up to one another.

The exorcism over, the "ta" (*pra*) begins: an omen of things to come. According to the Tibetans there are several ways to escape time's limitations and to look from the glittering heights of the eternal present down upon the passing show of things past and future. Such a vision is vouchsafed to men in a state of grace, possessed by a god or purified by penance from all earthly stains. But they think that the "accident of birth" may reserve a larger measure of that privilege to some people, and grant them larger gifts of spiritual sight. Such are the *delo* (*ạdas log*), usually women who have an unaccountable way of falling dead and rising, even more unaccountably, again among the living. During that interval their conscious principle, the kernel to which Buddhism reduces human personality, wanders in the realms of the thereafter, freed from the bodily fetters, and crosses the several purgatories where other conscious principles atone for their past misdeeds. When such persons come to, they relate their experiences, so that the living, hearing first-hand accounts of the punishments expecting the evil doers and of the rewards of bliss reserved to the wise, may scrupulously follow the Buddha's teachings. Still other people have prophetic fits, and their inner eyes are lit by the intervention of a god who, when properly evoked, sharpens and enlightens them above the common human standard.

In my previous journeys I had witnessed some "tas" ascribed to possession. After a due preparation meant to bring about the proper atmosphere, the deity is supposed to descend into the sorcerer, who shudders, wriggles and, in a trance-like state, starts speaking in a foreign voice, as if he had lent his body to a strange power.[7] Now, at Yatung, the "ta" was a woman in her early fifties, with an expression-less, commonplace, early-withered countenance bearing the marks of a hard climate and a life-long toil. She was ex-pected to read the future on a Chinese metal mirror, which was placed upright on a bowl full of rice. This bowl was laid in front of the altar where the exorcism had been per-formed, and a square wooden board bearing the image of Jampeyang and his symbols was set up behind the mirror itself. A silk scarf of the kind Tibetans exchange on visits was then wrapped around this structure. The windows were shut. The darkness in the room was only rent at intervals by the dim flicker of two wicks whose wavering lights fluttered dully in the mirrors. Gyese lama started uttering his spells anew. Beside the drum, the bell (symbolizing the secret knowledge of the world's impermanence) and the ever pre-sent, indispensable, thunderbolt-shaped Dorje (*rdo rje*; meaning the active intelligence leading to the above said knowledge), his stock-in-trade included this time also a "dadar" (*mda' dar*). This last is an arrow whose shaft is wrapped in a tangle of motley ribbons, and is also employed at weddings. The lama grabbed and waved it furiously while rattling off new formulas in a different rhythm. The god had taken possession of him. The drum rolled and rumbled again, pitilessly beating the time of the spells which slipped off the lips of the lama more swiftly now, as if driven by an inner force. Suddenly Gyese threw some grains of rice on the mirror and bade the woman speak. We too sharpened our eyes, only to make out our distorted images on the surface of the mirror: but the old woman, waving a sandal stick to outline the shapes her inner eyes beheld, announced that she saw three men walk towards Lhasa, and further a cuckoo singing thrice in the night, which was another token portending the entrance of three men into the forbidden City.

The message that reached us on the following day did not seem to bear out the magical forecast. In spite of my untiring insistence, the permit for Lhasa had been granted to myself only.

Apparently the prayers and the wishes of the several grateful patients treated by Dr. Moise had not reached the heavens either. Nor had the many photographs liberally distributed by Maraini and Mele cut any ice. Tibet was a door as tightly shut as it had been for years, not only for the reasons explained above, but on account of the glut of entry applications as well. Not all those who had been allowed to set foot on its soil in previous years had realized the need to respect the country's customs and beliefs, if for no other reason at least in acknowledgment of the hospitality that had been granted to them.

My safeconduct, which had been sent from Lhasa on the 7th May, reached me at Yatung on the 18th. It was drawn up in a thin, elongated handwriting regularly covering a large paper sheet, and sounded as follows: "All districts, villages, village headmen and subjects from Trommo (Yatung) up to Lhasa by direct route please note. Mr. G. Tucci, an Italian, has been exceptionally granted permission to enter Lhasa. On his way from district to district he shall therefore be supplied with fresh relays of four riding and 20 pack horses at the current prices, which shall be from time to time entered below and duly sealed. Moreover, accommodation, fuel, boats to cross rivers, eggs, milk etc. shall also be sold to him at the usual prices. Nothing should stand in his way towards Lhasa. This safeconduct shall be handed in on his entering the capital. In the years Earth-Mouse, 4th month, 4th day".

The safeconduct thus obtained, the date of our departure had to be fixed. My problem was not only to lay hands on horses, a commodity hard to get on such a busy thoroughfare, but above all to set out on a propitious day. Even in Italy there are some widespread superstitions on this subject: like the one earmarking Tuesday and Friday as unauspicious for weddings and journeys. I for one never paid any heed to it and made a point of setting about the most important business of my life just on those two days, and everything went all right. But things were different here. First of all, I was not alone. The caravan crew and the servants were persuaded that striking one's tents on an unauspicious day would be tantamount to asking for trouble.

A brave deed has often been born of faith in success. If I had not respected the beliefs of these people, I should have probably undermined their confidence and their good will. I therefore had recourse to the Tibetan calendar with the help of a Tsipa (*rTsis pa*) or astrologer, and found out that the most favourable day for our departure was the following Monday, the 24th of May. With great regret I took leave of my friends and set out, accompanied by Sirdar Tenzing and Van Tendsin. My Lama had previously left for Lhasa in order to pave the ground for me. On the "wool route", as I would like to christen this path connecting India with Tibet through Sikkim and conveying the most valuable products of the Land of Snows to Kalimpong, my caravan merged with the others. We met, along with the merchants, monks and pilgrims; at times abbots of great monasteries, people worth seeing indeed. When we were at Yatung, for example, the Dunkar monastery "incarnate", usually known as the Trommo theologian, happened to pass by. He resided at the monastery of Dunkar, half a stage beyond Yatung. I had already met him some years ago in Western Tibet: at that time he was a wizened old man already, and people held him in high esteem as one of the holiest men of Tibet. He subsequently died and was supposed to have been born again right away, by transferring his "conscious principle" into a fresh body in order to set forth his arduous task, which could hardly be fulfilled in one life in a frontier province where the "red caps" still predominated. He was said therefore to have taken up again his abode among the mortals as the child of a noble Sikkimese family. He was fourteen at the time, and in his self-control he betrayed already the harsh discipline to which his tutors pitilessly compelled him. But when Mele and Maraini photographed him, his youthful inquisitiveness got the upper hand over the mask-like impassiveness casting a pall of inhibitions on his cheerless childhood. The path of saintliness is indeed a hard one, everywhere.

3 On Our Way to Gyantse

I left with twenty horses, seventeen of which were meant for the baggage and equipment, and three respectively for the caravan leader, the cook and for myself. Tibetan farming resources are so scanty that any traveller who is not prepared to live on tsampa (a porridge of barley meal), Tibetan tea, mutton and yak meat, had better carry his own victuals with himself. As my stomach usually refuses to enjoy Tibetan cuisine, I am accustomed to carry with me from Italy the necessary provisions, as canned meat, vegetables, noodles and fruit preserves.

Sugar can be found in the largest centres like hari, Gyantse, Tashilhumpo, Tsetang. Liquors are a useless burden, and the bottles are apt to break on the bumpy Tibetan roads. Those who do not yield to the temptation of sipping some local *chang*, a kind of beer brewed from barley, and some *arak*, distilled *chang*, may make *arak* themselves with a still, as I used to do in Western Tibet, and grade it according to their taste, thus obtaining a pretty good brew midway between brandy and whiskey. At any rate caravans should be kept small as, in some months and some seasons, especially at harvesting time, horses and donkeys are hard to get; and even when there is a chance of getting them, the peasants, busy on the fields, are loath to part with them at once, which can delay the setting up of the caravan. I would not advise to buy pack animals, as the prices have gone up considerably of late and fodder being very scarce in some parts, the people attending those animals have a way of making extra profits for themselves. Besides, such journeys are very trying for the animals, so that, when attempting to sell off the surviving stock at the end, one would usually get very bad bargains.

For the fouth time I went by the "wool route" to Gyantse. Since the time that road had been opened after the Anglo-Tibetan war in 1904, it was placed under the control of a British trade agent, who had of course been replaced, since India had become independent, by an Indian agent. The two main centres on the route are its terminals, Yatung and Gyantse. In both places there were detachements of Indian troops who guaranteed the safety of the trade agent and of the caravan road.

It takes some nine stages to reach Gyantse, but whoever is in a hurry and disposes of good animals can do it in five or six days. A few miles before reaching Pharidzong (*P'a ri rdsoṅ*) the traveller gets his first glimpse of Tibetan landscape, a huge plain in whose very midst, perched on a lonely rock, the fortress of the same name rises, overhung by pitilessly barren mountains, where no single tree grows. On these blunt crags rises the sharp needle of Chomolari (*Jo mo lha ri*), in whose mysterious loneliness, according to the Tibetans, a goddess lives. Steep, unclimbable walls of sheer rock lead to the deity's abode. Even snow and ice cannot gain a foothold on its slopes, and heap up on the nooks, the ledges, the less steep sides and the peaks of the lower mountains, huddling, as it were, under the wings of the frightening giant. Abrupt parallel ramparts rise and taper off to keen edges, like the ranges of walls of a castle perched on the clouds. To the west, as if obeying a nod of the goddess, another Himalayan colossus towers up, the Pankanzi, the Sikkimese counterpart of the Tibetan peak.

Pharidzong was a very important village, headquarters of a district governed, according to the traditional Tibetan wisdom, by two commissioners, a clergyman and a layman, as four eyes can certainly see better than two, and the presence of a colleague is a constant warning. There is much to say for such a system, which, if I had any say in the matter, I should try to apply to some European offices, having care to put in charge two people who are not too close friends. At Pharidzong only the lay officer was on duty at the time, a young man from Lhasa who had already been elsewhere in the same capacity, and whose wife had been at school at Kalimpong and spoke good English. They were both educated and mannerly people, and it was a real pleasure to spend a few hours with them. Pharidzong is the market where the wool routes meet, and whence mountain paths lead into another forbidden country, Bhutan. Since 1937 and 1939, when I had crossed this area last, many things had changed. What struck me most were three fine buildings erected by wealthy businessmen who practically held the whole trade of Tibet in their hands. One of the three buildings, which had belonged to the late regent, had been transformed into a customs office.

Realizing that wool trade could yield a handsome State revenue, the government of Tibet had levied a duty of one rupee on every bale of wool leaving the country, the receipt of which had to be produced at Yatung; a procedure which gave many a headache to the smugglers. This made Pharidzong into a large business centre, where the cross rates of exchange between the Indian rupee and the Tibetan currency were usually established. These rates did not always hold good at Gyantse and Lhasa, and one Indian rupee drew 3 *sang* and 3 *shokang* at Pharidzong, whereas its rate could rise as high as 3 *sang*, 8 *shokang* and 5 *kamala* in Lhasa. On the Yatung-Gyantse road Indian silver and paper money was accepted by everybody, but elsewhere one had to carry a
. fairly good supply of Tibetan currency. Silver coins were called *tanka*, and the copper *shokangs* could usefully be kept

in reserve for alms to the beggars and pilgrims one inevitably met on the road. The government also issued 10, 100 and 1000 *sang* bills.

Past Pharidzong the road climbs the Tangla Pass, 15,200 ft., but the way up is so smooth that you would hardly realize you are climbing: just like the words of a dissembler, hoaxing you where you would not go yourself, and letting you down in the end. The road then leads down to Tuna, and reaches Kala by the Dochen bend. We had a very cold journey over there, as it usually froze at night and a high south wind rose at noon, stinging with the frost of the Himalayas, and blew on relentlessly up to sunset, till everything and everybody was shivering under its lashings. But the dismal dripping of rainy Sikkim and foggy Yatung was over. Cake-like white clouds sailed through the bright turquoise sky, and everything shone so garishly that each colour seemed to enhance the others by sheer contrast. Shortly before reaching Dochen the road skirts the Ramtso lake (*Ram-mts'o; mts'o* = lake), and after running along a moss-edged brook it reaches, in the neighbourhood of Kala, a twenty-five mile wide valley, dotted by another lake, the Kalatso (*sKa-la-mts'o*). On the Ram lake the Chomolari range, like a diamond-studded necklace pointing to the north-east, was mirrored in such a true-to-nature, still likeness, that, had we taken a snapshot of it at that moment, nobody would have been able to tell which side was the reflection in the picture. In the west we could see some hills bent as it were in a weary bow, crumbling away into gold-yellow sand under which other layers of iron-black glittered in the sun like freshly forged metal. At Dochen the lake took up life like an uproarious spring, where water fowls swam and cackled and fluttered filling the air with their near-human voices, and the mosquitoes swarmed buzzing around and bothering man and beast. We were at a height of 14,900 ft. now and the loneliness had nearly swallowed us up. In one day's march we barely met fifteen to twenty people: desert had succeeded Pharidzong's human beehive.

A few pilgrims, some itinerant lamas, riding merchants armed with Mauser guns and rifles, long caravans filing out, busy spinning or reciting prayers, yaks and donkeys loaded with wool. Religion had become an instinct to those people lost in a frightful loneliness.

On the high tableland a person can be seen from a great distance, like a meaningless black dot on the background of barren, lifeless rocks. Huge, overbearing cliffs crowd the landscape in the boundless waste, with the crushing majesty of nature. Man does not count: he is a tiny being moving along and disappearing without trace, even as the Chinese painters saw him in their metaphysic pictures where the mountains, the clouds and the water spread all over the canvas, and man seems to appear only to give the measure of his nothingless. He then defends himself against loneliness by filling with ghosts the emptiness surrounding and oppressing him. The air rustles with invisible presences; each peak, each pass, each landslide-ravaged bluff is inhabited by a mysterious being ready to harm or to help, easily won over by a prayer and as easily moved to crushing anger by an involuntary offence. Man walks through these surroundings loaded with forces he cannot see, which weigh on him like a nightmare.

The villages were few and far between, wretched and small. But the ruins dismally looking on to the lonely valley were the wreck of an ancient prosperity ended by the 1904 war. Life had never sprung anew from those relics, the fields had never grown verdant again, the canals had dried up and it looked as if the people had been engulfed by death forever, without any further chance to multiply.

As far as Gyantse, one could at the time still keep in touch with the rest of the world. The Indo-Tibetan agreement had led to setting up post and telegraph offices on the roads leading into Tibet from Sikkim, at Yatung, Phari and Gyantse. In many of the rest bungalows one could even ring up Phari or Gyantse, provided the line had suffered no damage, as it was often the case. The permit to stop in such

bungalows had to be obtained from the Political Officer of
Sikkim and the Indian Trade Agent at Yatung. They were
usually well kept, and the ones of Phari, Tuna, Dochen and
Kala, places often swept by a pitiless high wind, offered a
pleasant shelter, rendered further comfortable by a roaring
fire which the keepers liberally built and fed.

The artistically minded travellers could not feast their
eyes on much worth seeing, while on that road. Nearly all
temples had been destroyed during the 1904 war, and the
few which were preserved were subsequently entirely re-
built. The Tibetans do not lay a great store by art as such:
what most interests them is the subject dealt with, the
divine "cycle" represented in any work of art. Rather than a
blackened frescoed wall they would have the garish display
of a new arrangement of figures, gaudily painted by a
contemporary local artist. Supplying the money and the
work needed to do a sacred work is a meritorious act bearing fruit and wiping the sins away - therefore the religious
motive entirely replaces any thought of art. This is why
many masterpieces had become a total loss just in those last
years in the wealthiest provinces, as those of southern
Central Tibet used to be. At Phari in 1937, before entering
the town on my way from India, I visited a small temple
built in the 15th century by a famous ascetic, Tanton Gyal-
po (*Tstan ston rGyal po*), and saw remarkable remains of
paintings dating from the century in the cell. Now I only
found brand new frescoes.

On the whole road I only met three temples worth seeing:
the ones of Samada, Iwang and Nenying. I went to such
lengths describing them in the fourth volume of my "Indo-
Tibetica"[8] that I cannot mention them now without risking
repeating myself. The Iwang temple, hidden in a dale left of
the mountain road midway between Samada and Kangmar
on maps was the oldest of all. In the small cell, standing
Bodhisattva images surrounded the Buddha in the middle.
Both the sacred cycle and the layout of the building followed the oldest Buddhist Tibetan tradition, when such

chapels were built in the valleys, on the plains and along the road. As the times changed, and the strife between the feudal families and the convents actively participating in the political events grew harsher, the temples were built inside the monastery as its spiritual kernel, protected by its mighty constructions. There, entrenched in the turreted masonry bulk, the warlike monks defended the privileges of their sect and of their lay patrons. The Tibetan temple, not unlike its Indian counterpart, is not merely the place where the gods' images are on display and where the Lamas perform the right ceremonies at the right time. It is the projection of a given spiritual plane through the symbols of some deities after the prescriptions of the treaties dedicated to them. It is a whole world, magically limited and circumscribed, entering which with full awareness of its meaning and the proper mystical preparation, one enters a transcendental plane. It is at the same time a heaven and a *maṇḍala*. A heaven, inasmuch as its consecration and the presence of the gods, whose power was by force of the rituals made to descend into their statues, make it into a place quite different from the world we live in, a place whose aura has been thoroughly changed by those presences. It is also, as I said, a *maṇḍala* (Tib. *dkyil ak'or*, chinkor) and as this latter idea carries such a weight in the whole of Buddhism, I had better dwell on it a while.

The *maṇḍalas* are projective figures reproducing, by a manifold arrangement of symbols, the pattern of forces and stages along which the colourless light of cosmical consciousness, that fundamental essence of all that is and becomes, unfolds, scattering and sparkling back, through the endlessly changing aspects of creation. By thus unfolding, that essence realizes itself in the passing show of both physical and spiritual worlds. If, led by his master, the initiate reads the *maṇḍalas* and catches the sense of the patterns and textures displayed in them, he can tread backwards the way, retrace the steps, by direct experience, from the manifold to the One, reintegrate himself into the immovable principle of everything. A *maṇḍala* is therefore a soul-and-world-picture symbolizing that return and pointing the way to it, and is surrounded by a wall (*lcags ri*, pron. chagri). The Buddhists think likewise of the physical universe as girt by concentric chains of mountains, also termed *lcags ri*, which cut it off from non-existence. Just as the *maṇḍala's* centre and climax is essentially that consciousness, that principle which stays forever motionless, yet acts through its own radiations and shapes everything, so in the temple that fundamental essence is represented by the god in the middle (*gtso bo*) around whom the others are arranged according to the suitable pattern stated in the liturgical books. Some *maṇḍalas* are traced with coloured powders on the floors of the temples during the initiation ceremonies, that the disciple may see displayed before his own eyes the mystery of things and grasp the way to release which suits him best. Some are painted on canvas as a lasting blueprint for the seekers. Some are built into pavillions where the symbols and the images bulge out of the background in the fitting arrangement: those architectonic *maṇḍalas* are called lolang (*blo laṅs*).

At Iwang I could still see some paintings in the Khotannese style, which was introduced into Tibet by some Central Asiatic monks driven away from their country by the war turmoil and Muslim inroads. The main frescoes of Samada were in the entrance porch, but had been retouched. Some bronze statues were also to be seen, dating back to the 11th century and bearing the name of the artist carved on the plinth together with the name of the monk who had commissioned the work.

Nenying, also one of the main monasteries of that area, was surrounded by a mighty belt of walls and contained a great deal of cells and chapels, but had been seriously damaged in the 1904 war.

As we were getting nearer Gyantse the valley broadened and showed larger patches of green. The barley, recently sprung forth from the chilly soil, glistened in the sun like emerald. Within a few weeks the rain would swell it, then graciously yield the ground to the sun whose heat, enhanced by the surrounding barren rocks, would let the crop make up for the delay and ripen by September. Only the irises, which sprinkled with violet the endless green, would be no more within a few days. It was surprising to see how the peasants let such a large expanse of even, easily irrigable soil, be invaded by a pretty but awfully harmful plant, as if there had been a dearth of farm hands or the people's mind had wandered towards less ungrateful and more profitable work. The land usually belonged to the nobility; the landlords, called *gerpa*, made up the class from which the Government drew its officials. The peasants tilled, on their own, a part of the field alloted to them, to an extent varying from place to place, and the *gerpas* paid the taxes to the Government in their turn. The monasteries were exempt from taxes and usually possessed large estates bequeathed to them by the worshippers or entrusted to them by the State. The peasants' lot was a hard one, so that in lean years they preferred to abandon their fields and go begging about. But many fields belonged to the Government, and their yield made up the officials' pay, as hardly anybody's salary in Tibet was in cash. To each official a holding was alloted corresponding to the rank held, which he managed to his own profit for the duration of his tenure. In some cases he might get a governmental loan on his nomination, enabling him to live to his rank, or to collect a handsome interest by investing its amount.

The willows and the poplars seemed to vie in fresh greenness with the budding fields, and cast their shadows on the well-to-do houses and the gardens watered by purling brooks. In the hottest days the wealthy people used to pitch their tents by the cool streams and spend their time feasting with their families and friends. The river enlivening that valley turns NW towards Shigatse and flows by the hill whose top is heightened by the pyramidal Gyantse fortress, and crowned lower down by the town houses. The exact figure of the population of Gyantse is an open question. That town rated the third largest in Tibet after Lhasa and Shigatse; it could have counted between five and seven thousand people, a rough estimate as no census was held. Its highest official was the Kenchung (*mK'an c'uṅ*), a church dignitary who discharged the duties of a Tibetab trade commissioner and did business with his Indian opposite number, who also resided at that end of the wool route. The city and its vast district were run as usual by two commissioners, a churchman and a layman, who collected the taxes and administered justice. At the time only one of the two, a scion of the Ringang family, was present, certainly the youngest district commissioner in the world, as he was only nineteen. He was a bright and courteous young man, but perhaps he could not help feeling a misfit in that ancient fortress looking down at the town and the immense valley like a dismal old gentleman who had seen better times. The green valley is surrounded by the petrified surf of endless peaks, looking as tawny, as bare and humpbacked as rows of sleeping camels. But the grey monotony of rock was broken wherever a source squirted out of a ravine, lined by a few sheeny willows and tiny groups of snow-white houses, holding arms, as it were, for fear of the encircling desert. Those were the hermitages where the lamas spent a yearly retreat, in lonely conversation with the gods.

I should have liked to stop only a few days at Gyantse, but I had to stay longer. I had just come in the middle of celebrations: a troupe of actors was in the neighbourhood and the whole town had streamed out to see them. The shops were shut and there was no approaching the authorities. Gyantse looked like a dead town, as everybody had left for three days to see the show. The troupe had come from Kyomolung, a village near Lhasa; they were professional actors — *achilamo*. The Government granted them the income of tax-free land estates that they may ply their trade without worries. In August they would have had to

perform in Lhasa before the Dalai Lama. When the actors
come to the towns, all rejoice as for a sunny day in the midst
of bleak winter, as nothing uncommon or unexpected ever
relieves the dreariness of life in the towns. Only the religious festivals start spells of shortlived mirth dotting an
endless monotony. Obviously such actors would visit each
town at the right moment, during the fairs or celebrations,
or, as it was the case of Gyantse now, when they were
invited by the local authorities to honour an ancient custom. The performance took place on a large square outside
the town, and the stage consisted of two large tarpaulin
screens held by sturdy stakes. There was no scenery, but a
showy display of costumes. The populace was crowding all
around squatting on the ground in order not to hide the
stage from the people of distinction, who were seated in a
box sheltered by a large canopy. Whenever one of the
squatters stood up, policemen shouted him down
flourishing a whip which, to tell the truth, I never saw hit
anybody's shoulders. Near the stage, to the audience's left,
the monks sat at the place of honour, wrapped in their red
robes. Further right and left, there was a flight of white
tents with blue trappings, where the gentry enjoyed the
show while sipping tea. In the box of the authorities were
the Kenchung, the district commissioner Rinshe Dodi, an
owner of large estates in the Gyantse district, an abbott and
other prominent officials happening to be in town. As soon
as the news of my arrival spread, I was invited to watch the
show and to have a seat in the box. Thus I found myself in
the midst of the Tibetan smart set gathered at Gyantse for
the occasion. It was a feast for the eyes: the splash of the
blazing colours was as loud as in a summer garden. Everybody wore rich costumes of Chinese silk. Some had a long
turquoise ear-ring hanging on their left ear: it was the badge
of the officials. The height of the seats was graded according to the rank. The highest seat had been allotted to
Rimshi Dode, the Phari collector of the wool exit duty and,
as it was apparent from his name,[9] an official of the fourth

rank. Right after him came the Kenchung, then the district commissioner; the others followed each a peg lower. On the right, on a sort of bench, lay the hats, bearing a certain resemblance to those of the Roman Catholic clergy, but all of them yellow. On the top of the hats was wedged a piece of coral, varying in size according to the owner's rank, and precious and semi-precious stones were set in golden badges which the hats bore in front. There was a flurry of activity in a kitchen behind the box and frequent processions of servants offered tea and cakes. A new play was performed every day, from ten in the morning to five in the afternoon.

I watched the performance of Tsukyinyima, a Tibetan travesty of Kālidāsa's Śakuntalā, which Goethe's admiration has made popular in Europe for the last century.[10] But there was hardly anything left of the real Śakuntalā. The play staggered along through ex-tempore scenes poking fun at popular figures and entire peoples, at prophets, pilgrims, Muslims and Chinese, and often lapsed into ribaldry and coarse innuendoes. As it is always the case in popular theatre, the actors improvised after a set pattern, and as soon as they noticed that the audience enjoyed their quips, they improved upon them till they succeeded in shaking even the statuesque impassiveness of the highly placed ones out of their majestic self-control. There was an endless hustle and bustle. Whoever got tired of the show withdrew when he liked but, while passing before the officials' box, he crouched as low as he could and stretched out his tongue to its full length as a sign of homage. All the new comers brought with them a jug of tea or *chang*.

In comparison with 1939, when I had been there last, I noticed a greater wealth. The Tibetans are merchants born, and they seemed to have exploited nature's gift much to their own profit. A thrifty, hard, cunning stock, they know how to feather their nest. At Gyantse I saw many new houses built in those last years, large, comfortable buildings surrounded by gardens. The merchant class had grown, and prosperity with it, but the prices had risen accordingly.

The cost of living was then three times higher than it had been ten years before, which seemed to imply that Tibet had somehow kept abreast of the rest of the world despite its isolation. Farming had stayed what it had been, and I thought that if it should develop in keeping with trade, Tibet would be in for a boom.

Gyantse has always been an important town. In the 14th and 15th centuries it was the capital of a large feudal holding state as far as Phari and Kampadzong, and played a great role in that troubled age of Tibetan history. It then slowly declined after reaching its climax under Rabten Kunzang (*Rab brtan kun bzaṅ*).[11] This chief was a restless man, though his biographies, which I went to great trouble to copy, describe him as a pious person. Nowadays his waverings and trimmings between the setting power of the Sakyapas and the mighty lord of Yarlung are forgotten and his only extant works are a tribute to his faith and devotion, i.e. the Pekor chode (*dPal k'or c'os sde*), Gyantse's biggest convent, and the Kumbum. The latter is the current name given to large chortens (*mc'od rten*), buildings on the model of the Indian stūpas, an architectonic symbol of the Universe as conceived by the Buddhists, and at the same time a shrine for relics and the expression of the kernel of Buddha's teachings. Such buildings widened in Tibet until they could contain several chapels — the name Kumbum itself implies the presence of a hundred thousand, i.e. of endless images of gods — and grew up to a great number. Still, the Gyantse Kumbum is one of the most famous and its sight is said to be enough to purify a soul of all its sins and to help it on its way towards final release.

In its chapels world evolution is retraced backwards up to the towering peak of its essential nature, where the symbols of cosmical consciousness are displayed, from which everything stems. Frescoes on the walls picture the whole of the immense Buddhist olympus.

The images, now peaceful, now terrific, seem to jump up alive before your eyes, to crowd on you like ghosts and to engrave themselves mercilessly into the bottom of your subconscious so as to haunt your dreams as well. You would think that the painters have by some wizardry conjured up living forces and driven them into their work, and that these could float out of the walls, force their way into your soul and take possession of it by a magic spell. The religious spirit underlying those works is worlds apart from our own. Those are visions evoked with primordial force from the pit of a soul who had no eyes for anything but mystery and the darkness of abysmal depths, by a people still bent on chaos, on the indiscriminate bottom of things whence evil and good, hell and heaven, the lustful will to live and death's withering wings leap up still firmly clinging to each other. On one side the smile of Lord Buddha, suggesting unruffled peace and triumph over the conflicting opposites of life — on the other side, or rather side by side with it, the sneer of the demons reflected in the senseless turmoil of the human subconscious.

Here we are confronted with an elementary stage of being, where everything surges and swells, mixes and coexists, clashes and yet gets along together. That explains why in Tibet, and still earlier in India, the Yoga schools throve so much. Their disciples felt that inordinate throbbing in themselves and sought to check it or soar beyond it, towards that spotless light in which they saw the very hub of the universe, the beginning and the end at the same time, over and beyond the giddy whirlpools of the unconscious mind or of any troubled state of consciousness.

At Gyantse we reached the end of the rest houses. From there on we had either to rely on the Tibetan families' hospitality or on our tents. I had taken along some light tents of the Caucasus type, which the firm Moretti had kindly put at my disposal. A horse could easily carry two of such tents with the whole equipment of camp cots, tables and washing stands. Besides, they proved excellent in cold weather.

To the north-east, near the road leading to Shipta,[12] the

mountain inhabited by Gyantse's guardian spirit, is the spot where the human corpses are exposed. The dead are not burned in Tibet, but left out in the open that vultures, wolves and dogs may feast on the flesh. The bones are then collected, crushed and scattered away. Thus no trace remains of the mortal frame. The reason of that ruthless destruction is both a fear that the dead may regain possession of his body and the attitude of flight from life common to the whole of Buddhism. According to that religion all that appears and undergoes change is certainly a delusion, but it does not rise out of nothing. Our life is precisely what our actions in past lives have brought about. When our bodies succumb either to an illness, to an accident or to the wear and tear of age, neither extinction nor eternal heavens or hells expect us. We shall have to begin anew, loaded with the experiences of a past whose consequences we shall bear, and responsible for a future whose foundations we are going to lay. Surely there are a few who will not be reborn, who will not return either to this Earth or to any other world where life obeys the same laws and is subject to the same trouble. Such are the Perfect Ones, *trutob* (*sgrub-t'ob* in Tibetan) who on yielding up the ghost will plunge and vanish into the ineffable, boundless cosmical mind, as in the game of magic freedom, in which though others get ensnared, they have chained victory to their own car. Thus they transcend forever that sea of delusions which we call life and become one with the Absolute again.

But very few are those who reach such a degree of perfection or rather of wisdom as to reconquer the "Buddhas' essential body", that unsullied vessel which endures beyond the ups and downs of life's flow. Moreover, some of these Noble Ones renounce Nirvana of their own accord, in order to stay among people and help them by their words, their deeds, their sacrifice. Those are the Incarnates or *tulku* (*sprul-sku*), and the Dalai Lama is supposed to be the first among them. They are known as Bodhisattvas in India, the ones who, out of compassion for the sinning suffering world, have indefinitely postponed their final extinction in Nirvana.

But what of the others, who have not attained such heights — and how will rebirth take place even in the case of the Incarnates? What is re-embodied? Surely not the self, as for the Tibetans, and for all Buddhists, there is no such thing. They only speak of consciousness, thought or the mental make-up. That should be the mortal centre of the individual and, as it is responsible for every action of ours, it creates karma and is therefore the cause of our repeated births and deaths.

At any given moment thought holds in itself past experiences and the unlimited possibilities of the future, is the creature of what has been and the builder of tomorrow, and flows ceaselessly. The Tibetans imagine it as something imponderable yet physical, something that can act at a distance, move and influence other people's thought and be influenced by it, even force its way into somebody else's body and replace his personality altogether. A restless, curious being which cannot stand inactivity, thought rests, or rather rides, on breathing and, like breath, it cannot stay put, cannot stop on anything. At the moment of death, when the body starts on its way towards decay and breathing ceases, thought finds itself thrown away from its support. Then this centre of our being, as we shall see further, runs the greatest risk. Death therefore should not catch us napping, but in the full possession of our conscious powers. That is why a dying man's relatives in Tibet do everything in their power to keep him awake on his death bed. When I myself fell ill in the Rupshu desert in 1931, the wizard of a nomadic tribe near by did nothing but recite formulas aloud while bidding me not sleep.

Should one be conscious and see the signs of approaching death in himself, he ought to have recourse to Yoga and by sheer will-power effect the transfer of his conscious principle, or thought, on to the plane of the Absolute by plunging it back into that flashing stream of universal consciousness which is the only permanent reality in the passing show of dream-like things. Thought, the erratic rider of breath, ought to be forced into the middle of the three invisible channels in our being, the ones starting at the sexual organs and ending at the fontanel on the crown of the head, called in Sanskrit the *brahmarandhra*. Both the side channels open into the nostrils, and that is where thought flows in normal life, whereas the yogi drives it into the middle channel. Here it will turn into immaculate light, flow, spread and dissolve into the glow of universal consciousness. Should the one about to die be unconscious or unable to make that effort, either on account of his weakness or of past sins, his sluggish thought would rather cling to things earthly than soar towards the eternal truths, and rebirth could not be avoided, which is the lot of most people. How can one then help the dying, if not entirely to avoid the consequences of their evil karma, at least to alter and correct its course? There is a book, the *Bardo Todöl* (*Bar-do-t'os-gröl*),[13] often called "the book of the dead" teaching how to lead the listener to avoid existence between death and rebirth. If the consciousness of the dying person is benighted by illness or sin, the words of this book, read aloud, can awaken him and remind him that his next form of existence depends on those last instants. A lama or a friend therefore, as soon as his life ebbs, will have to stand by him and read passages of that book clearly and aloud, that he may learn what dangers lurk and what ways toward release he may tread. According to that doctrine, forty-nine days elapse between death and rebirth, if rebirth has to be. During this period the consciousness of the dead, wandering homeless, as it were, in unknown regions, may be beset by bewitching or threatening apparitions brought about by his karma, and these can prove his undoing.

A few, the elect, do not go through this intermediary stage. Even before they die, they see before their eyes a great light, blazing and dazzling so as no human words can describe: "it is like a spring mirage waving and swinging over a plain". With undimmed awareness they recognize in it a flash of cosmical consciousness, the only extant reality in the flow of short-lived dreams. Into it an immediate "transfer" of the conscious kernel can be operated, and can be keyed up by the rituals of specialized lamas. They let the moribund lie on his right side, as Buddha about to enter Nirvana is depicted, and firmly throttle the two lateral channels thus forcing, as said above, the conscious principle into the middle channel, where it will surge and rush to the top, spurt through the fontanel and flow out into that light. The very awareness that such light is the absolute principle of all things will blot out the delusion of life and spell eternal release. That is the first stage, called in Tibetan *chikai bardo* (*ac'i k'a'i bar do*), or "intermediate state at the moment of death". Less saintly or lively persons do not get release in one flash, but pass on through a second stage, in which that light does not appear so bright, but dulled, or anyhow harder to recognize. A greater concentration and the help of good forces, i.e. the guardian gods, first and foremost Avalokiteśvara, is needed here. But after these two favourable moments the conscious principle may flag and flicker away like one overcome by a swoon, and stay thus benumbed for three days and a half, or four. When it wakes up again, it will see its body doubled up and bound, ready to be cremated, and the funeral offerings of food near it. Close by it will see the weeping relatives, who will not pay heed to its calls. This will grieve and anger the departed, till he will realize he is dead, and be at a loss what to do. His past actions will conjure up before him frightening sounds and visions. During this lapse of time, which will last up to the seventh day, the reading of the *Bardo Todöl* will remind the dead that those sounds and visions are but the projections of his own consciousness flashing before him by force of karma. In this world, the book goes on, there is nothing real but one's own thoughts and delusions. The dead should realize that even these perturbing visions are nothing but images, and thus conquer them. Should he

on the contrary mistake them for something real and objective, then *Samsāra*, the whirlwind of births and deaths,
would sweep him off and he should have to begin all over
again. Two ranges of lights and colours appear before his
eyes: the ones shape up as the five supreme Buddhas, each
with his peculiar colour; the others, murky and dull, symbolize the different worlds in which he could be reborn.
Fear of the former's dazzling brightness may lead him to
plump for the latter, and life would have him in its clutches
again. A battle is thus engaged between the visions born of
good and leading gradually to release and the images conjured up by the evil forces which chain one to life. Only
awareness of their real nature, of the fact that they have
grown out of ourselves and been created by our own deeds,
can conquer and scatter them. From the eighth to the
fourteenth day the fight will grow harsher and more dangerous. *Samsāra*, the forces of *māyā*, of magic liberty chaining
us to life, tighten their grip and bully the dead by furious
and frightening apparitions. If he fails to pierce through
their masks, he will have to embark upon a new life and
first of all to appear, loaded with his offences, before the
god of Death. The good and the evil he did will now be
placed before him in the shape of white and black pebbles,
and the supreme judge will see all his life as faithfully
reflected in a mirror. For the evil he has done hell's tor-
ments await him. But even at that tragical moment, the
Bardo Todöl comes to his help by trying to awaken his
consciousness, by suggesting that those demons, those tor-
ments and his own body are nothing but embodiments of
his own thought.

"Thy body is an imaginary one, and it cannot really die
even if beheaded or torn to pieces. Thy body is unsubstantial, and thou must not fear. The demons of death are but
hallucinations due to thy karma. What is unsubstantial
cannot harm what is unsubstantial. What is attributeless
cannot harm what is attributeless. Beyond thy own hallucinations nothing exists objectively, not even the god of

Death. Realize this".

If the dead succeeds in realizing this, he can still struggle free. If he does not, he is born again in hell, where he experiences the most dreadful tortures, not because he has any real body or is subjected to any objective pain, but simply because he thinks so. Or he will be reborn among the gods, if he tried to do good and to respect Buddha's teachings on earth, not in order to get everlasting release from *māyā's* magical spell, but in order to gain rewards in the thereafter. Or he will be reborn as an animal if he sacrificed or killed animals in his life, or committed sins which abase man's dignity to the level of the brutes. In other words, he will get the lot for which he paved the way himself. Even if his conscious principle, straggling supportless, seeks a foothold somewhere, he still cannot really choose his state after death, and whatever state he thinks he has chosen is exactly what his karma, by an iron law he was unaware of, has matured for him. Should his lot be another earthly life, the wandering conscious principle will seek a house where a man and a woman lie together, "and feel love for his mother to-be if he was a man and hatred for his father, and vice versa if he was a woman". That is, the male offspring will hate the father and the female the mother by a natural propensity to be corrected later by upbringing and life.

Thus, the transmigration of the souls is, according to the Tibetans, but a chain of misunderstandings. The individual is nothing but thought, wrong and illusory thought, a thought which does not recognize itself for the mirage it is and does not realize that everything, beginning from itself, is but a phantom. This phantom wanders from life to life till cosmical consciousness dissolves it in its own light. The Tibetan Book of the Dead helps to see a flash of that light and reminds that nothing but it really exists.

Knowledge leads to release — and release means nothing else but extinction of life's phantom.

Beside this practice meant to avoid rebirth, other chances

unfold before the dead according to the Tibetans. The conscious principle, the departed one's personality, can for example be transferred into the Western Heaven, ruled in great splendour by Amitābha, the God of Boundless Light. There he will strike root as one of the lotus flowers basking in the God's glow and will thus be able to spend aeons in the contemplation of him preaching the Law. This transfer may be carried out by the dying person himself or, as usual, by a specialized Lama. In both cases the technique is the same, though in the latter case an exterior agent, as it were, takes possession of the conscious principle and leads it.

As I have said above, that conscious principle, the kernel of our mental make-up enriched by the karma of each of our previous births and forging anew the one of our next ones, rides the stream of our breath. In normal conditions, it flows to and fro along the two invisible side channels described above, winding from the bottom of the spinal column up to the two nostrils and embracing the whole body. Those two lateral networks are switched on in usual life, when people are engaged upon karma-producing activities, when they are bent towards the world, receive its stimuli and react to them. That is when the conscious principle scatters and fritters away its energies by pursuing different perceptions and nursing various desires, and is entirely out of focus. In order to free it from the fetters of the world and its appeal it has to be compelled to meditate on the symbol of cosmic consciousness Vajradhara, *Dorjechan (rDorje 'c'an)* in Tibetan, the favourite deity of ascetics. Self-consciousness is then lost and the meditator drowns into that god, who radiates his own light into the whole universe till the numberless Buddhas presiding over the infinite worlds dissolve in it. A live consciousness and a direct experience of the individual Self's identity with the Whole, not in its flitting outward appearances but in its essential, permanent kernel, is obtained through this meditation. Man, freed from the ties of impermanence, regains the boundless wonder-working possibilities of the Absolute.

When the mystic awakes from that vision and comes down to the plane of normal existence again, he replaces meditation by a mantra, that is to say a ritual syllable. Mantras have a great magic value. In their swimming into sight, growing, changing and disappearing, all things follow rhythms of their own as the universal energy of Creation by which they are swayed surges, throbs, quickens its pace and stops, like a mighty breath holding the key of life and death. The very sound of human words is a modulation of that cosmical breath, and therefore it counts more than their meaning. If a word is pronounced in the proper way and thus attuned to the different rhythms of that breath, its elementary magical power will be restored and it will range again among the forces of the Universe. Such ritual syllables, termed *mantra* in Sanskrit and *ngag* (*sṅags*) in Tibetan, enable the initiates to force their conscious principle into the middle invisible channel mentioned above, and throw it out of their own bodies at will, projecting it far away and exactly where they want. Continuing an Indian tradition, the Tibetans claim that such transfer can be operated not only at the moment of death but also in the fullness of life, not only in order to be born again out of this world, but to remain on earth. Thus the conscious principle can be moved from a person into another, or more generally from any creature to any other creature, as its transference from a human being into an animal is not excluded.

Moreover, the conscious principle may be transferred into an already lifeless body — a corpse — or into the body of a living person, in which case the latter's conscious principle must be driven away first, or, in other words, the other person killed. His soul will then follow the usual laws of transmigration and be re-embodied according to his karma.

Dealing with the thaumaturgic powers to be attained through its practice, Indian Yoga had also mentioned the faculty of forcing one's way into somebody else's body (*paraśarīrāveśa*). To this day, this practice is sometimes looked upon as black magic and therefore hardly mentioned at all, as black magic bestows demoniac power and great prestige on its adepts, but rather than guiding them to the conquest of truth plunges them into the abyss of evil. This is why popular tradition hints at it more frequently than the Yoga treatises, as fiction and entertainment are not too particular about truthfulness, add or subtract freely to their sources and merrily mix legend and science. Indian novel and short story have feasted on the subject of the change of personality due to a conscious principle's violent introduction into somebody else's body. But such stories, apart from the overgrowth of fairy tales they were burdened with later, rested on some well-known principles of Yoga.[14]

Anyway, the practice the yogis seem to care most for is what the Tibetans call *"drongjug"* (*groṅajug*) literally meaning "entering a corpse", i.e. transferring into it one's conscious principle. That naturally entails the transmigration from a body into another, but the transfer is operated volontarily, before natural death sets in. How a corpse, however fresh, can be used, is not at all easy for us to understand, as death means to our mind either the final breakdown ensuing upon a long wear and tear or the effect of a lethal injury rendering the body, even if young, unfit for further life. Should either of the two take place, we do not see how death can be avoided or life prolonged. But for the Buddhists death, rather than with the bodily conditions, is firmly connected with a moral force: karma; death's decay is but the ripening of karma, which brings about the break between the conscious principle and its provisional support — so that until the corpse has got into a state of utter decay it can still receive a new lease of life from a yogi's transfer into it. Death is not looked at as an irreparable end, but, less tragically, as a split.

The most famous example of *drongjug* in Tibet is the one of the Darmadoday (*Dar ma mdo sde*). He was the son of the great ascetic Marpa and, together with Milaraspa, his most prominent pupil. To him alone among all pupils Marpa had revealed the yogic meditation, liturgy and practice needed to effect the transfer. One day Darmadoday, who had been to a feast without his father's consent, fell from his horse on his way back, broke his head and was taken dying to his father's presence. There was no time to lose: friends and pupils entreated Darmadoday to practice the transfer. As no fresh human corpse was available, they brought him a dove some sportsmen had just killed: into it he forced his own conscious principle. The dove was revived and took wing towards India where, after fluttering about for a while, it perched on a hut where the death of a young Brahman was being mourned. Darmadoday seized the occasion, left the body of the dove, which fell dead to the ground in the sight of all, and revived the boy's body. The overjoyed parents were stunned to notice that their son had come back to life with a different soul and an unusual, baffling knowledge of the mysteries of Buddhism.[15]

After this tragedy Marpa was loath to reveal the secret of *drongjug* to any other pupil. That is how the knowledge of that esoteric practice imported from India came to an end in Tibet. The works of Marpa's master, the great thaumaturge Naropa, are extant and deal somewhere with *drongjug*; but the reader cannot expect much from such treatises, which offer but a scanty trail, show glimpses of inner experiences to which only a living master, having an eye on the pupil's aptitude and progress, can lead through the gradual steps of a suitable training.

Obviously, this practice of taking possession of somebody else's body has left a deeper imprint in the legends than in the doctrine. Nowadays the Tibetan masters still mention it as a real faculty which, however, cannot practically be exploited as the esoteric tradition is broken. The writers of novels and of the saints' lives have long made that subject their own and embroidered it in their own way. But they were drawing their facts from an ancient doctrine which for centuries had been giving the adepts a hope to be able to enter other bodies on their death, thus remaining indefinitely alive. Whatever the result may have been, many masters of India and Tibet delved more deeply into the study of man's mind and body in order to perform that miracle. They perfected the technique of breathing and devised subtle tricks with a view to awakening magical powers in us. What they found out still deserves the greatest attention of the scholars.

4 From Gyantse to the Brahmaputra

The road to Lhasa runs east of Gyantse. Along the Nyeruchu valley it skirts the green fields of Traring, a feudal holding of the Traring family, some small villages whose houses look like white clouds, ruins of cloisters and farms. This is where the Tibetans made a stand against the British troops who, after capturing Gyantse in the 1904 war, were marching on to Lhasa. That stand cost them dearly: even at that time I could notice how hard it had been to make a new start. After that reverse the Tibetans had left agriculture for jobs yielding an easier profit, or had settled somewhere else. Among those mountains each field has to be wrested from the rocky desert, carefully watered and looked after, without wasting a single day, as ploughing, sowing and harvesting all take place within the few months stretching from May to September. It was the end of June at the time and only the barley had sprouted, but the farmers were ploughing previous to sowing the peas (*trema*, written *sran ma*), with a primitive plough drawn by yaks festively bedecked with blazing red plumes. Those trappings, together with the propitiatory prayers which were said daily before work began, were meant to ward off the evil influences and to guarantee a bumper harvest.

As we went on, even those scanty patches of green grew scantier and were eventually swallowed by the sand and the rock. We were treading archaeologic ground of the greatest interest, an endless succession of ruins of villages and cloisters, especially the latter. We skirted Riboche and the two small monasteries of Ringan, and proceeded by the ruins of a huge *chorten,* around which the caravans respectfully turned clockwise: its name was "The Indian Chorten" (*rGya mc'od rten*).[16] Further on the left bank of the river the rows of 108 chortens surrounded the remains of a large monastery and of a tumbledown village, Piling. The neighbouring fields were a fee of the Depung convent in Lhasa (*ạBras spuṅs blo gsal gliṅ gi gźis ka*). We went through the small convents and pleasant villages of Gyaridon (*rGya ri gdoṅ*) and Gyatrak (*rGya brag*). The road was overhung by wrinkled rocks looking like crocodiles. Crumbling ravines, scars of incurable sores which the storms re-opened and deepened every time, furrowed the mountains from the tops. A new feeling of desperate loneliness set in, as we marched on and on under a scorching sun along the hot rocky wall, and the packmen dragged their weary feet stirring clouds of choking dust. The drowsy stillness was broken by the jangle of the bells hanging in plenty on the horses' harnesses and, in response, by the litanies of the lama accompanying me and the sing-song of the devout servants, like a grotesque funeral procession in the midst of a deafening carnival revelry. We made a halt at Gobshi, a hamlet of a few houses and a ruined fort. The place had been an important road junction, as its very name purported, meaning "the four doors" (*sGo bźi*), i.e. the crossing of four roads, the eastern one leading to Ralung being termed "the road of the Law", as it leads further to Lhasa; the southern one, running toward Nyinro (*gÑiṅ ro*), "the wood road", as timber comes from Bhutan in the south; the western Gyatrak road "the barley road", as barley is chiefly grown in the plain up to Gyantse; and the one leading north to Dochag (*rDo lcags*) being styled the "iron road". Until a few decades earlier Gobshi had been the seat (*rdsoṅ*) of a district governor. The population had subsequently dwindled down, the village lost its former importance and its rank. About one day's march southeast of Gobshi, in a mountain gorge, there is a chapel ranging among the oldest monuments of that region, named Nyinrodemogon (*gÑiṅ ro de mo dgon*). I found it lonely and abandoned, and its few extant paintings, though fairly ancient (14th century), could hardly be compared with the ones at Ivang. Worth seeing was on the contrary the Kamodon (*K'a mo gdoṅ*) monastery, belonging to the Nyingmapa red sect, and of the Serkim (*Ser k'yim*) kind, that is to say, inhabited by married monks. It is dedicated to Guruchovang (*Gu ru c'os dbaṅ*) of Lhobrag[17] and was placed under the supervision of a monk who was a direct descendant of that famous master. In the temple I did not find anything of interest but for a highly worshipped relic, a stone bearing footprints attributed to Padmasambhava.

The next halt, at Ralung, took us to a height of 14,800 ft. I could have spent the night in the house of a prominent citizen, which had kindly been placed at the travellers' disposal, but I preferred to sleep in my tent. That house swarmed with children, dogs and fowls, so that even less light sleepers than I was would have had no chance to get a wink of sleep. Moreover the court-yard was full of oxen, horses and mules and ringing with the din of their bells, a noise still resounding in my ears from the march. It was the house of Ralung's wealthiest inhabitant, who had not had a penny till a few years earlier, but only a few sheep. He had then gone into business and made a fortune in no time. While he was plying his trade his brother was staying home and looking after their estate, cattle and pack animals. Both brothers were sharing the same wife, polyandry still being practiced in a large part of Tibet. As the bride married, along with the man of her choice, all his brothers, it did not happen seldom that she ended by landing three or more husbands at a stroke. But custom and habit were guarantee of agreement, and soldiering and trade, by keeping one brother at home most of the time, took care of the shifts.

At some four miles from the village of Ralung and a height of about 15,000 ft. there is the Ralung monastery, rising at the foot of the Norjingangzang (*Nor sbyin gaṅ bzaṅ*) range which takes its name from a deity of the Nantose (*rNam tos sras*) cycle. On the barren stretch around the cloister wild goats were hopping undisturbed, and eagles were cruising overhead. Above it the cliffs bristled with sharp, jagged crags pointed like spears and as black as basalt, on which the gleam of glaciers glided. The convent, or rather the convent community, kept watch in the mountain stillness. Monks and nuns were praying and procreating here: and their children were from their births destined to be, according to their sex, either nuns or monks. This sect had had no sexual scruples at all, and ruled down that divine service and the gratification of lust could just take turns in the people's life. Even Marpa, the founder of this sect, was married, which however did not prevent him from being one of Asia's greatest yogis. As to Ralung, I could not say whether sexual love was firmly ruled by wedlock or rather left to the random choice of fancy. That monastery is one of the most famous in the area and was always regarded as one of the Kagyupas' citadels and the favourite residence of Gyarepa of Tsang (*gTsaṅ pa rGyas ras pa*).[18] One of the greatest masters of that school, Pemakarpo (*Pad ma dkar po*), a manifold writer and the theorist of Tibetan esoterism, lived there and wrote Ralung's guidebook. The cloister buildings crowd around the Tsuglakang (*gTsug lag k'aṅ*), the huge temple in the middle, entrance to which is gained by a broad porch supported by tower-like pillars, miraculously flown from Bhutan, according to the tradition. The figures of the custodians of the four cardinal points and the lives of the masters are painted on the walls. There is a flight of imposing and majestic chapels in the interior, and a huge statue of Tsepame (*Ts'e dpag med*) in the first one on the left.

The names of the Buddhist gods to whom the temples are dedicated will recur again so often in this book, that I think that a few more words for the non-initiates on the meaning of the main deities will not be out of place here. I said above that, according to the kind of Buddhism Tibet has adopted, all things visible and invisible are the emanation of a fundamental source, a cosmic consciousness, a spotless brightness which, owing to its own inner law, must expand into a manifold universe while gradually darkening and disintegrating in the process and becoming other than itself, viz. matter. I added that release was viewed as a return to the initial unity. As to the gods, they are just taken to be symbols, supports for the meditation enabling one to retrace the steps of the lost way back to that initial unity. According to that doctrine, the human mind is so shaped that it needs the help of outward signs to get a glimpse of the mystery hiding behind things and a guide on the path leading to it. The human mind must realize the meaning of those signs, not by a theoretical knowledge, but rather by an inner, lively experience of that truth, by a dramatic struggle capable of bringing about a revulsion from this to that plane. The root of all things, that spotless brightness, is often represented, in its first bent towards emanation, as Dorjechan (*rDo rje ạc'aṅ*), "The One possessed of the Diamond", a god whose name hints at the purity and unfailingness of that state; which, however, can be represented by other gods, like Namparnangdzechenpo (*rNam par snaṅ mdsad c'en po* = Mahāvairocana), the sixth cardinal point, the climax or zenith. In the next stage, this multiplies and irradiates through the five ways, which are the springboards to infinite expansion and are symbolically arranged in the form of a maṇḍala, viz. with one centre and four sources at the four cardinal points. They are the five mystical headings (ringa, *rigs lṅa*), under one or the other of which fatally all existing things will fall, and to which the archetypes of bodily and spiritual evolution correspond. That centre will take the shape of the god Namparnangdze (*rNam par snań mdzad* = Vairocana) or Mitrupa (*Mi ạk'rugs pa* = Akṣobhya) or Heruka, or Hevajra or Dukikorlo (*Dus kyi ạk'or lo* = Kālacakra, the wheel of time), Sangduba (*gSań ạdus ba* = Guhyasamāja) and more. All round will be arranged in the east Mitrupa if Namparnangdze is in the centre, or vice versa; Rinchenchoungden (*Rin c'en ạbyuń ldan* = Ratnasambhava) in the south; Tsepame (*Ts'e dpag med* = Amitāyuḥ) in the west; Donyodrupa (*Don yod grub pa* = Amoghasiddhi) in the north, each represented with his colours and attributes. Some of these gods have had a particular fortune, like Tsepame, the god of boundless life who, with his twin Opame ('*Od dpag med* = Amitābha) the god of infinite light, rules the "Western heaven", a heaven where those who do not attain Nirvana may enjoy an everlasting bliss in that god's contemplation. Man, as usual frightened by the appearance of void, is also scared of Nirvana and dreams of evading that impersonal existence and gaining the peace of serene heavens.

The sacred images of those gods and their acolytes are either carved or painted and made of several materials — wood, stone, metal, cloth — and meant to survive natural decay. But the Tibetans also carve them in perishable substances, like meal kneaded with butter.

When man gives the mysterious forces ruling the universe a shape he can understand, he likes that shape to be durable, as the god's image is his appearance and only the enlightened minds can distinguish it from the god himself who is supposed to inhabit it. Therefore using perishable stuff to reproduce godly countenances may seem to hurt man's inborn yearning to be lastingly sheltered by the protective nearness of the god.

But things are different with the Tibetans. The image does not always imply the deity's presence, as both statues and paintings are nothing but lifeless matter unless elaborate rituals called "rabne" (*rab gnas*) have led the divine spirit down into them and chained it to them with the unbreakable fetters of mighty formulas.

Nor does it ever happen that the Tibetans, as we often do, should only look at the beauty of a sacred image when this is also a work of art, and be so overwhelmed by that beauty as to stand in awe before it. Our attitude, on the other hand, may seem irreverence but it is not, as even the worship of beauty in which we forget ourselves is a revelation of godliness and a purifying ecstasy of the soul.

Tibetan art is a kind of liturgy: nobody sets hands to it who has not attuned himself to the divine worlds he wants to represent according to the traditional symbols; and it is closely connected with the ritual act. One could say it is a treatise of theology in pictures, rather a subtle construction of the intellect than a work of phantasy.

The artist is first and foremost an evoker, then a geometer and last a priest. A geometer he certainly is as the image he creates does not spring at random from his fancy, but is laboriously built according to a carefully laid-out blueprint. Outlines and proportions are inviolable: they are what they are and cannot be changed. There is no room for improvisation or individual change, as the God would not recognize himself, and man's work to compel him into an image that could not receive him would be purposeless and sacrilegious.

This goes to show that the image is the god's provisional or permanent abode, the one he or she inhabits owing to the ritual's liturgic force. But the god may as well leave mortal planes and dissolve into the mysterious realms beyond space if other rituals are performed.

The human and divine planes are neatly kept apart — the former being impermanent, the latter eternal. There is no possible contact between the two worlds. That the gods may be present among us is just due to a meteor-like breakthrough conjured up by magic — but the gods as such cannot mix with earthly caducity. That is why if the god's presence is only required for the short span of one ceremony, he is released after it and the charm which compelled him into one of his or her images is broken and the statue itself, deprived of that might, is nothing but lifeless matter again.

So do they do in India. One of the greatest feasts of the Indian calendar is devoted to the Great Mother. In her twofold form as Durga and Kali, peaceful the former, terrific the latter, she symbolizes the ups and downs of life passing through death in order to renew itself, the rhythm of cosmic change scanned by the succession of birth and decay. At the end of the rainy season the goddess is invoked to descend for a few days into the earthen statues elaborately prepared by the priests, rejoices the mortals by her sacred presence and, on the tenth day, she leaves her temporary abode again and vanishes into the throb of all living things. Then the praying crowds seize the god-forsaken image and throw it with untold of grief into the waters of the river, that the earth it was made of may dissolve and return to its original state.

The perishableness of the matter some images are made of entails therefore a parting ceremony whose liturgy should release the god. Which is quite natural, as the gods only descend into the world of men when compelled by the magical power of formulas, and the spells fetch them down from the lofty spheres where they invisibly float. In a certain sense we create the gods ourselves as they, being the boundless powers evoking from nothing all things which are, and containing in themselves the seeds of those which shall be or will never come to light, have no shape. They are impulses, vibrations, forces which weave the warp and woof of the moral and physical universe. In order to catch them, man imagines them in such aspects as are not too far away from his own experience. The form of the symbol through which we represent them is an embodiment of that which has no body, a victory of man's stubborn will over the realms of mystery; but a short-lived one, a fleeting ascendency of time over eternity, an ephemerous contact with the cosmic powers bound to fly away again soon.

On the other hand, if the sacred images carved e.g. in

butter — like the Tormas — are not likely to last long, nonetheless the Tibetans model them with great care. The reasons stated above still hold good: if the god's aspect does not correspond to the symbolic patterns which make it understandable to human beings, the god himself cannot recognize his temporary embodiment in the image and will not make it his own abode. Hence the painstaking accuracy of Tibetan sculpture and painting, that endless repetition of images being, as to colours and symbols, the deadspit of one another and giving anybody entering a temple the impression of the prodigious multiplication of numberless forms of gods, now placid and unruffled, now threatening and dreadful.

The powers these images express run like a ground swell, pervade the world like an invisible tracery. The artist, who knows the secrets of their symbols and the formulas summing up the mysterious essence of their beings, compels them to hover into sight, to take that shape under which a century-old experience has imagined them, to flash alive before him in the rapture of ecstasy. At that moment the artist's concrete personality vanishes and he is no more this or that creature afraid of human paltriness and torn by the turmoil of human passions, but Cosmical Consciousness itself, in its infinite possibilities of creation.

But the accuracy of the lines making up the inner structure of each picture or statue is not enough. Colours are as important. Most Tibetan images are painted, whether they are made of stucco, of wood or of butter, and even the bronze ones, which get a resistent coat of gilding: and gold is looked on as the synthesis of all colours and means them all.

Thus each image entails a world of ideals of inextricable complication and of religious feelings of unfathomable depth, born of subtle self-analysis, being the embodiment of an enlightened and constant meditation, the result of an insatiable eagerness to lift the veil of universal mystery.

Tibet, like India, confronts the traveller with an absurd

coexistence of conflicting features. Grim faces and sullen countenances often hide a spiritual refinement you can seldom find in Europe. You can hardly take Tibet at her face value. If you enter a temple and let your sight get gradually accustomed to the darkness, you will discover on the walls, the altars, and even hanging on the ceiling, an undreamt-of jumble of images of gods and devils which may let you think you are in the realm of gross idolatry. Tens, hundreds, thousands of deities teem and surge before your eyes, as if they had been born of those copulating images so dear to esoteric iconography, as endless as the stars on a midsummer night. They are hard to count and will at first look all alike, but a trained eye will detect subtle differences in the attitude of the hands, in the garb and the colours; and the newcomer will feel thoroughly puzzled and nearly overwhelmed by that avalanche of gods jostling him on all sides, as if every aspect of creation had perforce to be either a god or a demon. If he does not lose heart, if he talks to the monks and reads the sacred books, those images will melt before his very eyes, those gods will dissolve and that religion, which struck him as the height of a devilish polytheism will abruptly shed all its idols; the whirlwind of sacred figures will vanish like night's darkness at daybreak, and the motley crowd of dancing monsters will fade into dull emptiness. There are no gods any more. That revelling, macabre Olympus will leave its place to a religion without gods, nay, without God, to a serene contemplation of void, the revelation of impassive, mercilessly dazzling light in whose immovable blaze everything evaporates without trace. Man finds himself alone, though he is everything: as he is himself that light, not any more an impermanent being with its limitations, its daily sufferings and hopes, but an unshakable reality in its quintessential purity. When a religion dissolves even the gods, man proves to be even less than a dream-like shadow, like the moon's orb reflected on the ruffled mirror of a lake. Tibetans live and die in the certainty that truth is not in things they see, in the things that frighten, trouble, charm or delude them, but just in that nothingness blowing its frosty breath on all wordly phenomena. Asked what is at the bottom of the universal mystery, any Tibetan will answer: "Tompanyi" (*sToṅ pa ñid*), i.e. the void, nothing. That answer will be on everybody's lips, the priest's and the packman's, the prince's and the peasant's. That is why the ascetics who do not expect to be born again after their present embodiment do not seek the sacred images nor pay them any homage: they enter the temples without bowing and regard the holy things as profane, as the fire of knowledge has burned away all dross of ignorance in them. They are "soulless bodies", as their conscious principle is supposed to have vanished into nothingness already. Images will be of help to the others, who have not yet ripened and are still enmeshed in the struggles and ordeals of life, wavering between renunciation and the appeals of the world, tossed right and left by the storm of passions, craving for God and afraid of the devil. Images are a suggestion, a challenge, a hint: they remind you of that nothingness, but lead you gradually up to it. The great truth of void cannot be proclaimed all of a sudden to everybody, as it implies a fundamental upset of all accepted standards and an overthrow of all usual feelings and perceptions, as if day were turned into night and night into day. The truth of "nothingness", if taught to those who are not yet spiritually trained to accept it, will rather harm than help, just like trying to catch snakes without knowing the formula to charm them: one would catch them and be bitten to death. One could easily picture to oneself the result of such a blunt statement to mankind: nothing really exists, everything is void, vain, short-lived. Such a naked formulation of that truth would lead to wantonness and anarchy, to a ruthless enjoyment of the present in the firm belief that there is no tomorrow, instead of paving the way to renunciation, collectedness and contemplation. That goal has to be reached little by little, by a ladder provided with many rungs — and the rungs are those gods, those images and symbols which one is likely to take at their face value at the outset of one's spiritual training. Later, as one has mounted higher on that ladder, those gods will vanish. Everything is void (*tompa*).

It goes without saying that each human being's attitude towards that conception is different. For the humble pack-man it is an arduous doctrine on which he entertains no doubts, as the masters have taught him so, but whose mechanism baffles him. For the lamas, especially for those who face the hardships of ascetic life, *tompanyi* is the absolute truth, it is reality, a certainty which the daily experienced materiality of things cannot discount. And as the world is apt to trouble one's mind with its sensuous appeals and the renunciations one has to force on oneself, those lamas have recourse to a practice meant to give them a direct, concrete experience of the vanity of whatever belongs to the world of change and appearance. In the dark fortnight, when night's mystery and terrors are deeper, they retire to the fields where human corpses are exposed, beat a drum made of a human skull, play a flute made of the shin bone of a sixteen-year-old girl, put on a robe plaited with human bones and patiently painted over with images of terrific gods, and shout at the top of their voice evoking those monstrous deities and rousing deep, long echoes in the lonely darkness. They have long realized intellectually, through their books, that no such gods exist. But any idea is a reality in itself if it has only been thought of, and those gods are present in their traditional shapes in the minds of the evokers. No wonder if the power of suggestion in that dark, silent desert is such that the images of the gods actually appear before the hallucinated eyes of the lamas made of less stern stuff, and if quite a few cannot bear the sight of those ghosts and are driven mad with fright or die in a fit of terror. However, most of those lamas get properly accustomed to that training of giving a concrete form to the images of a phantasy not yet bridled and purified by esoteric knowledge. The next step in the training is to dissolve them again, thus realizing that everything is mirages and dreams and that the human mind is but the source of all images. Only the wise ones can tame it and put an end to the pageant of phantasms the mind arouses and creates according to its whims. The ascetics devoted to that practice, which is styled "chod" (*gCod*), i.e. "cutting off" the cosmical delusion, always wander in loneliness or retire into hermitages. One cannot live in the world and look at it in that way. No midway solutions are possible: living among people will make short work of those heroic strivings — and the ascetic will either succumb to passions or, even worse, strike a compromise.

But to return to the Ralung temple. Near Tsepame I saw Dugparinpoche (*ąBrug a rin po c'e*), the founder and master of the Dugpa sect. On the right was Śākyamuni (the historic Buddha) between the two disciples Śariputra and Maudgalyāyana and the gods of medicine, who appeared again in a smaller chapel behind the latter. At the further end, in the centre, was the main cell, devoted to Champa (*ąByams pa*), i.e. Maitreya, the future Buddha. Eagerly, the guides suggested I should also visit the temple of Drolma (sGrol-ma), dedicated to the compassionate goddess supposed to succour anybody who invokes her in danger, and the one of Dorjechan (*rDo rje ąc'aṅ*). One of the most precious objects kept there was a gilt bronze lamp shaped like a lotus flower, on each petal of which an image was carved. When the lamp had to be put out, the petals could be folded up as in a real flower, by the means of hinges. It was of Indian origin and dated from the 12th century or thereabouts. On the upper floor the images of the Dugpa (*ąBrug pa*) lamas were worshipped: it was a regular gallery of statues constituting the "lamegyü" (*bLa mai rgyud*), the row of saints, of earthly people in whom the highest master embodies himself. In the vault or cupola upstairs, called Utse (*dbu rtse*), I saw Dorjechang in the aspect of the one truth transcending its ephemerous, if endless, manifestations. He too was surrounded by "lamegyüs", as only the master can make the redeeming knowledge bear fruit.

The Gonkang (*mGon k'aṅ*) is the innermost recess of all monasteries, where the *yi dam* of any sect is worshipped, i.e. the terrific aspect its main deity assumed in order to fight the hostile powers that might try to defile the purity of the place. Around the *yi dam* crowd all the guardian spirits of the convent, those whose anger should not be roused, and whose favour is constantly prayed for by specialized lamas alternating in round-the-clock services, in a dismal singsong dotted by drum beating. On visiting a convent it is first of all advisable to make a money donation (*shaldep*, *źal adebs*) in keeping with the number of monks. Besides, the visitor should perform the pious ceremony of lighting a lamp (*mar me* or *źu mar*) on the altar of each chapel, either by buying the clarified butter personally in advance, having one of the sextons pour it in a large vessel, and dishing out a spoonful into each of the votive lamps, or by paying the Konya — the keeper — to do the above. It will moreover be proper to purchase the ritual "katag" (*k'a btags*), a homage scarf to be reverently placed on the most worshipped statue. In a Gonkang, a "serkyem"[19] had rather be offered for the propitiatory ceremony of the gods who have been disturbed from their solemn quiet, at the end of which the keeper offers the visitor some holy water or some *chang* from the *bum pa*, a long-spouted, round vessel, into the hollow of his outstretched hands, that he may quaff the sacred beverage and sprinkle the last drops on his own head. This will secure him the *chinlab* (*sbyin rlabs*), the blessings of the conciliated deity. Some alms should besides be offered on the plates full of barley or rice lined up on the altars. The Gonkang is Ralung's oldest temple, and a chorten in its centre guards the mortal remains of Chorje Shonnu Senge (*C'os rje gŹon nu seṅ ge*). I saw some largely deteriorated but important frescoes depicting the lives of a few masters of that school. Of a Tibetan temple the Gonkang is the part most likely to impress the traveller, as everything there breathes mystery and fear, and the terrific images prevail to such an extent as to weigh like a nightmare on anybody entering into the chapels. A thrilling, but uncanny tenseness grips him as the flickering lamps suddenly elicit from the darkness improbable figures bristling animal-like with arms, with several heads, devilishly sneering, dancing in lustful copulations, shaking with destructive rage. A deadly shiver seems to be running through those images, though on closer scrutiny they do not really prove frightening. Some Egyptian statues, in whose mysterious stiffness there is the glint of a ruthless cruelty, can really haunt your dreams, as those steely features conceal an unflinching will baulking at nothing and ready to bend anything. Their expressionless silence and their numbness will chill you.

In the Tibetan images there is the rhythm of dance, a sense of movement, of death paving the way to renewed life: their destruction will create again. There is an echo of dancing Shiva, of that cosmic power alternatively dealing out death and life and offsetting both in its embrace. If those images therefore had baffled you first, your impression may improve on acquaintance, as you will feel they have a meaning, and a bearing on the fabric of the universe. You will be able to understand them and, in doing so, to see through them. They will dawn upon you for what they are, the outline of an elemental world where things have not taken up yet any final shape but are still struggling for it, with sudden repentances and recoils, where the human and the beastly, good and evil are co-existing in bud. You will then feel nearer this people, who still lives so close to the hub of things and disposes of a clairvoyance shedding light on the riddles of the subconscious and discovering there "armies of angels that soar, legions of demons that lurk", a foamy turmoil of powers only Buddha's word can set at rest, by dissolving those images into Nirvana's peace. But until this comes to pass, man always find them standing in front of himself, because he himself is bringing them to life; those images are the projection of his innermost individuality, the active fragments of his interior life, the shadow of his thoughts that follow him until he dies out in the mystery of that nirvana.

Another remarkable temple I saw was devoted to Dorjesempa, with paintings showing the succession of masters and, on the door's side, the protectors of the cardinal points, the four Gyalchens (*rbyal c'on sde bži*) — all of the 18th century. Some five hundred yards further from the monks' city a great isolated Kumbum rises, slightly smaller than the Gyantse one but, like the latter, full of frescoed chapels inside. Their date is known, as in one of the upper chapels, devoted to the eleven-headed Avalokiteśvara surrounded by the school's masters, one could see the picture of Sonamtobgye (*bSod nam stobs rgyas*), Tibet's regent from 1728 to 1747. He was a liberal patron of religion, and he had the Kangyur and Tangyur, the two main Tibetan Buddhist sacred books, printed in more than three hundred volumes at the Narthang monastery, near Tashilhumpo.[20] He too hailed from Tsang, from the Drungpola (*Druṅ po lha*) valley which turns west from the Gyantse-Shigatse road; he was named Pho lha nas from the name of his fee. His picture was to be seen in the frescoes as well as in the wood prints illustrating the stories of the *Avadānakalpalātā*, a chain of Buddha's life stories, which he had engraved at Narthang. An inscription to be read under the pictures hails him as "the exalted, saintly king, through whom the creatures' happiness and welfare are promoted and the teaching of the Buddha's law gains ground in the whole Jambudvîpa", i.e. in the whole world.

The way from the upper floor leads through the chapels of Śamvara, Hevajra, Guhyasamāja and Kālacakra, gods who, though worshipped by other schools as well, are the particular *yidams* of the yellow sect. Clearly, when Pho lha nas reconstructed the Kumbum, he endeavoured to leave in it lasting imprints of the sect that had won and made him its patron.

The guide then took me to the other chapels, to the one of Tsepame, the god of infinite life, recognizable through the vessel of ambrosia he carries on his joined palms; and to another Gonkang, its walls dark with black and yellow figures ascribed to Pemakarpo by tradition but, for the reasons stated above, likely due to a later hand.

After visiting the Kumbum, a lonely guard to the lonely slopes sagging further down to the Nyinro gorges furrowed by a short cut to Phari, nothing was left to see but the Potrang (*P'o braṅ*), the building where the abbot lived and where images of Tsepame, together with the ones of Pemakarpo and other masters of the sect were kept.

We left Ralung by a road winding around the Norjinkangzang, climbing the Karola (16,800 ft.) and squeezing through huge expanses of glaciers hanging over it as if they were ready to collapse at any moment, and yet quietly reflecting glimpses of the blue heavens. An endless road, on which we had to do two days' march in one, twenty-seven miles at a stretch, as there was no fodder for our pack animals.

Gentle downward climbs were followed by a long succession of flats all looking alike, all dusty with the slow crumbling into sand of the humped mountains standing guard over them. Distances were measured by the postmen's relays, amounting to five and a half miles on a good road, and five miles only on a bad one. At such various intervals stood the postmen, armed with spears festooned with mules' bells and ready to take over the bag from their comrades and to carry it up to the next station (*dak*), thus ensuring a round-the-clock forwarding of the mail. We stopped for two days at Nangkartse (*sNaṅ dkar rtse*), a dilapidated fort watching over the unruffled mirror of the Yamdrog (*Yar ạbrog*) lake and the surrounding flooded meadows. We had to change horses there, and I could not leave the place without seeing the Samding[21] monastery, built by Potopa Chogle Namgyal (*P'yogs las rnam rgyal*).[22] That convent is famous on account of the incarnation of the goddess Dorjepamo (*rDo rje p'ag mo*), "the hog-headed One", supposed to dwell there uninterruptedly changing her mortal form. Never fear: the god-

dess' mortal mirror does not look that dreadful and was, at
the time, a pretty girl of 13. The pilgrims were just gathering for the feast which was to take place within a few days
(the 11th, 12th and 13th day of the fifth month). Three
garishly caparisoned horses stood patiently in the sun,
listening to the monks' chant and smelling the incense
being burnt in their honour, as they were supposed to
impersonate the protecting spirits of the place (*gži bdag*)
and had to be propitiated twice a year. They were known as
"luntangonpo" (*rLuṅ rta sṅon po*) and their respective
names were Phurburagpa (*P'ur bu rags pa*), better known as
Trashi obar (*bKra śis 'od ạbar*), the most important of the
three, Shinkyongbapa (*Śiṅ skyoṅ lba pa*), and Dritsangshag-
pa (*Dri gtsaṅ zags pa*).

The goddess, to whom I was presently introduced, received me very affably and, laying her hands on my head,
bestowed her blessings upon me. We exchanged scarfs and
gifts. The central image of the largest temple represented
Śākyamuni (the historical Buddha) surrounded by eight
standing Bodhisattvas, in a style like that of Iwang, though
certainly later. Some faded paintings between the statues
dated from the 16th century. The Gonkang resembled an
armoury, its walls and pillars bedecked with swords, spears
and armours. According to the tradition, they had all been
captured from the Dsungars when, on their invasion of
Tibet, they tried to plunder the temple and were driven
away with great losses.

The monastery was a flight of smaller and bigger temples. Huge silver shrines set with semi-precious stones held
the relics of the goddess' various incarnations, the bones
and the dust of illusory bodies harbouring an eternal spirit.

All around, in the endless plain slumbered the black tents
of the Drog pas, nomadic shepherds roaming about with
their herds and flocks, who speak a peculiar dialect and
have no home. At Nangkartse I found an old acquaintance
of mine, who was a mere child when I met him first in 1935,
the son of the then district commissioner of Davadzong. He

recognized me at once, as meeting a European is an event those people never forget. Nangkartse had been a small feudal holding mentioned in the local chronicles, its main claim to fame being its relationship with the Chongue princes, whose descendant, the daughter of the Nangkartse prince, gave birth to the fifth Dalai Lama. A baked-earth statue of her is kept in the fortress temple, built above the ancient palace; a likeness with strong, marked features pointing to a bold nature, like the one of her son, who was undoubtedly one of Tibet's outstanding personalities. But the Nangkartse temple has much suffered from ravages and wars. Only a few gilt bronze statues of the golden age of Tibetan art had been saved. Some were doubtlessly of Indian origin. In the Gonkang I could see some ancient painted scrolls of the 15th and 16th centuries on one of which the image of the donor, probably one of the Nangkartse princes, was painted. The guide showed me a room in the fort where the fifth Dalai Lama allegedly lived and left his foot prints. The Lundup (*Lhun agrub*) temple, built on a crag two and a half furlongs from Nangkartse was also worth seeing. It belonged to the Kagyupas, or rather to their branch, the Potopas. The Buddhas of the Three Times (*dus gsum sans rgyas*), viz. Dīpankara, Śākyamuni and Maitreya, were worshipped there. The gilt wood halo of the middle statue reminded me of the ones I had seen at Narthang. In the temple and in the Dukang (*adus k'an* = assembly hall) I saw several good bronzes, some of which were certainly from Nepal.

The Lundup monks officiated in the Samding convent. The family of the Nangkartse princes was already extinct at the time like all other families who had ruled over the several provinces of Tibet at different times.

Past Nangkartse we skirted the Yamdrog lake for two days. The lake was as still and as deep blue as the sea can be at Naples on one of those days when heaven and earth seem to clasp each other in an embrace of love. The gentle lapping of the waves on the pebbly shore and the sea-like

smell, so unusual in that pitiless ocean of mountains, roused
subtle memories of home and left me dreaming. Between
Nangkartse and Pede a road for Tashilumpo branches off
and heads for Rimpung (*Rin spuṅ*), once an important
feudal state ruling over the whole of Tibet. At Pede, where
the ruins of the fort are reflected in the large expanse of
water, two caravan roads for Lhasa branch off. The one
crosses the Kampa la and is blocked on the 15th June, when
the river swells with the rains and the ferrying becomes
dangerous. The other one crosses the Nyapso la. I was still
in time to follow the former, and went by way of the Kampa
la, leaving the gleaming lake at Tramalung, a small village
resounding with the cackling of ducks and coots. The road
made for the Kampa la pass, short and easy on the south,
steep and endlessly long on the north side. We met more
frequent caravans now, and all of them armed, as they
expected unpleasant encounters. A wedding cortege also
came our way. The bride, entirely wrapped and hidden in
her garments, as if to join her one or many bridegrooms
incognito, was going to Nangkartse accompanied by her
mother and the bridesmen carrying the ritual arrow festooned with white ribbons. Her horse strutted in a silken
yellow shabrack embroidered with blue dragons, the other
horses had less showy red harnesses. I could follow them all
the way from the pass, as their gaudy colours brought them
into relief against the barren rock as soon as they started
down from the top. The cortege spent the night at Tramalung and would be at Nangkartse on the next day. Then the
bridesmen would intone the traditional songs and sing the
girl's praises in front of her house, and the bridegroom's
family would retort singing their own glories from the window. The bride would eventually enter her new abode and a
banquet would seal the wedlock.

5 On the Road to Lhasa

Beyond the Kampa la the landscape began to change little by little, and at a bend of the road the Brahmaputra appeared. The Tibetans call it Tsangpo (*gTsaṅ po*). Its course is slow, as if the river wanted to stare admiringly at the green fields dotting the yellow expanse of the sand banks. The stream emerges into the valley from a narrow gorge guarded by the Karag massif (18,000 ft.), its steep, black rocky face crowned by gleaming glaciers and white clouds. In the two highest tops, confronting each other across the valley, ancient mythology saw and worshipped a divine couple.

I pitched the camp and lay for a rest on the bank of the river which I was seeing for the second time since August, 1939, when I rode its blustering spate from Lhasa to Puntsokling, entrusting my life rather to Tibet's tutelary gods than to the yak-leather coracle. Now the same river was as peaceful as a child's dream, though the rains would swell it again to a furious torrent in a few weeks. That valley is engaged in a relentless struggle between life and death. The water streaming from the mountain slopes and seeping underground from the river pours lavishly into the earth's veins and feeds liberally the green hopefully glittering in the sun, but the lurking rage of floods and sand storms threatens its life at any moment. Swift whirlwinds would suck up that sand now peacefully resting on the rocks and pour it down to form dunes again elsewhere. The mountain peaks were staring impassively around, as if nobody had ever climbed them and only the daring of the Western mountaineers could violate them. Yet, on every peak there was a *lhabtse*, a heap of stones on which the prayer banners fluttered, where the *shidag*, the mountain god, was supposed to live. If not properly appeased, he could shatter the rocks and hurl them down with frightful booms. Thus, in order to build the *lhabtse* and to worship the demons, the Tibetans do some mountaineering too.

At Chaksam (*lCags zam*) we crossed the Brahmaputra on a thick raft. Once there was a suspension bridge from which the place draws its name,[23] the wooden planks resting on two thick chains hooked on two pillars. Now the planks were gone. Such a piece of engineering still filled the Tibetans with admiration and pride. It had been the work of a Tibetan who lived in the fifteenth century: Tanton Gyepo.[24] He must have been a practical and active man, especially an excellent engineer: but in Tibet, where everything turns to religion, even the technician became an ascetic. Tanton Gyepo is now known to history as a saint and a worker of wonders. Anyway, Tibet owes her largest bridges to his initiative — not a little merit in a country where the number and the violence of rivers are one of the greatest obstacles to communications. A picture of Tanton Gyepo the ascetic is treasured by the Chaksam monastery, built to keep watch on the river. The central body consists of the Dukang, the assembly hall, where there was nothing special to be seen. It had been often repaired and often botched, but in the chapel on the far end the Buddhas of the Three Times attracted my attention. They had been recently restored and repainted and, as Tibetan art sticks faithfully to its iconographic patterns through the centuries, the groundwork of those figures preserved a certain primitive force which is seldom seen nowadays. The same applied to the images of Tsepame and Chenrezig on the right wall. The best piece was a splendid Bodhisattva statue standing behind and right of Tsepame. It had all the grace, the composure and the delicacy of a Ming Chinese statue, and its expression and features were Chinese as well. Chaksam, an unavoidable road junction, had been the theatre of many battles and the monastery had suffered in consequence, and it was sheer luck that such a statue should have been saved to bear witness to the ancient splendour of the place. I could not see anything else worth of note in this Nyingmapa convent, and even the small Kumbum dedicated to Tanton Gyepo did not contain much of artistic interest, but only brand-new paintings and recent images. After visiting the four chapels on the first floor, the visitor may take his life in his own hands and mount to the cell in the cupola by a shaky staircase in order to have a look at the portrait of a man with a swarthy face and a pointed beard like a Chinese: that is how tradition represents the great engineer-ascetic. But there was nothing else, and the convent had no printing press.

After crossing the river the road ran towards Chushul (*C'u šul*) in a succession of endless screes and green oases, which took us down to 11,600 ft. Near Chushul the Kyichu river (*sKyid c'u*), flowing down from Lhasa, joined the Brahmaputra. There were a handful of wealthy houses, willow and poplar thickets, gleaming expanses of barley and wheat, a luxuriant growth of mustard, sprinkling its yellow on all that greenery, and on the fields rows of women busy husking rice. High up, on the inaccessible ridge of a mountain spur, were the ruins of the fort. Chushul had been an important and therefore disputed place: as the key of the roads leading into India and Bhutan it had changed hands very often. Following that path must have meant courting death at every step, as it leapt from rock to rock and squeezed through between the boulders the fury of the river had torn from the mountain. Instead of building a passable road like the present one, the Tibetans of old thought it enough to cut prayers or invocations in the stones or to carve the images of helpful deities in the larger rocks, and to appease or check the mountain demons responsible for the fall of those boulders, that good may prevail on evil. Not unlike them, the Italian peasants used to stick a rough wooden cross into the soil in order to ward off hail.

The inhabitants of Chushul had all gone to a neighbouring monastery for the yearly celebrations and I found the village empty. As it is well known, religious festivals are not always just the occasion to lift up one's soul to God. People often keep the recurrence as if it were a relative's birthday, they put on their best things, eat, drink and make merry; and the spiritual rapture is soon drowned in more earthly enjoyments. At Chushul too people started laying offerings on the altars and ended by drinking. A brawl ensued and a monk was injured. Soon the rumour went around that he had died, but it was subsequently ascertained that he had merely been stabbed in a buttock. The culprit was apprehended and led to the district magistrate office while the crowd clustered around eagerly looking on. He would be kept in jail for about a week and eventually get a hundred lashes on the back. Frightened by the impending punishment, he squealed the whole night.

I was some twenty miles away from Netang, the last but one stage of that pilgrimage. The narrow path squeezed on among the threatening boulders carved and inscribed with more images and prayers, still skirting the Kyichu river in whose whirlpools the azure sky was reflected. But in spite of that plentiful stream the sand banks prevailed on the fertile soil. Villages were rare and farming scanty, with the only exception of Tsa. Netang appeared soon, and at last a range of mountains hovered into sight which seemed carved out in the sky. They were the mountains of Lhasa. With my field glasses I could see the hermitages above the Sera convent. A few snow-white clouds look like immovable canopies spread to protect the Holy City.

Netang is a famous place in Tibetan history. One of the greatest apostles of the Buddhist renaissance died there on his way back to India. His name was Dīpankara Atīśa, and he had been born of a noble family in Western Bengal, at Vajrayogini, where I was myself in 1926, a small village in the exuberant plain, near a pond on whose banks rises a ruin overgrown with moss, perhaps the remains of a Buddhist temple where Atīśa moved his first steps in that religion. Later he became one of the beacons of the famous Buddhist university of Vikramaśīlā and his fame reached Tibet. A prince of Western Tibet invited him into his own kingdom that he may preach and spread the Buddha's word. His worship of Atīśa went so far that he refused to ransom himself, as the highwaymen who had captured him demanded, with his own weight in gold, and had this sent to the Indian master instead, to induce him to come to Tibet. After spending some years in Western Tibet, Atīśa moved to the central part of the country and died in old age at Netang in 1054.[25] Three temples are extant there, but the wars which raged so often around Lhasa and in that valley did not spare them.

The first temple one ought to visit is the Dolma Lhakang (*sGrol ma lha k'aṅ*). In its first chapel Atīśa's robe is preserved in a gilt bronze *chorten*; in another one the mortal remains of Marpa, Milaraspa's master, are shown. A chapel dedicated to Goddess Tārā's twenty-one manifestations follows. All statues are of gilt bronze, seated in the position prescribed by iconographic rules, and covered with a silk drapery. In that chapel, dating back to the great master's times, his guardian goddess, whose worship he spread in Tibet, could not be missing. In the middle of the same chapel I saw a standing statue of Maitreya of the late Pāla period; behind him, and still at the centre, a large Buddha, brought from India according to tradition, with a wooden halo carrying visible traces of Nepalese painting reminiscent of manuscript miniatures. The third chapel is devoted to the Buddhas of the Three Times, each of them flanked by his acolytes. Eight standing Bodhisattvas like the ones of Iwang, four of them on each side, look on impassively. Though the Netang images cannot be ascribed to the same age as the art of Iwang, they are fairly ancient despite restorations.

The Kumbum Lhakang, two and a half furlongs off the village, is a middle-sized, yellow-washed building. It was erected to guard two large *chortens*; the former on the right of anybody approaching Netang from Chushul, topped by a rounded cupola, is the older and the better preserved one. Large festoons are painted in dark colour around it, with thickly drawn outlines like in the Gyan Kumbum I studied in my 1939 expedition.[26] The *chorten* on the left is more irregular. According to tradition, each *chorten* should contain some *ts'a ts'a*, baked-earth cakes moulded with the images of gods.[27] But it is not to be excluded that those contained the great master's mortal remains. In the middle there is a chapel where pictures of Atīśa and his favourite pupils, Dronton (*qBrom ston*) and Nagtso Lotsava are worshipped. On the walls all around were displayed endless pictures of Drolma, portrayed green with jet black hair and sharp red outlines. There is a third temple nearer the village, dedicated to the 16 *arhats*. In its middle I saw statues of Śākyamuni flanked by two standing Bodhisattvas, fine bronze works whose graceful composure left no doubt as to their being of good Indian school. One statue had lost its feet, and it was easy to surmise that the whole group must have been the remains of a larger cycle involved in the destruction of the temple. Stucco images of the 16 *arhats* of the old cycle, to which were added as usual the figures of Hvaśaṅ, a Chinese monk, and Dharmatala, all of a much later production, surrounded the former.[28] In the Gonkang there was a picture of Shenyen (*gŚes gñen*), a pious person the tradition connects with Dharmatala.

The temple keepers were two devout old folks, simple souls to whom God spoke directly through the images and symbols they were capable of understanding. One was a monk of the Depung monastery, and candidly stated that his mind felt lost in the subtleties of the doctrine. "I am a poor block-head," he used to say, "as my brother keeps telling me all the time. He is very learned and has read many books — but I cannot do anything but pray". Pray he certainly could, as was shown by the collected light shining in his eyes — and he was perhaps nearer God than his theologian brother. He would not discuss God's attributes, but only gather His blissful light into the depths of his soul.

There was something idyllic and serene in the air of that green plain. The sky larks were warbling, and the shepherds escorting their flocks to the sound of flutes. Just a spot to forget the world and sink into meditation.

6 Arrival in Lhasa and First Calls

The road from Netang to Lhasa runs up and down the rocky slope leading to the banks of the Kyichu river and comes further to rest on a water-logged, sand-strewn plain. At a bend, a hill-like heap of stones marks the spot where the adoring pilgrims can get the first glimpse of the Potala's gilded spires. Each pilgrim is supposed to say a prayer at that moment and to throw a stone to raise the heap. We turned clockwise round the heap as it is done in Tibet when skirting anything sacred. The packmen took off their hats, loosened their long pigtails fastened in top-knots on their heads and let them hang before their chest, on the left side, just as they did when they entered a temple or spoke with people of rank. We went by the Takta monastery, whose incarnate was the Regent of Tibet at the time, and by Depung which scatters its convents and chapels by the dozen, in close formations, to conquer a narrow valley. On the green plain we could plainly see the monks, the apprentices and the servants of the convent sunbathing or swimming where the river widened and slowed down in canals, backwaters and ponds. The red robes discarded on the ground looked like big ripe mushrooms. European books harp on the subject of Tibetan dirtiness, but I know other countries whose inhabitants could vie with the Tibetans without having the extenuating circumstance of the climate on their side. Also in Tibet cleanliness depends on temperature and height, but when it is hot people are not water-shy and splash lustily in it like ducks, which reminds one of India.

Towards noon we reached the Potala. Rather than a palace, this is a hill in itself, an outgrowth of the rock underlying it, as irregular and whimsical as nature's work, yet built with such inner consistency that each corner and each line falls in with a necessary plan, as it were, and gives you the impression of order where waywardness prevails. It has grown with the stone like a diamond sticking to its matrix. Its main body is red, framed in a white setting and crowned by glittering golden cupolas and pinnacles above. Our caravan filed off past the Potala, reeled to and fro and broke its ranks at the sight of an elephant, a gift of the Maharaja of Nepal, which put in a sudden and solemn appearance, turned towards the river and stopped in the Gyavolinka, a shady park of willows and poplars.

The town of Lhasa spreads west of the Potala palace and stretches up to the line of trees fed, and sometimes uprooted and wrested away, by the river. Soon after my arrival, I was met by young Namgyal Traring, a relative of the Maharaja of Sikkim, who had been detailed by the Government to be my official guide during my stay in Lhasa. He had been educated at Darjeeling, spoke excellent English and had the lordly, refined manners of Tibetan aristocracy. He was a "senampa", i.e. a son of noble family. He wore a dark purple robe of Chinese silk, a long gold and turquoise ring on the left ear and on his head the *bokto*, a small yellow wool headwear, narrow at the rim and broader in the dome, a kind of pan-shaped cap fastened with an elastic ribbon under the chin, and swinging with each movement on the top of the head, the officials' headgear of daily use. At variance with the private citizens and the populace, their hair is not left hanging on the shoulders or plaited into one tress, but parted in the middle and braided into two pigtails right and left, which are clipped and held together by a gold and turquoise brooch over the crown. Off duty, the civil servants wear a simpler robe, the cloth and colour being left to their personal choice, and the *bokto* is replaced by a fur-brimmed hat whose high dome is covered with Indian or Chinese damask. European hats were forbidden in Lhasa by a Government ordinance meant rather to preserve the custom than to protect local industry. The civil servants were therefore often followed by a servant carrying the garments to be worn and discarded according to the occasions and circumstances. As respect of the local fashion had been prescribed to the ladies as well, these too were accompanied by maid servants carrying, like a trophy, the *patruk*, i.e. a kind of triangular diadem fitting the nape of the neck and sporting large coral and turquoise beads on a lacquered frame. The *patruk* being, however, too cumbrous, many ladies would rather do without it.

The house allotted to me consisted of two rooms looking out into a yard, the kitchen on the front, on the left the keeper's quarters, on the right the servants' quarters. From the window I could see Mount Bompori overhanging Lhasa, but as soon as I left the compound I could admire the Potala's grave majesty and the Sera settlement enlivening the mountain north of the town with its rambling white hermitages. On the day of my arrival everybody was singing and making merry: Lhasa had been changed into a playful city, the atmosphere of worship having given way to a wordly abandon. It looked like a fair. The meadows and the river banks were bristling with Chinese tents of all kinds and sizes. From time immemorial, the people were keeping the fifteenth day of the fifth month and pouring out of doors to celebrate, followed by a motley crowd of ownerless dogs, a stray, hungry second town living, barking and dying in the shadow of the first. It was like the camping place of a people on the move towards new dwelling grounds, noisy and happy-go-lucky. They were having baths, playing dice, drinking *chang*, dancing and singing. Even a casual visitor had to share this fresh, childish joy unknown, for instance, to India, where a pall of dreariness weighs like summer heat on everything, and the sun burns but does not shine, drowned as it is in a haze of dust. Here the sun made itself felt for a few hours, but then one could breathe again; it cheered but did not scorch, it played tricks with light and shade on the mountains and frisked on the golden domes of the temples.

I had to stay indoors for one week as the gifts I had purchased for His Highness the Regent were still on their way. As one's visits to the Dalai Lama and the Regent had to take place on the same day and one was not supposed to go empty-handed, there was no other course to adopt than to shut oneself in and wait. It would have been a breach of respect to go about town without having previously been blessed by the country's highest spiritual authority and granted an audience by the temporal power. Namgyal Traring and I took advantage of this forced delay to draw up lists of the people to ask for an interview and of the gifts to make to each. Though mine was a private visit, I could not disregard custom, and each visit called for the offer of a scarf and various gifts according to the visited personage's rank.

There are at least three kinds of scarfs, called respectively *nangdso* (*naṅ mdsod*), *ashi* (*a śe*) and *doshe* (*mdsod śe*). The first is of the finest silk and this was the kind I intended to give the Dalai Lama and the Regent; the second is silk as well, but of a lower quality; and the third of a coarser cloth. They were so much in use that they were sold by the bolt, and all came from China. The price varied according to the quality. Some *nangdso* cost up to twenty rupees, i.e. about £. 1/10, or some four dollars. On visiting the person meant to receive the scarf, this is rolled up, to be unfurled swiftly on the very moment of the meeting so that its middle lies on the outstretched palms, from which it glides into the host's palms, likewise outstretched. Host and guest bow gently as the scarf changes hands. The gifts are laid aside on a platter and never handed over directly. Particularly appreciated are guns, especially revolvers, watches of good makes, cameras and wireless sets. The Indian and Chinese missions had their own engines to feed the wireless stations, but a central power house was being built at the time some six miles east of Lhasa, meant to supply the whole city with electric light. For the time being they were working at the water reservoir. The machinery had not yet arrived and the power house was expected to work within two or three years. The old power house, entrusted to the care of the late Ringang, one of the four young Tibetans Col. Bell took to London to study many years ago, was out of commission by the time. The building of the new power house was supervised by the wireless operator of the Indian mission and by one of the two Austrians who fled an internment camp in India during the war, crossed the Himalaya, roamed adventurously for two years in Tibet and reached Lhasa, where the Government, after some hesitation, gave them employment. In the meanwhile, short of electric current, the sets owned by the wealthy people were kept going on batteries bought in India. To close the list of welcome gifts, also fountain pens and field glasses were appreciated. I regretted not to have brought fingernail rouge and lipstick, which were in great demand with ladies. Anyway, the upshot of my long huddle with Traring and my Geshe was that, after having been received by the Dalai Lama and the Regent, I should visit the former's two tutors, the chamberlain, the Regent's treasurer and the Shapays (*Žabs pad*), the three cabinet members. Then I should, of course, pay my homages to both foreign secretaries, as I explained above that there were two of all public officials, one being a monk and the other a layman. The monk belonged to the special class of church officials, Tsetrung (*ts'e druṅ*) and the layman to the Kuta (*sku drag*), the aristocracy, who had the right and the duty to participate in the administration. Even the army's commander-in-chief had as his colleague a monk whom I met some years ago at Gyantse in the capacity of Tibetan trade commissioner. All offices were shared like this, in keeping with the duality of forces ruling the country, monkhood and the feudal gentry. Moreover, the discharge of religious or civil duties was not thought to be conflicting with trade, but on the contrary as conducive to it. Therefore everybody traded in everything. Wool was exported into India, and from India came cotton cloth, damask, household equipment and chiefly aluminum vessels, which were gradually replacing copper ones and threatening to deal a death blow to ancient craftsmanship and its masterful achievements. A few goods, like hats, corals and cloth, came through India from Italy.

Though trade was still flourishing, its peak had been reached during World War II, when Tibetan caravans had been carrying cotton and all kinds of cloth from India to Likiang in Yünnan. A great deal of cotton was still at the time going to Sining, two or three months' journey northeast of Lhasa, thus crossing a great part of Central Asia, from where silk, much in use for the clothes of the dignitaries and their wives, was imported into Tibet. The Kham and Yünnan roads were still open to the traffic of tea, a coarse, leaf-and-stem kind, welded into heavy lumps by a jet of steam, which the Tibetans consumed in amazing quantities. The three or four millions of them, whatever their precise number was, swallowed up more than twenty million pounds of tea per year. I could notice that time that tea was also often drunk in the Western fashion in the houses of the gentry and of the high church dignitaries.

Thus engaged in various palavers with Namgyal Traring and with the Geshe my week of seclusion was soon over. Its monotony was also broken by some visitors. Kukula, the daughter of the Maharaja of Sikkim, was a young woman who to her prettiness and personal charm joined a remarkable education, spoke English and French fluently and had a smattering of German. She lived in Lhasa as the wife of one Punkang, a member of a *Yapshi* (*yab gži*) family, viz.

one of the families into which a Dalai Lama had been born. Whether such families were rich or poor, as soon as they were blessed with so happy an event, they were granted an estate to be held in fee, which would secure their welfare ever after. There were five or six such families in Lhasa: Punkang being the one of the eleventh, Lhalu of the tenth and twelfth, Samdub Potang, Landen and Yutok of other Dalai Lamas. The holdings of the present Dalai Lama's family were at Chayul (*Bya yul*) in the South and at Drongtse (*ąBroṅ rtse*) near Gyantse.

Another pleasant visit was the one of Major Kaisher Bahadur, the Minister of Nepal, whom I had met at Kathmandu in 1935 when he was an official of the Ministry of Education. He had shifted to diplomacy now.

The Kipug (*sKyid sprug*), the official interpreter, also came to see me. He would join Namgyal Traring to accompany me on my official visits and look after the etiquette. He was another one of those young Tibetans Col. Bell had taken to London to be educated, and spoke therefore excellent English. He was on half pay (*zur pa*) now, which did not quite imply that he had retired from active duty, but rather that his effective position had been taken up by a younger colleague.

I only allowed myself one breach of my voluntary seclusion, on the occasion of the summer festival, *linka*, which had begun on the fifteenth day of the fifth month, with everybody streaming out to have a good time in the gardens or on the bank of the river. The celebrations started with a ceremony having the *Chokyongs* as its main actors. *Chokyong* (*c'os skyoṅ*), which should literally mean "guardian of (the Buddhist) Law", is actually a person into whom a god is supposed to descend for the occasion in order to express his will, to give advice and to forecast the future. The most renowned *Chokyong* is the State one, residing in the Nechung monastery. But the two *Chokyongs* present at the Lhasa celebrations, where I ploughed the sea of people under the escort of Traring, belonged to another convent.

The more authoritative of the two sat on a higher dais and most of the people thronged around him. He was wrapped in drapery of Chinese brocade and wore on his head a golden tiara on which human skulls were carved, with eyes of ruby. His assistants were liberally ladling *chang* down his throat off golden goblets. He was in a trance, and alternately snored, panted and rolled his eyes. The scarves the people offered him he returned at once, as if he had been in a hurry. He mumbled some strained, hardly audible words, gave his advice and foretold the future through vague signs and dark hints. If anybody handed him some barley he would puff on it groaning and hand it back. All the while he sweated as if under a heavy strain. The people were admitted to his presence in small groups, while the crowd shuffled and surged impatiently. The precedence was given to the carpenters and bricklayers, who held in Tibet the rank of public officials, as could be seen from the yellow *boktos* they wore. The state mobilized them, whenever needed, to carry out public works, but they would have had to stay idle till the end of that year as the ban on building had not yet been lifted. This was due to the Nechung *Chokyong's* and the astrologers' forecast that that year would be an unlucky one for the Dalai Lama. Building implies digging and therefore disturbing the quiet of the *Lus* (*klu*) and *Sadags* (*sa bdag*), the powers watching underground. That is why it had been forbidden to undertake any new construction work till the end of the ominous astronomic conjunctions.

Oracle-giving was followed by a restless, violent dance, atwitter with shaking fits and sudden jerks as if the *chokyong* had been tossed by an inner invisible power.

7 Visiting the Dalai Lama

Paying a visit to His Holiness was a complicated affair. The ceremonial to be followed was far from being simple and I was afraid that, in my instinctive disregard of routine, I would make a mess of it. Before reaching the age of eighteen and starting personally to rule, the Dalai Lama did not usually grant formal interviews. My visit had been fixed for 9 a.m., as he was expected to attend school at his two teachers' one hour later. The apparel I should wear for the occasion had been the subject of a long argument between the Geshe and myself. He would have liked me to wear the Chinese tunic and the Mongolian boots, but I am a born enemy of any masquerade. Though I had come into Tibet in a spirit of devotion towards her religious traditions, I could not forget my Western birth and could not, without feeling hopelessly ill at ease, discard my usual clothes, even if they were not so fine and showy as the Tibetan outfit. That is why I paid my call on the Dalai Lama in European dress, wearing the best suit I had taken along.

At eight o'clock we were all riding towards Norbulinga, the summer headquarters where the Dalai Lama would stay till September. Before us rode the servants carrying my gifts. The Norbulinga was a great park shadowed by willows and poplars and surrounded by a seven ft. high fence. The main entrance was guarded by two stone lions and some sentries who ranged themselves on one side as they sighted us and, at the command of an officer, stood at attention. They were clad in khaki with a wide-brimmed hat like the one of the Gurkhas. A few days later I saw the police march past to the sound of a Scottish march. Past the gate we entered an alley at the end of which the Dalai Lama's palace could be seen. A new palace was being built at the time, taller and more sumptuous, with great display of gold and garish colours. All around straggled the houses of the officials and the servants; further, the Regent's palace could be seen. First to meet us was the Gronyerchenpo, His Holiness' chamberlain of the private household. He descended of one of the most noted families of the Gyantse area, the Palhas, most of whose goods were seized and most of whose members executed towards the end of last century because they had received and favoured Sarat Chandra Das, who was clandestinely touring Tibet at the time with a view to collecting facts for the *Geographical Survey*. The Gronyerchenpo was in his forties, a tall, distinguished, lively man wearing spectacles, a rare sight in Tibet. He was the highest official of His Holiness' private household, comprising a large number of dignitaries, from the Zim pon (*gZims dpon*) and Sö pon (*gSol dpon*), looking after dress and food, up to the Tsedronyer and Shaptopon. He conducted us into the waiting room, a kind of open verandah on one side of the Dalai Lama's palace. Traring, the four servants and I sat on a row of cushions. Shortly afterwards we saw the monks celebrating their daily office file out into the same verandah. One lama was reading aloud in a book and others followed him intently. Those were monks destined to the higher ranks; some would become the abbots of great monasteries, others church officials. Crouching among the psalmodizing priests was also the commandant of the guards, clad in khaki and wearing a sun helmet. After some twenty minutes' waiting, and many cups of Tibetan tea, we

were sent for. We fell into line with the ranks of church
dignitaries waiting for admission to the Dalai Lama's, crossed with them some chambers lined up with the lamas
reciting their office and streamed out into the audience hall,
in a blaze of gold. At its further end, on a throne reaching
up to a man's shoulder, in statue-like immobility, the Dalai
Lama sat, wrapped up in silk and damask drapery. On his
side was a low table holding a cup, a lamp and some flagons
for holy water, all of them of fine gold. His eyes were gazing
with sharp inquisitiveness at the foreigner whose unwonted
garb was set off against the red of the lamas, but his eyes
were the only thing about him that moved at all. We laid
our hats on the ground, bowed thrice, put our hats on again
and fell in with the rest. The servants had already presented
the gifts by handing them over to some assistants. When my
turn came and I found myself in front of His Holiness, I
promptly unfurled the gift scarf so as to have both ends
hang for an equal length from my hands turned palms
upward and holding it right in the middle. A monk on my
left handed me in succession a statue, a book and a relic
holder, placing them on the length of the scarf resting on
my hands. In my turn I handed them over to the Dalai
Lama, who took them from me and passed them to an
assistant on his left. This ritual, followed by all those who
were admitted to the Dalai Lama's presence, was meant to
establish a mysterious contact between the visitor and him.
The statue, the book and the relic holder symbolized the
three planes any human or divine being consisted of : the
bodily, the verbal and the spiritual ones, supposed to be
respectively localized in their transcendant essence in the
head, the throat and the heart (*sku gsuṅ gtugs*); their changing hands pointed to the two people's mystically meeting
beyond the flow of changing things. Having handed them
over, I took my hat off and bent my forehead. The Dalai
Lama blessed me by laying his hands on my head and
binding a red scarf around my neck. I then proceeded
towards a lower throne on the Dalai Lama's right, on which

the Regent was seated, the Takta Incarnate, Tibet's effective ruler till the Dalai Lama would come of age. The Regent was over seventy years of age and his impassive appearance contrasted with the fourteen-year-old Dalai Lama's glistening, inquisitive stare.

I could notice the strikingly clever expression of that boy, who had already given proof of a remarkable brightness in the logical disputations, a subject in which his tutors were training him. He hailed from Jyekundo, in the Amdo district towards the Chinese boundary. They had gone all the way to Reting to fetch him and had escorted him with great ceremony and merry making to Tibet's religious and political capital, into that many-storeyed palace bearing the name of Potala, the paradise of compassionate Chenrezig, the god who succours the creatures drowning into the whirlpools of life and especially protects Tibet, his favourite country.

The dignity of Dalai Lamas is not a very ancient institution. On paper it began in the 15th century, but it asserted itself in practice a hundred years later, when the old military aristocracy collapsed in Tibet and the religious sects began to dispute the country, till the Yellow sect outstripped them all. Supported by the Mongols, that sect succeeded in securing political power, and its head, formerly just another monastery abbot, woke up to be Tibet's spiritual leader and temporal ruler. To increase his prestige, the support of the scriptures was invoked to maintain that the Dalai Lama, viz "the master of the ocean-wide wisdom" was the earthly manifestation of Chenrezig who, though staying in his heavenly abode, projected on earth ephemerous reflections of his remote majesty, just like the sun which heats and fecunds the earth from its unattainable heights.

He is therefore supposed to be the temporary embodiment of a god, one of his projections, called upon to lead, comfort and improve sinful, suffering mankind, and to teach the way to release. It is throughout the same being who sits on the Lhasa throne in successive embodiments. The secret person, the spiritual reality of the Dalai Lama, is immutable and only his body changes, a perishable vessel employed to reach down to the lowly human level and to make the dazzling light of the truth he embodies accessible to our limited understanding. When the Dalai Lama falls ill and passes away, the Tibetans do not say he has died, but "he has shown the way how one dies". God is absolute life; but by the decay of the flesh, which gave the divine spark a temporary abode, he reminds man of the destiny of everything created and undergoing birth, that man may turn his thoughts towards eternity.

But one should not believe that the Dalai Lama is the only incarnate. Tibet is brimming over with them, even as truth reflects in a thousand lights spreading it everywhere and kindling everything with its flame. There is no monastery of some importance where such epiphanies are unknown, and though they are less noted than the one of the Dalai Lama, they are not held to be less holy. They are Bodhisattvas too, that is to say, they have renounced extinction in Nirvana's remote peace to help and comfort by their presence mankind hardened in its evil ways and wrapped up in the darkness of ignorance. On my journeys into Tibet I met dozens of them, heads of centuries-old monasteries, supreme leaders of sects in which the secret wisdom of India and Tibet is still faithfully handed down from master to disciple and, to tell the truth, I always had the impression I was confronted with people out of the common. I was not so much struck by their doctrine as by the spiritual gentleness of their judgements and by their detachment from the world. They were worthy specimens of a noble race of men growing in the shade of convents, amidst the barren wilderness of the Roof of the World.

But any incarnation is limited by the natural end of human life. As that god is supposed to embody himself over and over again, how would people recognize him when he has discarded the old vessel to select a new one? First of all, he is not certain at all to re-embody right after his previous death, and several years may intervene. There was for example a gap of three years between the 13th Dalai Lama (the last) and the present one.

During the gap Tibet mourns temporary desertion of the divine presence; prayers are said and divine services performed in all temples to invite its descent. Then experienced monks go in search of the boy. He must bear the Buddha's own tokens on his body, which, according to the traditional lists of the bodily features of the Enlightened One, are thirty-two main and eighty-four secondary ones. In practice only a few are heeded, especially the following: the legs' skin ought to be striped as a tiger's; the eyes wide and the brows turned outwards; the ears large; two fleshly excrescences should be found near the shoulder blades, as a token of the two extra arms of Chenrezig, the god whose earthly embodiment the Dalai Lama is supposed to be; last, the palms should bear the pattern of a sea shell. The presence of such features, which is tested, tried and checked by the most authoritative lamas, is a first guarantee and should bear out the forecasts made beforehand by the Samye and Nechung oracles, when the famed wizards of those two temples fall into a trance and, possessed by the divine spirit, give the first dark and blurred hints as to the time and place of the new incarnation.

When the boy's identity is proved beyond the shadow of a doubt, he is solemnly conducted to Lhasa, where the final test awaits him: among numberless objects of the same kind shown to him he must pick out the one cup, the one book and the one liturgic instrument he used in his former embodiment. This custom, whose positive result is confirmed by many eye witnesses, has nothing miraculous about it, as the boy is probably helped by the thought of some of the lamas attending the test. Transmission of thought is an art in which the Tibetan masters are very proficient as they train themselves in it also in order to convey mysterious doctrine and initiation secrets to each other without having recourse to writing.

When the last test has been stood, the boy's education begins. As a God he is doubtlessly omniscient, but once he has assumed a human body, he must adapt himself to human customs in everything. Nothing is hidden from him, yet he too must conform to the hard training of school as any mortal body.

Those children wrested from their families, subjected to the strict supervision of elderly wardens, compelled to parcel their day between the attendance of rituals and the recitation of holy formulas, led through the endless maze of lamaistic liturgy and dogmatics and plunged forcibly into the ponderous works of their former embodiments, certainly do not know the blissful astonishment of childhood: the destiny weighing upon them as heads of a church and rulers of a people shuts them off from that free world of fancies and dreams any child creates and destroys like a wizard around itself. Renunciation is easy for elderly people, as it means giving up what one knows already, more often what one is fed up with. The persuasion is then easily reached that many things are of no use, that many a desire only contributes to make life more bitter, that quite a few hopes wither into disappointment. But when we are young we are led by a nearly physiological instinct to figure the world different from what it is, as the whims of our fancy would have it, and renunciation looks extremely hard to us as it implies giving up things which may never come our way again. Such strict discipline, such statue-like immobility as the dignity of that office imposes, the daily intercourse with gloomy, elderly people, look to me like a violent, ruthless suppression of childhood. That is why I actually believe there should be something exceptional in those boys, born as they are with the dreadful burden of a saintliness which must be reached and lived up to at all costs.

Sometimes the monkish upbringing and the pitiless strictness of the wardens do not however succeed in curbing a fiery and rebellious nature. When the fifth Dalai Lama,

Lobzang Gyatso, died at the end of the 17th century, the Regent kept his death secret for many years and spread the rumour that the holy personage had withdrawn into retirement to meditate. His purpose was to keep the reins of government in a moment fraught with difficulties for Tibet, when the Mongolian and the Chinese threat loomed large on her horizon. In the meanwhile and with the help of faithful advisers he had the new incarnation secretly traced up and saw to the boy's education, ready to announce the event as soon as the political circumstances would allow. But the situation took a turn for the worse. The Emperor of China heard of the plot and asked for explanations. The Mongols, allied with the Regent, were collapsing under the blows of the Chinese armies, and the sixth Dalai Lama, then in the prime of his youth, was compelled to ascend the throne of Lhasa against his will. He had no bent whatsoever either for politics or for religion. None of his predecessor's virtues had been renewed in him. He loved merry fellowship, preferred pretty girls to learning and love songs to liturgy. To the wardens' and subjects' shocked surprise, instead of devoting himself to meditation he wrote poems in which his worldly passions found a fresh and immediate expression and flowed into a stream of melodious verse.

"Was this girl born of her mother? Wasn't she rather born on a peach tree? But her love withers even sooner than a peach blossom. Though I know her slender body, I cannot fathom her soul.

"Yet we hardly need trace a few lines on earth and the distances of the stars in heaven are thoroughly reckoned".

The Tibetans were at a loss what to think. True, as our scriptures say, the ways of Providence are endless and unfathomable, but one could not very well understand how the Potala's austere precincts could shelter a god with such an unusual, whimsical character. Astonishment soon grew into rebellion and poor Jamyang Gyatso, who would have gladly discarded those draperies and struggled free of a discipline dampening the ardours of his soul, in order to

enjoy life and attend to his poetry, was soon done away with
by the Chinese. But that was an exception. Some of the
Dalai Lamas, devoted to things spiritual, spent their years
in meditating or writing on theology and liturgy, turning an
altogether deaf ear to political events; others, when Tibet
fell under China's control, were a mere tool in the hands of
the Chinese *ambans* and were all mysteriously made to die
before they could grow into riper years and dream of independence. The fifth and the thirteenth soar above the
others not only as writers of sacred matters, but also as
politicians.

After the ceremony described above we sat for a few
minutes on a row of damasked cushions in front and on the
left of the Dalai Lama. We were offered tea, and rice to be
carried home — sacred food, as the child sitting in front of
us was not a common mortal for the faithful, but a god. It
should not be overlooked that just on account of that blind
faith of many millions he represented a force to be reckoned
with, as it had centuries ago, in the history of Asia. The
god-like atmosphere surrounding him was, as it were, the
concretion of his follower's worship, who came all the way
from Tibet's extreme boundaries and from Mongolia, not
walking, but prostrating at every step. They had been lift-
ing their joined palms to the height of their forehead, their
throat and their chest, meaning the three planes I have
mentioned above, then falling flat to the ground and tracing
with their hands a sign where their forehead had been.
Then rising again and placing their feet where their head
had been they had prostrated again, and again, and again
for hundreds of miles, walking for months, protecting their
hands with wooden boards strapped to their wrists, uphill
and downhill.

Namgyal Traring rose, walked to the middle of the hall,
placed his right knee on the ground and, bending his left
one, drew out of the folds of his robe the bowl in which the
Tibetans drink their tea. Calmly, he unfolded the length of
coloured silk in which it was wrapped, handed it to a monk

who poured some tea into it, then slowly lifted the bowl to the height of his head, as if to offer it to His Holiness, drank up, replaced the bowl into his robe, laid his hat on the ground and kneeled thrice. It was the survival of an ancient rite, when the officials had to taste in turn the food destined to the Dalai Lama in order to ascertain that it was not poisoned. In spite of this precautionary measure, after the first conquest of Tibet at the hands of the Chinese nearly all Dalai Lamas died inexplicably and at a very young age.

Thus the ceremony came to an end and we filed out of the hall, where the four gigantic *zinga* (*gzims bgag*) stood behind, the guardian lamas, towering with their huge bodies and watching with the might of their muscles over His Holiness' safety.

8 Civilian Authorities — Temples and Bazaars

The Regent, the effective head of the State till the Dalai Lama comes of age, was usually chosen among the abbots of the four greatest monasteries (*gliṅ*) of the Yellow sect in Lhasa or in the immediate vicinity: Muru, Kundeling, Tsomoling and Tsecholing. Those abbots were entitled to the Mongol style of Hutuktu. There were exceptions, as the Regent then ruling Tibet had been the abbot of Takta, not too old a convent a few miles west of Lhasa. Of course he was an incarnate too, namely the same being who, after each body's natural decay, descended on earth again and again in a new one. Like all incarnates he bore the name of his own monastery followed by Rinpoche, meaning "the gem", and being due to them only. He lived near the Dalai Lama and above the Norbulinga's great chapel, full of glittering golden statues.

The ceremonial of my visit to the Regent was very simple. After the usual prostration I sat in front of him and on his left and answered his questions. He wanted to know about my country, our opinion of Buddhism, the books I had read or translated, the number of people spiritually interested in Buddhism in Europe. They were the precise questions of one accustomed to think clearly and schematically about everything. Obviously he was a ruler who had given proof of his ability to cope with difficult situations when serious events had troubled Tibet in the previous year.

It was a strenuous day. After being admitted to the Regent's presence we went to see the two *yondzins*, the Dalai Lama's tutors. One of them, the Ganden Trichanrinpoche, was the Ganden monastery incarnate, a slender, tall, ascetic figure. He was one of the greatest authorities in logic and theology. As his title reveals, he was a Tipa (*K'ri pa*) viz. he sat on the Ganden abbot's throne, and a Chanchubsempa (*byan c'ub sems dpa'*), a Bodhisattva. Besides, having attained the peak of human perfection by dint of self-discipline and study, he was one of the seven Tsannyishabchis (*mts'an ñid žabs p'yi*), or one of the seven masters teaching the young Dalai Lama logic. He was a very learned man, and I could only wish he had had more leisure in order to be more often with him. The other *yondzin* was Yondtsinling, the greatest incarnate of Depung, His Holiness' main teacher, the one on whose shoulders the heavy responsibility of his education rested. As learned as his colleague, he was, however, more in touch with the world, and I could sense that beside his knowledge of sacred things he was possessed of political cunning and sharpness of judgment.

Our day ended by a visit to the Chandsod (*p'yag mdsod*), the Regent's administrator, who did not fill a very important position but, on account of his daily intercourse with Tibet's supreme authority, naturally had a big say in the matter. And it was quite a pleasure to meet him, as I found him an open and hearty, educated and affable fellow.

On the next day I went to the Shapays (*žabs pad*) "the feet's lotuses". They formed the Kashag (*bka' šags*) or Cabinet, and there were three of them, as the fourth had been sent as a Governor to Eastern Tibet. The eldest was Rampa Kalon Lama, a church official with a commanding appearance and a Chinese-fashion scrubby, white beard. He wore a monk's robe and a red tunic under which a Geshe's yellow doublet could be seen. The second Shapay was the Kapshupa and the third, the youngest of the three, was the Surkhang, both laymen. The Shapays were the highest officials of Tibet, only topped at times by the Silon (*srid blon*), the premier. But that office had lately shrunk to a mere name and the Shapays were directly in touch with the Regent, to whom they reported on each single question after dealing with it. The final, irrevocable decision lay with the Regent. Sometimes, when matters of great consequence were being discussed, also the Chikyab Chenpo (*spyi k'yab c'en po*) took part in the proceedings: he was an intermediary between the Dalai Lama or the Regent on one side and an ecclesiastic chancery, *yig ts'aṅ*, on the other, a body of four men dealing with all church affairs, appointing the different monks to the ranks to be bestowed by the Regent and the Chikyab and holding a supreme control on all monasteries, only Depung, Ganden and Sera excepted. The members of that church chancery were styled Trungyig Chenpo (*druṅ yig c'en po*).

The management of finance was entrusted to four Tsipon (*rTsis dpon*), who looked after the revenue in kind, revenue in money falling under the control of another office. There were also four Tsechags (*rtse p'yag*), three of them monks and one a layman, administering His Holiness' treasury; and four Lachags (*Lha p'yag*), likewise mixed, managing church property. The Foreign Office, in Tibetan Chigyalekung (*p'yi rgya las k'uṅ*), was a fresh institution, consisting of two ministers called Dsasa, one a layman (the Surkhang Shapay's father) and a churchman the other (styled Lyushar), assisted by a monk (*mk'an c'uṅ*), one layman (*rim bži pa*) and three lower officials. My visit to the Shapays took some arguing and planning, as I wanted to find out whether it was more advisable to see them together in their office or to visit them separately at home. The latter course was chosen, as we thought this would keep the conversation informal. The Shapays lived all in large, many-storeyed houses looking out into wide courtyards lined with stables and saddled horses. The horses are Tibet's motor cars: dignitaries never walk, but always ride, followed and preceded, according to their rank, by one or several servants wearing a large, basket-like hat with red woollen fringes. The interior decoration of those houses was after the Chinese fashion, but along with the large, damasked cushions and the Chinese beds and tables also European furniture and equipment could be seen. The officials wore broad tunics of yellow Chinese silk embroidered with dragons and girt by a red sash at the waist. Their way of gesturing and talking was lordly and refined. They spoke softly, in a flowery language, sometimes hardly understandable for a foreigner. In Tibet there are about three languages, or three degrees of the same language. There is the common way of talking among friends of the same rank, the honorific form of speech and the very honorific one, this last being used among others to address the Regent and the Dalai Lama. Asking e.g. a person of rank how he was, I should have called his body "kutsu", but talking of myself simply "ku". For my servant my hand was "chag", whereas his hand for me was "lag"; while asking the same servant to go, I would say "dro", but "peb" would have been proper for a nobleman, and "chibgyunang" for somebody of an exalted rank. This made any conversation with Tibetans very complicated. If a foreigner should feel out of his depth in that welter of words and idioms, he had better employ an interpreter. Conversation is not only a way to exchange ideas, but an exercise of rhetorics, which cultured people enjoy like a work of art.

Those visits were a sort of test for me. But after passing it, I felt surrounded by friends, at home, as it were, and was considerably helped in my research work.

Lhasa means in Tibetan "God's own country" and it certainly is a blessed spot compared with the barren rockiness of most of Tibet: the town lies in a wide, well-irrigated valley, green with luxuriant fields, dotted with willows and poplars. The mountain at its back protects it from the north winds, and in the winter the houses looking south drink in, through their heavily screened verandahs, all the light and warmth of a sun sailing in a blue sky. In the summer, with the exception of a few hours, it is never too hot. In July, the weary tail of the monsoon comes over from India, discharges plentiful rain and turns in a few days the desolate yellow rocks into an emerald scenery, with the help of the lively sun shining between showers. Lhasa was not a very great town at the time. It was hard to say how many inhabitants it could have: probably between twenty-five and thirty thousand. But a continuous come and go of caravans, pilgrims and beggars trickled into the city and out again, like an irregular flow. Some of them had come to stay. A very mixed crowd could therefore be met in the streets and, beside a majority of Tibetans, Lhasa counted some three thousand Nepalese, two thousand Chinese and several Ladakhi Muslims who had settled in Lhasa in full religious freedom since many generations and were called Kache. Among the Tibetans themselves you could find a variety of types: the Dokpas and Horpas, nomadic shepherds of the northern table-lands, the southern Bhutanese and the inhabitants of Kham, each with their own costumes and their own finery. All this crowd filled the bazaars and kneeled in the temples. Bazaars and temples were the skeleton of the city, and life, incongruously embracing earthly profits and heavenly rewards, moved and throbbed around them. Above the houses, soaring as high as the sky above the earth, gleamed the golden spires of the Tsuglakang and the Ramoche, ascending heavenward like a prayer.

The Tsuglakang is Lhasa's cathedral: the Jobo is worshipped there, an image of Buddha which, according to tradition, was presented to the first converted Tibetan king by a Chinese emperor whose daughter that king had married. Actually, it is not that old. Some writers reported that the Jobo was a hideous image, but one should not forget that statues get a new coat of paint every year in Tibet and thereby lose their original design. An endless, three storey high flight of chapels surrounds it, decorated with the smiling and sneering Buddhist pantheon. Blissful and terrific gods fill the shade of the cells and peer unexpectedly out of their mystery. But for the finely carved pillars of the porch, obviously the work of Nepalese craftsmen of the golden age, one would think at first sight that the Tsuglakang was a modern building. The frescoes decorating the walls of the circumambulation corridor and showing one hundred and eight stories of the Buddha's previous and latest life according to the very popular Kashmiri poet Kṣemendra's *Avadā-nakalpalatā*, as well as the cycles of the thousand Buddhas of the Bhadrakalpa, or the picture of Gusrikhan, the Mongolian prince who consolidated the power of the fifth Dalai Lama, are all modern. In fact, they were commissioned by the thirteenth Dalai Lama, but very probably after the trace of pre-existing pictures. Beside the Jobo, whose frame, pillars and throne are stylistically very interesting, the statue of Champa (Maitreya), worshipped on the top floor, is worthy of note. Remains of the older paintings could be found on closer scrutiny in some of the chapels. They are mere fragments, like the ones to be seen above the lintels of the Nepalese porch. But for the most part, and even in that case, the coat of smoke laid by a few centuries may let those paintings look older than they are in fact. I had as close a look at them as I could in the scanty light of torches and came to the conclusion that they could not date further back than the 15th or 16th century, perhaps to restoration works undertaken by the fifth Dalai Lama.

Among the relics, I was shown a bowl which is said to have belonged to the great king Srongtsengampo, kept in a kind of silver pitcher on which the date *16 rab ạbyuṅ me k'yi* (1946) could be read. The Tsuglakang was as crowded as the railway station of a large city. Pilgrims were kneeling in the porch before throwing themselves to the ground hundreds of times with their arms wide open, hitting the floor with their foreheads.

The Ramoche is the second temple in order of importance after the Tsuglakang. According to tradition, it should also have been founded by one of the wives of Srongtsengampo. There may be something in it, but then both temples should have been at first much smaller. When the temples were widened, or in other words when the two front porches supported by the massive wooden columns with the Nepalese carvings were built and the two main statues consecrated, is still an open question left to future research. In the Ramoche I discovered a gilt-copper plate inscription on the facade of a Sedon shirine. The plate was divided into several embossed squares, one showing the tree of life rising from a vase filled with the water of deathlessness and a few others some stories from Buddha's life. It is a Nepalese work I should attribute to the 15th century. The inscription could confirm or discount my theory — but I was not allowed either to copy it or to make a cast of it: I could only photograph it, and the very unfavourable light and the lack of the distance needed to get a sharp focus made the inscription illegible in the picture. Anyway, from the study of the statues and their halos, which I made on the spot in the dim light of the flickering lamps, I brought back the impression that the Jobos were far less ancient than tradition would have it, and I think that neither the Nepalese sculptures nor the statues date further back than from the 12th century A.D. The Ramoche is built on the usual pattern: from the front porch, on which the four protectors of the cardinal points are painted, one's way leads into the main hall, on whose walls frescoes not earlier than the 18th century are displayed. On the wall to the right of the visitor is painted the likeness of Pholhanas, the Regent mentioned above. On the far side a Jobo not unlike the one of the Tsuglakang is enthroned, to which homage is rendered by turning clockwise around it in the circumambulation corridor.

Not very far away is the temple of Tsepame with a statue of the god in the cell and, on the wall, the thousand Buddhas of the Bhadrakalpa, all alike.

While touring those temples, it would be advisable to have a look at the Gyabum Lakang (*rGya ạbum lha k'aṅ*), a temple built, as its name purports, where a great battle was fought between the Tibetans and the Chinese and the latter, according to tradition, lost some 100,000 men (*ạbum*). But the temple is also known under the name of Shitro (*ži k'ro*) as it is devoted to the peaceful and terrific gods appearing to the dead person's conscious principle in the interval between death and dissolution into cosmical consciousness, in the case of saints, or rebirth among men, beasts and devils, as it is the lot of the sinners. The temple had been restored when I visited it, and was dominated by the statue of Padmasambhava, whereas the walls showed the frightening procession of the Naragtondus, the powers of hell assisting the god of death.[29]

Another temple worth visiting is the Muru, devoted to the Chokyongs (see above), to whom the safety of the whole of Tibet is entrusted. As such, the temple is officiated by all three sects, the Reds, the Yellows and the Saskyapas. When the destiny of the country was at stake, theological strife was put aside and all schools agreed on the necessity of placating the tremendous forces lurking everywhere.

Its upper floor, the Dsambhala temple, displayed a great Śākyamuni with a stucco halo on the central wall and the eight Bodhisattvas standing around him on the right and left walls. Those works were carried out at a not very early date on the model of ancient statues, after a pattern repeated without change everywhere in central Tibet and obviously in the trail of a remote tradition whose oldest specimens are found at Iwang and Nenying. The standing Bodhisattvas, solemn, wrapped in a broad drapery often reproducing Iranian designs, pointed to artistic currents which were introduced into Tibet from Central and Western Asia, at the time of the conquests in the 7th and 8th centuries, and further enhanced by the presence of artists from Sinkiang, whom the political events had forced to seek sanctuary in Tibet.

Sight-seeing around Lhasa may be concluded with the Chakpori, on the top of an isolated hill between the Norbulinga and the Potala and looking north at the Kundeling (*Kun bde gliṅ*) monastery. It is consecrated to the gods of medicine and is, at the same time, a medical college. The path leading up to it is as steep as the ascent of heaven, but the sight from atop is an ample reward, as the eye can scan the whole Kyichu valley, down to where the river widens and flows slowly between its green banks. The town of Lhasa can be embraced at a glance, stretching down from the Potala and resting in the sun. Like other convents, the Chakpori, too, lends itself to defence and has been therefore the middle point of many a battle, thus losing most of its art treasures. In sculpture, only a few good pieces have escaped destruction. Medical college though it is, the Chakpori inclines to cure illnesses rather by prayer than by real therapy. The intervention of the gods is invoked to restore the balance of the humours.

The Potala palace is way out of town, on the hill from where it dominates Lhasa while shimmering with its numerous domes in the dazzling sun, as if to belittle with its brilliancy the dull yellow rocks below. It was built about two and half centuries ago, in troubled times, when Tibet was threatened by two dangers: the Mongols and the Chinese, till the latter prevailed and conquered her. It is as mighty as a fortress, and one is filled with awe when looking up at its cliff-like ramparts. Great flights of steps force their way into the forbidding walls, the doors gape like wounds opened into those masses by an unflinching determination, relenting further on into broad yards, and spending itself like a weary stream into a myriad of steps, stairs and alleys which cross the whole building from the ground floor to the top and violate the mystery of the chapels and the mausoleums harbouring the mortal remains of the thirteen Dalai Lamas in a splash of gold and in pompous grandeur. The people's devotion has materialized into gold. Tibetans are fond of gold and money, yet, as the most coveted and cherished things, they sacrifice it on the altars, a solidified prayer, as it were. Obviously this surfeit of glitter and finery bewilders and distracts one's attention, and the welter of enticing details, flashy arabesques and profuse tracery is not conducive to that thoughtful collectedness which bids the visitor bend his forehead before the tombs of saints.

Yet, the crowds of pilgrims daily ascending the stairs of the Potala were a tangible proof of devotion. Rich or poor, dignitaries or peasants, they kneeled before each image: faith and ecstasy could be read on their faces. Holding copper pitchers full of clarified butter, they went to feed the temple lamps. I could notice again that religion was felt there as nowhere else on earth: it swayed the whole life, it controlled the calendar, inspired art left its imprint on each thought and in each work. So must have been Europe in the Middle Ages.

By a lucky coincidence I happened to vist the Potala on the fourth day of the sixth month, when all chapels were open. This only happened once a year: otherwise most temples were shut or even sealed. The Dukang, the assembly hall, as huge as a city square, has a solemn, impressive air. Mighty pillars mark out a square opening in the ceiling, from which the hall draws hardly sufficient light. Curtains of Chinese silk cast slanting shadows on the floor, where long rows of cushions lie waiting for the monks to gather for the ceremonies. As the Dalai Lama was not there everything was desert and looked like the inside of a mysterious tomb, lit at times by the flicker of the gilt pictures. The guide led me from chapel to chapel, particularly lingering in those which sheltered the remains of the past Dalai Lamas. But the Potala had been plundered several times in the first half of the 18th century, when Chinese and Mongols fought for Tibet's control under pretext of securing peace and protecting her spiritual leaders, and little was left of the palace's fabulous wealth or its ancient monuments. In the chapel guarding the mortal frame of the fifth Dalai Lama a small silver chorten is said to harbour the relics of Chan-chub Ö (*Byaṅ c'ub od*), the king who invited Atīśa to preach the Buddha's word in Tibet in the 11th century. Another chapel sheltered the most precious works of art contained in the whole Potala, three statues from the Kirong (*sKyid sgroṅ*) temple on the border of Nepal, transported to the Potala in order to protect them against Nepalese inroads. Unfortunately I could not pass any judgment on their age and value as they had been entirely swathed in cloth wrappings, which was usually done with very precious or highly worshipped statues. Near one of Potala's ends the cave opens where according to tradition King Srongtsengampo (*Sroṅ btsan sgam po*) retired to meditate. A Nepalese statue of Maitreya watched over the darkness of the place.

The richest chapel was the one of the thirteenth Dalai Lama, who died in 1933. The lamps were massive gold, the holy water bowls gilt silver, set with precious stones. The whole of Tibet had sent her tribute to this exceptional man, the most outstanding in her history after the fifth Dalai Lama. In his youth he leaned towards Russia and was open to the Buriat monk Dorjeief's influence, a policy which led to the Anglo-Tibetan war of 1904, when the British entered Lhasa and the Lama took refuge in China. In 1912 he took advantage of the collapse of the Chinese Empire to proclaim Tibet's independence. From then on, though following a strict policy of isolation, he leant upon Great Britain but trimmed so successfully as to wrest a high degree of autonomy for Tibet. China, on her side, never gave up her suzerainty over the Land of Snows.

At variance with what other travellers reported, I found the Potala clean and well-kept. Some chapels were so smart and spruce as to remind me of Japan. Yet, as I said, but for a few exceptions the Potala does not harbour many note-worthy monuments and would disappoint the archaeologist and the art historian. Too often had the Mongol hordes led their inroads from the Penbogo pass in the north, beyond Sera, to plunder Lhasa. It is the destiny of all capitals, especially the religious ones, where the faithful seem to heap up treasures only to entice the unfaithful to come and loot them.

The bazaar surrounds the temples on all sides, most of the shops being run by Chinese and Nepalis. Tibet is indebted to India for her culture, religious life and literature, but civil life showed already a deep Chinese imprint.

The garments, most of the furniture, the household equipment and even table manners had been borrowed from China. Some streets of Lhasa could have been mistaken for quarters of Shanghai or Hongkong.

I went to the bazaar the first time on the day when I paid my homage to the Dalai Lama. Even at that late hour, the bazaar was full of bustle and din: people were running after one another with pitchers and vessels full of water, dousing and drenching everything and everybody around among loud peals of laughter. The monsoon was late, the whole country was tensely waiting for the rain, and that was a way to attract the downpours by sympathetic magic. The monks had begun reading the sacred texts and the Gaton (*dGa'gdoṅ*) oracle had been consulted, had fallen into a trance and forecast rain for the next day. Twenty-four hours later the monsoon crossed the mountains and a violent cloud burst soaked the parched fields.

9 Life in Lhasa

After crossing such a bulk of mountains, the monsoon reaching Lhasa is a weary one. Violent downpours are followed by bright clearings and idle barrages of clouds sail around the sky dampening the light, without breaking into rain.

The people seemed to enjoy that warmth, and the river banks were snowed under white tents from which smoke rose. Everybody plunged into the waters, work being reserved for the winter. The merchants — and all seem to be merchants here — were having their rest. It was too hot for them and their animals, the rivers were in spate and fording was risky. They were waiting till cold would set in order to set out for India or China again. The wealthy were having a good time and inviting one another for five or six days at a stretch.

Sometimes such social events were compulsory: every official at the outset of his career was expected to give a party of four or five days on end to all other officials present in Lhasa. The celebrations would of course start in the morning and end in the evening. One could count on an average of two hundred guests and, as each of those would at least bring two servants, some six hundred people had to be catered for, which entailed such an expenditure that many families could not afford it. Another ceremony prescribed by custom was a public riding test where the young officers had to hit given targets with a spear, an arrow or a sword while in full gallop: the name of such a practice was *drunkor tsalgyu* (*druṅ ạk'or rtsal rgyugs*). Originally a military exercise, like the hard ritual ceremony of hunting, which nobody could escape, this had become a kind of pageant meant to give those present a pretext to display their best clothes and the young officers an opportunity to show their skill. That had also been an old custom with the Mongols and the Turks, with whose habits ancient Tibetan institutions had much in common. A great merriness marked all those events, but there was no breach of the respect which the young owed to the old, the lower to the higher officials and the laymen to the monks.

The guests were expected to come early in the morning and to stay till late in the evening. Tea with cakes and candies was served at 11 a.m., and a Chinese-style lunch between 12 and 1 p.m. Bone or ivory chopsticks were used to pick morsels here and there from the innumerable plates the servants juggled on to the table: vegetables of all kinds, hot sauce, shark's fins, clear soup with noodles and rice. Tea was served again at 3 p.m. with all kinds of cakes. Between five and six dinner was served, starting with monkey and cashew nuts, pumpkin seeds and pickled fruit, having as its main dish yak meat or mutton cooked in various ways, and ending with fish, rice and sweets. The whole was washed down with *chang*, tea or orange juice.

Such meals were like a liturgic service and the dishes were presented with the same care as the offers on an altar. In saying this my purpose is certainly not to mix wantonly sacred with profane things, but rather to point out again how everything revolved around religion in that country. The intervals between meals were spent in the garden playing dice or mahjong, quite a risky game, at which I saw some people lose hundreds of rupees in a few hours. This merry way of life did not keep anybody from doing his duty. The monks held their services in the morning, the dignitaries paid their homage to the Dalai Lama, the officials went to their work, but everything was done unhurriedly, with frequent recesses. However, the echo of world events spread a dark cloud over such a serene atmosphere. It began dawning upon Tibet that it was not enough to shut one's doors in the foreigners' faces in order to feel safe in the gathering storm. The threat of World War III seemed imminent, malignant ideas were troubling the minds and spreading like wild fire. Through a budding but still vague consciousness of a connection with the whole world and what was going on in it, Tibet was no longer indifferent to what happened outside her frontiers. Till a few years earlier, she had been vaguely conscious of a flow of "chilimpas" in the world beyond. Chilimpas were the foreigners, the people foreign to the Buddha's word, foreign to the land of Tibet, a faceless, nameless crowd among which emerged like islands some countries to which closer political association gave sharper outlines: Great Britain, China, Russia. Now the world map had taken a much concreter shape in the mind of Tibet's political leaders and the news, however stale, leaking through from the rest of the world gave raise to a certain apprehensiveness as to what would come next. What would Tibet's lot be in the case of a new world conflict? Would her isolation be respected? Just in those days a great collective prayer had been offered in Lhasa to ward off the threat of war. The three great monasteries of the yellow sect: Depung, Sera and Ganden had sent one thousand monks each for the occasion. An immense pile of aromatic herbs had been laid on the main square, ready to burn for the exorcism meant to drive the evil spirits away, a ceremony which was sure to remove the danger of war at least for the time being. Towards 2 p.m. a stream of red-clad monks started flowing slowly and solemnly from the cathedral, preceded by one of the Depung rectors, reached the square and squatted silently while the votive offer was laid on the pile by the rector, clad in flaming red and wearing a yellow mitre. Shortly afterwards the old Ganden abbot appeared in yellow drapery, sheltered by a great sunshade of the same colour and followed by a group of incarnates of the several monasteries. He sat down under a white canopy and the ceremony began. After half an hour a motley crowd moved from the same direction dancing and swaying multicoloured standards: they were the followers of the Nechung seer, the State oracle foretelling coming events and controlling the spirit world. He approached the pyre in a trance, now running, now halting suddenly, propped and guarded by his assistants, and wearing on his head a huge golden tiara surmounted by a crown of ostrich feathers. At a certain moment he stopped short as if he were looking for something. A bow and an arrow were handed over to him, he grabbed them and shot the arrow into the pyre, his hand shaken by violent fits. The pyre took fire at once and the flame, swiftly destroying that dry brushwood, scattered the grim powers waylaying world peace. The oracle fell in a swoon and was carried away on a stretcher among a cheering crowd, while warriors in ancient armours and mail coats were shooting away at random from old harquebuses.

Magic mentality still dominated Tibet, by which actual being and imagination were looked upon as one, and a sense of mastery and subjection at the same time was derived from the possession of the key opening the doors of mysteries or from the knowledge of formulas and rituals governing the play of cosmical forces. That induced a quiet confidence that everything would conform to ones' wishes, that human will would triumph over the whims of malignant forces — a world entirely different from ours, where a hopeless battle is raging between man's demiurgic aspirations and the dumb unresponsiveness of matter. The shadow of mystery, gradually dispelled from the rest of the earth by swift and frequent means of communication, was still lingering on Tibet. Scientific certitude, of which we are so proud and solicitous, makes the air so thin that it can hardly be breathed, spreads a light so bright that our eyes are dazzled. But when the shadow of mystery is removed and the blossoms of dreams nipped in the bud, the tree of life withers and dries up. Thus, almost unconsciously, we ended by confining the miracles our science discounts or laughs off to this Tibetan loneliness forbidden to Western inquisitiveness, and assumed that there, even nowadays, man can escape the limitations of time and space and subdue the laws of matter to his will. Actually the Tibetans are not far different from us: only they were long ensnared by a religious and magic outlook on life, in which the boundaries between the realms of reality and possibility, of truth and imagination were not clear-cut ones. The intellect in them had not yet reached such a degree of freedom as to stamp out the dreams of the soul. The brains were not the all-in-all of life like in the West where the eagerness to rationalize and the craze to "do something about it" have strangled in us the child and the poet bent to sound the mystery of things in the language of myth.

In Tibet man had not yet disintegrated: he still sank his roots fully into that collective subconscious which knows no difference between past and present. In that uniformity of feelings and thoughts you could hardly expect a full-fledged personality, a rugged individualist to strike out for himself, discarding that indistinct background. That would require a self-sufficient, lonely soul having its isolation as its only guide. In Tibet on the contrary greatness had always been measured in function of conformity to tradition. That people followed the beaten track, keeping its links with the past. There was no dearth of cultured people, but culture was of a religious nature. The State did not look after the citizens' education, but it did not put obstacles in its way either. All villages of some importance had schools where the three Rs were taught and, if I am allowed to judge from the correctness of the spelling with which even minor officials could write a language rendered harder by the chasm between the written and the spoken word, that primary education was efficiently imparted. The gentry went to a boarding school in Lhasa where a greater store was laid by arithmetic. Higher education was given in the convents, as only those acquainted with the sacred scriptures were rated as really educated. Specialized colleges were under the direction of Lamas, like the Mentsikang (*sMan rtsis k'an*) college of medicine and astrology, directed by Lobzang Tenpa.

Medicine is based on the doctrine of the four humours, and for Tibetan traditional lore the earth was square and the sun turned around it. Still, the Tibetans are accurate enough in foretelling eclipses, clever in diagnostics, and past master in herb lore. In Lhasa I suffered from a bowel trouble which gave me fever just in the days when I should have been in the pink of health to cope with the work to do, as I had to take leave of the Dalai Lama and make the arrangements for my departure. The director of the medical college healed me with such efficient pills that I took a liberal supply of them on my journey. In that college the students were monks. They had in their keep a huge collection of drugs and herbs manipulated according to the instructions of the masters, who had all been the official physicians of the Dalai Lamas. That kind of medicine rests on a subtle lore expounded in some famous treatises of Indian origin: the Gyushi (*rGyud bži*) = "the Four Medical Tantras" and the Yanlaggye (*Yan lag brgyad*), the Tibetan translation of a famous Indian work written in the 9th century.[30] But those are of course only the sources which gave rise to an immense indigenous literature of commentaries, explanations and glossaries. Outstanding among those is the Vinduryangompo (*Vai du rya snon po*), a work of the famous Regent Sangye Gyatso (*Sans rgyas rgya mts'o*), an outstanding figure both in Tibetan politics and education. The study of this ponderous work is simplified through large coloured plates offering a pictorial bird's eye view of its principles and applications, which make them much easier to learn. The same system is also adopted for the study of Tibet's greatest astrological work, the Vindurakar-po (*Vai du rya dkar po*) which was written by the same author. The director of Mentsikang college showed me a superb collection of such colour plates holding in them-selves all of Tibet's medical and astrologic lore, which one can thus see unfold under one's eyes in a gallery of express-ive paintings, as it were. The Tibetans believe that medi-cine is, of course, a revelation, the great physician being Lord Buddha, who inspired the masters and led them to lay down the medical principles in a literary form. The dispens-ing of drugs goes therefore hand in hand with the treat-ment of the soul, not so much because the physician will have it so, but rather because of the patients' firm belief that the pills and mixtures are not mere chemical subst-ances, and cure chiefly on account of the wonder-working virtues infused into them by prayers, rituals and spells. Many drugs were dispensed together with pamphlets in-structing the patient what prayers to recite and what cere-monies to perform before taking them in order to secure recovery. In a word, substances are powerless when not supported by that spiritual counterpart. The sick, who knew those principles and firmy believed in them, prepared themselves to take a drug with the same faith as they would receive a sacrament. In hopeless cases it was assumed that the patient had to atone for his karma and that this had to run its course anyway, or that he was a victim of evil forces, the *sadag*, the *lu*, of the unwittingly offended underground powers, or of the naturally ominous planets (*gza'*). In these cases recourse was had to the choral recitation of the sacred scripture by the monks, as such books, the word of the Buddha, were the Master's verbal plane and wielded there-fore a wonder-working power. Another way was to have the exorcists build a magical image of the world, *do* (*mdo*), consisting of a cross in the middle around whose arms motley threads were wound and re-wound. The evil spirits were magically transferred there and tied up.[31]

But the West was already creeping in with all its gadgets. The Tibetans were growing fond of cameras, fumbling about with wireless sets and field glasses as with strange toys, the vanguard of stranger and less harmless curiosities which would follow, like an expanding grease slick. Till that time, however, Tibet had displayed a surprising determination to stay aloof, like a floating island of antiquity, from the violent currents shaking the new world. An island of great culture, of inborn taste and refinement, of profound humanity, but of no modern comfort. There were no roads and nearly no bridges. The only post offices were on the highway to India and at Shigatse. As soon as we strayed from the main caravan route, we were compelled to entrust our mail to occasional pilgrims or merchants crossing our path, and many a letter was mislaid. Most machines were still unknown. The Tibetans felt the allurement of machines but still gave them a wide berth, as if they had realized that, once they had taken to them, they would not have been able to dispense with them any more. The leading class had successfully maintained their isolation, though some Tibetans had already had a foretaste of Western civilization while on pilgrimage or on business in India. But that isolation was doomed to be short-lived. One could already foresee that Tibet would be hard put to fall in line with the other countries once the partition walls had collapsed. In the meanwhile the rumblings of the storm about to shake the world could be heard at Tibet's very door.

As I have said above, China, which conquered Tibet in the 18th century and kept her under her own control till 1912, when the empire fell, never officially gave up her suzerainty; nevertheless, being aware that Tibet, after proclaiming her independence, had placed herself more or less covertly under Great Britain's protection, never pressed her claims further. But it was clear that the Nanking Government's fall and the advent of Communist China would greatly jeopardize the independence of Tibet and that the latter, unable to defend herself by her own means, would be compelled by the very circumstances to strengthen her ties with India, the natural heir of British policy in Asia.

Then the amenities of politics, the whirlwind of parties and the pageant of politicians would commence for Tibet as well, and the people would lose their detachment and engage in strifes which would enslave them in the name of freedom, as actual freedom belongs to man alone, to man left alone with God, and all the rest is treachery and trash.

I loved the medieval aura still enshrouding Tibet and found that, in spite of appearances, it allowed man a greater self-mastery than the Western way of life. The State was not an anonymous tyrant poking his nose everywhere and controlling all you did, you had, you said and, according to some ideologies, even what you thought. In Tibet the State was a few people you could get personally — and humanly — in touch with, and not the shapeless red tape tying up and squeezing everything and threatening to shatter civilization. Those rulers were supposed to be the masters of their subjects' lives and goods — but what was happening in those very days under our very eyes in such a great part of the world? Give me a personal master any time rather than an abstraction named State or democracy or what not, in whose hands I should feel as hopelessly enslaved. Man has indeed been born under an unlucky star, and only the saint or the poet can somehow struggle free from it.

10 The Monastic Cities

Near the lay city, yet separated from it, are the two towns of Depung and Sera, entirely inhabited by monks.[32] The former was supposed to accommodate 7,700 and the latter 6,600 monks. Some thirty miles further to the East, the town of Ganden, topping a 14,000 ft. mountain peak, was said to be inhabited by 3,300 monks. They are real towns, as the abbots, friars and disciples live, single or in small batches, in huts and houses hugging each other as if to keep warm, and clustering meanderingly towards the temples. The temples, the spiritual centre of the monastery, are the gate into another world, the door-step leading to Nirvana for those alive to its meaning. Huge, gold glittering statues sit there in endless meditation, exploring the depths of the soul from half-closed eyes. Their frozen masks are unruffled and they wear the expression of a bliss beyond any movement or any feeling, like a colourless, heatless light. Such is the remoteness of detachment they inspire, that anybody watching them feels desperately lonely and willing to plunge into the mystery they point to in order to escape that solitude. Such was the ideal of the old ascetical schools. Convent life is, on the contrary, like a retaliation of associate life over estranged confinement. Left alone, a hermit swings precariously between the kingdom of god and the world of demons, and is likely to get frightened both by the peaks and the depths. The isolated hermits will therefore join hands against their common fear. Thus the cells are welded into convents and the convents into monastic cities, a society of recluses ruled by strict laws and an iron discipline.

Life in Tibetan convents is anything but comfortable, and the monks anything but an idle, lazy crowd. At the bottom, as in any community, are those doing the hardest chores, like cleaning and cooking — people rather endowed with brawns than brains and better suited for menial work — as even in Tibet men are not all equal; and life rests and thrives on diversity. Those better mentally gifted engage in study and meditation — still another kind of work, which can perhaps only be rated higher because it is not immediately polluted by any practical purpose.

Two inspectors supervise the discipline of a monastery. Their sturdy frames are enhanced by their shoulders, wrapped by a scarlet shroud, a garb conferring upon them a commanding, martial air. While on inspection they are preceded by two lictors bearing heavy iron maces, on whose points their yellow hoods are hoisted. To top it off, these are preceded in their turn by other attendants who let loose beastly yells at regular intervals. The Tibetan mind identifies the dreadful with the beastly, i.e. with a nature not controlled by reason, a world prey to the furies, a return to the origins. Such inspectors last in charge one year and have to stand an examination in the presence of the Dalai Lama; a good memory and a powerful voice being indispensable assets to pass it. Whenever they make their round everybody vanishes from sight and goes into hiding like marmots into their dens at the sight of a sportsman. The convent looks then like a dead city but for the students who, powerless against curiosity, peep through every key hole, from every window and peer from the street corners, to vanish in their turn into the shadows as soon as the slow procession of the inspectors draws near.

As to the monks' work, there is no making light of it. Prayers, offices, study and the choral recital of sacred scriptures succeed each other uninterruptedly since the early morning. Whenever I spent the night in the monasteries I was regularly awakened at 3 a.m. by the thundering of drums, followed by clarions and later by trumpets, the concert being topped off again by a deafening, alarm-like rattle of drums. The whole thing lasted an hour, and would have certainly awakened the dead. Everybody rushed into the assembly hall for the morning choir and stayed to recite the office till broad daylight. In the evening the monks did not retire early but stayed up late to recite litanies in small groups in the houses and the students in their colleges.

Most of such education is based on memory. Strict exactitude and a meticulous care of detail pave the way to the study of logic, the most cherished subject of the Yellow sect; it is formal logic, a tricky, pettifogging structure of syllogisms embroidered around the most obvious truisms, but a good guide to a precise expression and accurate analysis. A third step was dogmatics, an inextricable maze in itself. After twenty-five years' study, tests and public disputations, the student may graduate in theology. But that is a dead end, a given, received knowledge, where only further commentaries and deeper explanations are possible, no further spade-work on unknown ground, as nothing more can be learned after the Buddha's revelation, and any change or addition would be heresy.

The real hermits live outside the convents, in mountain wilderness; but all monks of the better sort feel at times the instinctive urge to struggle free from the fetters of ritual and the dullness of texts, to leave the convent and go into lonely meditation, thus facing directly the unfathomable mystery whose symbols they have been seeing so long in temple imagery. Every year the élite — those monks in whom theology has not killed the longing after the Infinite — withdraw for some months into the hermitage unfailingly built in the neighbourhood of each monastery (*mts'an k'an, ri k'rod*) but isolated, like an eagle's nest, on the top of steep rocks. In a loneliness librating between heaven and earth, the soul is more likely to be flooded by God's light.

As I said already, the largest monastery is Depung, thus named after a well-known place in Southern India where, according to esoteric tradition, an important treatise of Buddhistic gnosis, the "Wheel of Time", was revealed to Lord Buddha. Among the monks inhabiting that town some fifty are "rinpoche", i.e. Incarnates or Bodhisattvas, being reborn continuously in order to keep the Buddha's doctrine alive in the world. Depung rises some four miles West of Lhasa and scatters its lively white, yellow and red buildings along a valley framed by mountains on three sides. I was received by the inspectors and the lictors and went at once to see the abbots, kenpo (*mk'an po*). The convent is divided into four sectors or seminaries called Tatsang (*Grvats'an*). Their abbots last in office twelve years, after which they go into retirement and are styled *zur pa*, but still hold the paraphernalia and privileges of their rank. The kenpos are usually Incarnates, whose constant rebirth in a new body represents spiritual continuity surviving the flow of time. Their mortal remains are collected in huge, silver and gold-plated chortens, because the perfection of their minds has wiped off the impurity of flesh. Thus the worship of relics is born. In the innermost shrine of every monastery I could see flights of such monuments, like solidified waves of time on the ocean of eternity.

The abbots were not concerned at all with convent discipline. They were usually great ascetics who had sacrificed everything to their religion, and not out of a merely intellectual interest. While talking to several of them I had discovered a deep, loving concern for suffering mankind at large. They were persuaded that the Buddha's word could relieve all pain and wipe out all sins — the gentle delusion of pious souls who seemed not to know that no word can work the miracle if the spirit is not aglow with faith.

We spent much time arguing. Such arguments were a kind of test I was subjected to, in order to ascertain whether I was not masquerading in borrowed plumes. We mostly talked about the *Lam rim c'en mo*, a kind of *Summa Theologica* written by Tsonkhapa, the great reformer of the Yellow sect, a subtle summary of the doctrine and, at the same time, a guide to the conquest of suffering and delusion, a path leading beyond the human stage. The whole of Mahāyānic Buddhism is summarized in it with a precision of language and a subtlety of reasoning making it into one of the greatest monuments of Asiatic thought. Each school has of course its own dogmatic handbook: the Nyinmapa have the Kunzang Lama Shalung (*Kun bzaṅ bla ma žal luṅ*), the Kagyupa have Gampopa's *Lam rim*, the Saskyapa the treatises on the *Lam dre* (*Lam ạbras*), none of which is however so famous as the *Lam rim c'en mo*.

My interviews with the abbots over, I went for a round of the monastery, and walked first of all into the great assembly hall (*ts'ogs k'aṅ, ạdus k'aṅ*) where a great statue of Maitreya, especially worshipped at Depung as its protecting god, rose against the main wall, and where, according to custom, I fell thrice on my knees. In the same hall I admired two ancient statues of Padmapāṇi, good pieces belonging to the same set. I then proceeded to visit the first college, the Ngagtatsang (*sNags grva ts'aṅ*), devoted to the study of the Tantras. The Yellow sect does not lay such a great store as other schools by esoteric literature and restricts its study to four fundamental cycles: the Kālacakra, the Guhyasamāja, the Śamvara and the Dorjejiche.[33] Many chapels opened into the walls of the Ngagtatsang's solemn, sturdy-pillared main hall. In its centre, the Buddhas of the Three Times were surrounded by eight Bodhisattvas, and high up on the wall the sixteen Arhats appeared in paintings of the 17th century. In the Losal Tatsang (*blo gsal grva ts'aṅ*) college I was shown the picture of Sonamtagpa (*bSod nams grags pa*), one of the greatest scholars of the Yellow sect. In the garden of that college, shaded by century-old trees, the Geshes were trained in discussions of logic, in which the Dalai Lama himself participated sometimes, when he took up his residence in one of the college buildings. I then visited the Gomangtatsang (*rGo man grva ts'an*) where the Buddha's 108 deeds are depicted, and the fourth and last college, the *De yan*, dedicated to the gods of medicine. In its Gonkang the dreaded Gonpos, enshrouded in the atmosphere of redoubtable mystery common to such places, watched over the purity of the building. Pe har and the other Chokyongs were worshipped there and constant prayers were offered to them. According to custom I assisted at the Serkyem, the ceremony of propitiation of terrific deities, which was performed with *chang*. We took leave of the guides who had accompanied us and went down to Nechung, on the Lhasa road, where the state oracle resided. Everything was modern there. A small pillar in the yard reminded of the ancient pillars of the kings' age, but there was no trace of an inscription.

The Sera convent was N of Lhasa and divided into three colleges or seminaries: Sera che (*Sera byes*), Sera me (*Sera smad*) and Ngag pa (*sNags pa*).

But the most venerable of the three Yellow sect convents around Lhasa is Ganden (*dGa' ldan*), thus named after the heaven where Maitreya, the future Buddha, expected to redeem mankind in a few thousand years when it has reached the depth of evil, is supposed to reside now. Ganden is some thirty miles off Lhasa, built on the top of a hill S of the Kyichu river. It is held in high esteem on account of its strictness in keeping the rules, and chiefly because Tsongkapa died there and his mortal remains are kept in the convent.

Going to Ganden gave me the opportunity to see Yerpa, one of the most ancient stations of Tibetan Buddhism. It is another monastic town carved out in the live rock overhanging a fertile valley bounded by mountain ridges some eight miles E of Lhasa. Padmasambhava, Atīśa and other great Buddhist missionaries from India spent some time there in meditation. The road runs through verdant barley and wheat fields heaving around wealthy, gay villas. I had to stop at several villages for a change of horses, as the Government had ruled down that mounts and means of transports had to be changed at every village on the road. Obviously this caused the traveller great trouble and loss of time, but secured an equal share of gain to the peasants. In the village of Garga the sacred scriptures were carried in procession around the fields (*on k'or*). The exorcist, the priests, the village headmen, men and women wore their best clothes for the occasion, and the garish colours were set off against the green background. The exorcist proceeded pompously under a large red canopy. The ceremony aimed at drawing a kind of invisible, magic furrow around the fields, preventing hail, and securing a good crop. At that time of the year, when any sudden hail storm could jeopardize the harvest, there was hardly a village which did not perform such a ceremony. Painted tablets were stuck into the ground at the four corners of each field. Formulas were recited on them by the exorcist, thus marking out the bounds the evil spirits were not allowed to overstep.

Yerpa appeared suddenly before my eyes at a bend of the road, a cascade of small white buildings along steep, green overgrown cliffs. One could have thought one was not in Tibet. Giant junipers and tufts of rhododendron topped a thick tangle of undergrowth, brushwood and grass victoriously fighting the hard barrenness of rocks. The cliffs were riddled with burrows and caves, some of which were so high up on the face of the abrupt hill that it would have been risky to climb up to them. Temples and chapels had been built in the bigger ones. We reached the place at dusk and were greeted by a warbling and twittering of birds conferring upon the hermitage an air of unexpected merriness. No wonder that the Indian missionaries chose to stay here long. In few other places in Tibet could they have found a recess so charming and restful as to remind them of the lovely exuberance of Indian hermitages. The people in charge of the convent town met us on our arrival and led us to the main temple. I was accommodated in a roomy hall whose door went out on a large terrace. Under me was the temple where the monks assembled for collective prayers. Before my eyes the whole valley was lulled into sleep by the litanies ascending to heaven from the chapels scattered around. I felt ensnared in the charm of a country where of the outside world there was but a sweetly blurred recollection left, and life was stripped back to its essential meaning of impersonal communion with the cosmic rhythm.

Traring, the man detailed to accompany me by the Tibetan Government, was busy working out the details of the ceremony for the souls of his parents, which he was going to perform in that sanctuary, by offering one hundred Torma (*ts'ogs* = cakes) and lighting 108 lamps (*rgya mc'od*) on the altars. At dawn we began our pilgrimage through the chapels. We saw the one dedicated to the three Guardians of Tibet (*Rigs gsum mgon po*) viz. Avalokiteśvara, Vajrapāṇi and Mañjuśrī, which did not contain anything remarkable; Atīśa's cave, where a statue of Atīśa was displayed; the chapel of the sixteen Arhats, adorned with terracotta statues of these and some 18th century frescoes covering part of its rocky walls; and the Pukar Rabsal (*P'ug dkar rab gsal*) where I had a long conversation with an ascetic who had been living there for seven years. In another cave nearby I had a talk with a hermit who had spent nine years there. On the front of their caves both had built pretty verandas full of flowers, and their store rooms were heaped up with holy images and books. They were poring over their treatises, meditating on the mystery of life and endeavouring to overcome its sufferings by lighting an everlasting flame in themselves. I had met many such people on my Tibetan journeys. The one who impressed me most was a sage I met beyond Saskya in 1939. He had been living walled up in a cave for twenty-seven years and his only outlet on the outside world was a small window cut into the wall. A stone slab hanging on a hemp rope was fixed to the wall, and the

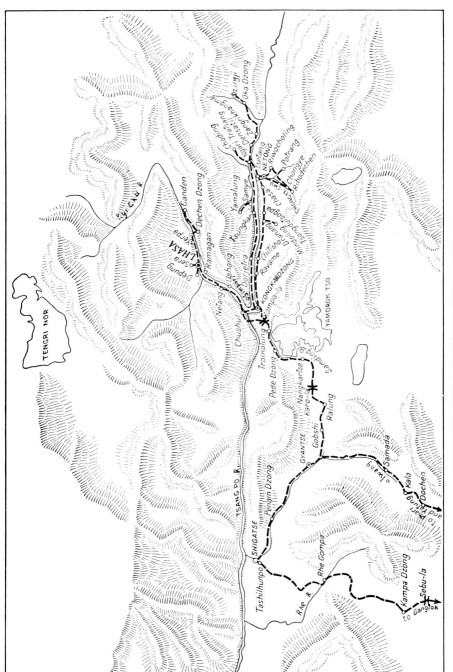

MAP OF THE TUCCI EXPEDITION TO CENTRAL TIBET, 1948

TENGRI NOR

KYI CHU R.

Ganden

Dechen Dzong

Sera Sera

Depung

LHASA

Ramagan

Ushang

Tsunghar

Dorgelra

Nelang

Chushul

TSANG PO R.

Tamalung

Tumpa-la

KONGKARDZONG

Rayame

Chilshol

Ratodogopa

Gongkar Chase

Danang

Chushul

Chonye

Chongye Khodechen

Potrang

Riwocholing

NETONG

Tsetang

Zangden

Tsethankhamar

Chongye

Oka Dzong

Samye

Chongye

YAMDROK TSO

Tramalung

Pede Dzong

Nangkartse

Gobshi

Karo-la

Ralung

GYANTSE

Penam Dzong

SHIGATSE

Tashilhunpo

Rhe R.

Rhe Gompa

Samada

Kala

Dochen

to Phari Pe

Kampa Dzong

Sebu-la

to Gangtok

Taichi Zomphud, Governor of the Shigatse and his wife. On his left: *The author and Mele;* on the far right: *Col. Moise* (Photo Mele)

The garden of one of Lhasa's high officials

Jigmed Traring (Photo Mele)

The great temple of Samye (Photo Mele)

View of Potala Palace and Shol

General view of the monastery of Samye from Mount Haspori (Photo Mele)

View of Tashilhumpo (Photo Mele)

General view of Lhasa: the author with Namghial Traring

Fort of Kampadzong

Preparing an offering

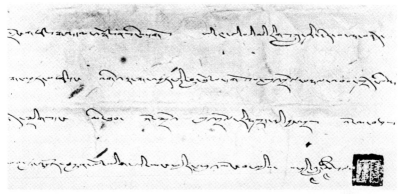

Passport to Lhasa delivered to the author by the Tibetan authorities

Images of Dolma in the temple of Netang

Crossing the Tsangpo

Dromo Geshe Rinpoche II

The Kapshupa

Trijang Rinpoche Lobsang Yeshi, the Dalai Lama's spiritual guide (Now the Dalai Lama's junior tutor)

General view of Ganden

The hermitage of Yerpa

A pilgrim (Photo Mele)

The Himalaya seen from the north, on the way back (Photo Mele)

visitors announced their presence by banging on it with a rock. The words of that sage, who did not belong to our world any more, drove straight to one's heart with winning sweetness. He was a man some fifty years old, with bright eyes and an easy flow of speech. He explained that his isolation from the outside world was not meant to help him alone. The spirit's sublimation born of steady discipline would be worthless unless others could draw some profit from it. "But you are not preaching" I told him "and while staying up here walled up into the mountain you have not the slightest idea of the world's sufferings". "Should I really not know them" was the answer, "I would not lead such a life. By lighting up a great fire at the dead of night you rend up the darkness all around and those who had gone astray can find their bearings again. You are coming from far, far away, yet you too felt the urge to climb up these crags in order to see me. But for the little spark of good in a few people, the world would exist no more, as evil is death, even if it sometimes takes the shape of an over-whelming, lustful craving for life".

The hermit went on talking for a few hours through that peep-hole of his cave by way of which the villagers brought him food and drink. His words were the mirror of a candid soul, and of noble thoughts. Once more I had to remark how wrong it is to judge the culture of a people through its outward appearances. We sometimes look at the Tibetans as if they still were in the darkest of Middle Ages, unaware of the prodigy of machine and of science's ingenious con-structions, aloof from the heroic struggle for life. But that people finds in contemplation a poise which we are seeking in vain. While acting, man takes several shapes, as the aims of his action are manifold and conflicting. As what one reaches never satisfies one's purpose and human volition is driven from one wish to another, dissatisfaction follows like a shadow upon the work of man and discards it again and again as disappointing, while producing a renewed wish for action. Contemplation instead is a backward path leading inward from outside, but it is so hard that very few reach the innermost shrine. Those who hang on long enough reach a point beyond which it is hard to go. They find inner peace and feel they have achieved a realization many have achieved before in the same way, thus coming to rest upon something eternal.

I reluctantly took leave of the hermits and went on. In the Champalakang (*Byams pa lha k'an̄*) a statue of Maitreya was surrounded by eight standing Bodhisattvas. The images, of Chinese school, had been recently retouched, but they could well have been ancient. Beside the Bodhisattvas, the statues of Champa's (Maitreya's) mother and father, Drolma and Namse (*rNam sras*, Vaiśravaṇa) could be seen, together with the one of Mar ston, the master of Mar, who commissioned the largest statue for which the chapel is named.[34] There was hardly any ground to doubt tradition. The works were most probably of the 13th century, had suffered in the wars and had been lately restored.

In the Chogyalpug (*C'os rgyal p'ug*), thus named from a legend which, anticipating later events, has it that King Srongtsengampo spent some time there in meditation after his conversion to Buddhism, a great statue of Chagtongchantong (*P'yag ston spyan ston*), Avalokiteśvara with one thousand arms and hands, was worshipped. The statue was of no artistic value, and neither were some traces of paintings apparently of the 16th century A.D. In some niches in the wall of the main cave I saw a few images of Srongtsengampo with his two wives, the Nepalese and the Chinese one. In another chapel my guide showed me the images of Begtse, of Pandenlamo (*dPal ldan Lha mo*), the protectress of Lhasa, and other terrific deities. A small, dark-stone pillar, its top knocked off, attracted my attention. It was obviously the stump of a *linga*, the manly symbol Indian esoterism takes to espress Shiva's inexhaustible creative power. It had probably been carried up there by some Indian tantric master. On the walls I could make out some scattered letters, among others "g s j", but I did not under-

stand their meaning. In the same cave was kept the hat Lha
luṅ, the murderer of the apostate king Langdarma, wore
during the dance in the course of which he shot the deadly
arrow. Thence I proceeded to the innermost recess, where
in the middle of the cave sat, on a large throne-shaped
plinth, four Buddhas whom I easily recognized from the
attitude of their hands as Akṣobhya, Amitābha, Amoghasiddhi and Ratnasambhava. In their midst sat Vairocana
wearing a five-sided diadem on whose each face a Buddha
was carved. It is an old, well-known five-Buddha cycle
depicted in all Tibetan temples contemporary with the
second wave of Buddhism which Atīśa led into Tibet. On
the walls of the cave, figures of Buddhas and Bodhisattvas
could be seen: Dīpaṅkara, the latest Buddha before the
historic one, on the left; Maitreya, the next one, and Lokeś-
vara, on the right. The statues were of a remarkable mastery. They had the graceful suppleness of Indian pieces of
the golden age, and I incline to think they were carved by
Indian craftsmen who were perhaps in the retinue of Atīśa
and his companions.

In the Davapug (*Zla ba p'ug*) temple I paid homage to a
statue of Padmasambhava, who was said to have spent some
time there in meditation, and had to drink some *chang*
offered to me in a human skull. The other temples, the
Treumarserpo (*sPreu dmar ser po*), the Lamalakang and the
Tsogkang (*Ts'ogs k'aṅ*) with its 18th century paintings were
nothing to write home about. A little lower down was the
cell of Atīśa (*Atīśa gzims*) and the Tsepamelakang (*Ts'e dpag
med lha k'aṅ*) chapel, against whose walls stood the statues
of the eight Bodhisattvas. The doors were guarded by the
two *chokyongs* Hayagrīva and Acala. All these statues had
been recently restored. In the open on a small plain, in the
midst of that wonderful natural scene, was the throne of
Atīśa where, according to tradition, the apostle of Buddhism used to preach to his disciples. Higher up, and separated from the chapels by a dell, rose the barren, round
cone of Lhari, the holy mountain where the tutelary spirit

of the place is supposed to dwell. Traring, my companion, climbed its top to perform the propitiatory ritual by the offer of incense and prayer flags.

On July 24 we climbed down to Dechendzong and up to Ganden again. It was a regular ascension. After leaving the Kyichu river, the road made for a wide valley where a few villages watched over some meager fields belonging to the convent, then rose steeply and deliberately toward the monastery. The bodily exertion in conquering the stiff gradient was suggestive of the soul's hardships on its way to God. On the ridge overhanging the Kyichu valley the smoke rose from Drokpa camps and herds of yak spread their dark masses. Further, as far as the eye could reach, an ocean of peaks hove into sight. Against that grandiose background, Ganden was set off in the trim spruceness of its freshly whitewashed walls framing the blazing red of the temples and the garish gold of the roofs. It was a sight out of this world. The huge buildings looked bodiless, a mere outline silhouetted against the spotlessly blue sky. Mace bearers came towards us carrying gifts of eggs and milk. I was assigned a suite of two red-and-gold lacquered rooms, so large that I felt lost in it. On the next day I started on my round of the temples and buildings. I was first conducted into a chapel which was Ganden's sanctum sanctorum. There the relics of Tsonkhapa and his two main disciples were kept in two large gilt bronze shrines. Remarkable frescoes ascribed by tradition to Ketrubje (*dGe sgrub rje*), one of those two scholars, but perhaps painted two centuries later, could be seen on the chapel's walls. In the Yan pachen Lakan I was shown other monuments holding the relics of some of the most famous Tripas (*K'ri pa*) or rectors of the Ganden monastery.

The convent authorities had been so kind as to grant me permission to see the Nangtens (*naṅ brten*), viz. the particularly sacred objects only special visitors are shown. The occasion called for the lighting of lamps and a money contribution to the convent's maintenance. I could see a *maṇ-*

ḍala of the *lolang* kind built, according to tradition, by Ketrubje; his hat and some bronze statues, the most interesting of which represented Dorjejiche. Then I was led to the cell where Tsongkhapa died in 1419. The wall paintings were, as far as I could judge, of the same age. The throne (*k'ri*) on which he had sat was a good Nepalese handiwork of the 15th century.

In the Champa Lakang there were two statues of the future Buddha, the one representing him seated and the other standing. The former especially attracted my attention: it was a fairly old Nepalese work. I was then led into Tsonkhapa's quarters, low-ceilinged, dark rooms, their walls coated with frescoes darkened by time and smoke, presumably of Nepalese hand, with gilt stucco reliefs. I could not help feeling a certain emotion at the sight of those rooms. Whatever one's faith, one cannot stay indifferent to the great work the founder of the yellow sect did in reforming Tibetan church, up-to-dating Buddhistic thought and liturgy and thus starting a current of moral force which was to leave a deep imprint in Tibetan history. I like visiting the places where the great religious souls lived, as they, like the great artists, rose above the flow of time which sweeps everything off into oblivion and annihilation. Those modest, dark rooms on whose walls the gods of esoteric Buddhism filed off, revealed a meditative, steadfast nature, deaf to the blandishments of the world, a soul that had to bend over itself in lonely confinement to draw upon fresh sources of strength and be ready to pour upon the world its new load of energies. From the austere, sombre silence of that cell we were led again into contrasting surroundings: into the seminaries where the already grown-up church paraded its power, lavishing the wealth in which temporal power prides. The Ganden monastery included two colleges: Shartse (*Śar rtse* = the East point) and Changtse (*Byaṅ rtse* = the North point). Arabesques, tinsel, imposing pillars and hundreds of painted scrolls hanging on the ceiling between the columns were their apparel. The guide pointed to some

embroidered *tankas*[35] which Srongtsengampo's Chinese
wife, Gyaza (*rGya bza*), was supposed to have painted. But
they were more recent works either carried out in China or
after Chinese models.

Rest houses were usually built around the convents for
the pilgrims, and hostels for the monks who came to complete their education in the convent. As the latter were often
of customs, traditions and language other than Tibetan,
they were accommodated in special houses where they
could feel at home with their countrymen and suffer less
from homesickness. Women were not allowed to spend the
night in the monastery. Dogs were not admitted either.

I left Ganden with some reluctance. I had spent some
days in one of the most venerable sanctuaries of Tibetan
Buddhism as a welcome guest, and had enjoyed the spiritual serenity radiating from that place. It was like living on
timeless Isles of the Blest where the days flowed on in a
changeless rhythm, the events of history stopped at the
doors, and the hectic agitation of our age was left far behind. There was no more question of a man-to-man relation. It was a man-to-God relation, with a different pulse.

I climbed down to Dechen and on my way took pictures
of the Buddhas, Bodhisattvas and saints the devotion of the
faithful and the danger of landslides had carved on the
rocks. A powerful fortress had once risen at Dechen: now it
was ruined and its walls were hardly distinguishable from
the sharp mountain crags. The whole village had become a
fief of Ganden. There was only one remarkable temple
devoted to Champa, where a huge statue of the God, seated
European fashion, watched serenely over the cell. The statue was of Nepalese style, and so was the halo protecting its
shoulders. According to tradition the temple was built by
Ketrubje, Tsongkhapa's pupil. Past Dechen we left our
horses and, as we had attained the upper reaches of the
Kyichu river, we hired a boat, which would take us back to
Lhasa in less time. We skirted Tsekungtang (*Ts'al guṅ
t'aṅ*), once the capital of a feudal holding which played a

great role in Tibet's history. Then, under a stormy sky which shook our flimsy craft, we landed at Lhasa.

My departure from Lhasa was now drawing near: my days, always busy, were getting even more strenuous. My friends, who had swollen to a crowd by now, came to see me at all times of the day and dragged me hither and thither, asking me to tea, dinner and supper. But soon I had to begin to take leave of everybody, and was flooded with parting gifts. Most of the times I got lengths of wool, one of the main products of Tibet's home industry, and a great deal of books. By now they knew what I had come for and met very kindly my wishes. His Holiness the Dalai Lama set the example. He had heard that for many years I had been after a book I had heard about, but I could never lay hands on. It was a twenty-six-volume collection of esoteric works, the Nyingmagyubum (*rÑiṅ ma rgyud ạbum*), a translation into Tibetan of Indian gnostic treatises. The original Indian books had long been lost, and the work survived in that collection painstakingly assembled through the centuries in the Land of Snows. It is a complex, liturgic, secret doctrine in which Indian initiation schools allegorically expressed their urge to escape world contingency and associate life and to merge into the impassive light of cosmical consciousness. I termed such treatises "gnostic" as you can find in them nearly the same attitude and ideas as in the Western gnostical schools. The same anxiety, even if expressed in a different form, seems to have gripped the world about the same time from the banks of the Tiber to those of the Ganges. It is a very rare book: there were only two copies at the time in the Potala palace. Such books are never given to foreigners, as every scripture treatise represents the Buddha's word, and is therefore something holy to be laid on altars and worshipped in chapels, just like an image eternally blessed by the god's presence. I was summoned to the Dalai Lama's presence one day and presented with a copy of the Nyingmagyubum from his own hands. Never had religious books been so showily presented to foreigners.

It was like a consecration from Tibet's highest spiritual authority, the recognition of the work I had been doing for decades, a personal homage to the Buddhist scholar who, on pilgrimage as it were, had crossed the Himalayas eight times. As soon as the news spread — and all Lhasa knew of it in a few hours — the natives shed their natural reluctance to give away their sacred books. One of the top officials gave me some works he had purchased in Eastern Tibet. The Church Foreign Minister, pious, gentle Lyushan presented me with some religious books and begged that I or my pupils should translate them and spread them around to help the human mind in this troubled age. For my part I bought all the books I could lay hands on and my money could purchase, by sending around to the convents or the private houses some people selected for the purpose. Collecting books in Tibet is no easy proposition. An actual book market exists only in Lhasa, but it has on stock only books for pilgrims, monastery guides, lives of saints and miracle tales. Each convent has its own printing press. To have a passably complete library, therefore, one should in theory make the round of all convents in Tibet. Those printing presses were placed under one or a few monks' supervision. Wood-print, which is carried out by stamping wood-engraved negatives on native paper, is an age-old art in Tibet. The types of books, or rather the hard-wood blocks bearing the reflected-face text of a whole oblong page neatly carved on each of them, are ranged volumewise and kept on shelves there. To buy a book means to have a new copy of it printed on order, and as Tibetan convents are usually devoid of paper, one had better bring along the necessary amount of thick, rugged paper and, on finding the blocks of the desired work, hand over the paper to the monk in charge of the printing press. This latter would cut the paper to size, spread the thick, greasy ink on the blocks, lay and squeeze the paper on it by means of a small roller. The neatness of the print depends on the quality of the paper and the thickness of the ink, which has a way to run and clog alternatively, thus blurring the point and putting the reader's eyes to a great strain. Tibetan books are usually printed on 8″ to 16″ long sheets of paper. Each sheet has six to seven lines of print on its front and reverse side. Printing costs the equivalent of 6s. each hundred pages, or roughly one dollar a hundred and thirty pages. There were two main printing presses in Lhasa: one in the Depung monastery and the other at the Shokang (*žol k'añ*) under the Potala. But the smartest and most prized books were brought out in Eastern Tibet, where copper blocks instead of wood carvings were used.

In the collection I made there was a little of everything: historical and theological works, liturgy and grammar, books on rhetorics and divining. But I had also found two small living beings which would fill my loneliness and follow me to Italy: Tsering and Damema, a couple of cute Lhasa pups.

11 A Hundred and Twenty Miles by Boat on the Roof of the World

Leaving Lhasa is not like leaving any town. It is easy to return anywhere else, but Lhasa is so inaccessible as if it were out of this world. Departing from it is like seeing a dreamt of image vanish, without knowing whether it will ever appear again. The rehearsals of a big show to be staged in the Norbulinga palace before the Dalai Lama were being held, attended by a large crowd. But when I left, all the crowd poured on to the banks of the river to see me off, as I had planned to travel down to Samye by boat, and further if possible, first on the Kyichu and then on the Tsang-po. This would allow me more freedom to engage in research on the spot whenever I felt like, without depending on the caravan, crossing at leisure from one to the opposite bank. I had hired three of the usual Tibetan coracles made of yak leather fastened on a hulk of willow-wood. They were over-loaded with luggage. As if that were not enough, the boat-men hauled on them three sheep meant to transport their meal and food supply when, carrying the coracles on their shoulders, they would start on their return march. There was a brisk current, but the water was scanty, and we had to

152

see that the boats did not scrape their flat leather bottoms against the gravel bed of the river. My servants, used to riding and unfamiliar with that means of transport, were nervous. From the time we weighed anchor they kept their eyes longingly glued to the banks, while casting suspicious glances at the water from time to time. We held an average speed of four miles an hour. Slowly and steadily the Holy City receded into the background. The gilt spires of the Potala disappeared, while Depung hove in sight. At a hair-pin bend of the river we suddenly debouched into the Netang valley, with abrupt cliffs on our left, on which ruined castles perched. The sunshine was reflected in myriads of sparks on the waters shimmering like molten metal. The boatmen accompanied the beat of the oars with a slow whistling, and songs overflowing with sadness. I might have been ploughing the shoreless, dreamy waters of an Indian river. There was the same sense of an endless lull, as if time had ceased to flow. Those songs sounded like an invocation left unanswered in an inexorably vast loneliness where everything lost its outlines, its limits and vanished away like the fathom in a silent, bottomless ocean. Nobody said a word. Only the dogs were whimpering.

I should have liked to put in early in the afternoon, because about 3 p.m. a fresh southerly wind arose, which made the going rough and not quite devoid of danger. Short, but lively waves started rolling on the river. The boatmen stopped singing and tied the three boats together that they might better stand the onslaught.

We had left Lhasa at noon. After about two hours' sailing against a fresh head wind we landed at Ramagan. At some two km. from the bank a village rose on the ruins of a famous building: the Karchung temple built by Tisrongdet-sen (*K'ri sroṅ lde btsan*). Only four huge chortens were extant where the four corners of the temple had been. At the NE corner of the enclosure was also a pillar bearing a long inscription remembering the king's devotion and his founding the temple. On the dilapidated chortens gaped some openings which might have been abandoned chapels.

As we could not land at Samda, we made for Magda and pitched our tents there. The place was lonely and desolate: there was only one hut on the river bank. I spent the night at Magda and early in the morning walked to the Samphu monastery, one of the most notable in Tibet. The road skirted the tomb of its founder, a small temple with dark blue roof tiles. Much as I tried, I could not find its keeper nor, therefore, visit its interior. After two hours' uphill walk I reached the convent, which looked as stout and compact as a fortress, and rose on a green hill, behind which was a wooded mountain slope. As the legend has it, those woods were born of the hair of the founder. Both the Sakyapas and the Yellow sect officiated in the convent, though the latter had a bigger say in the matter. Neither of the Gonkang, into which we were admitted to come in touch at once, as it were, with the gods protecting the place, contained anything of historic or artistic interest. In the largest temple, the innermost cell opened into the back of the main hall and was separated from the rest by a circumambulation corridor. In front of it rose a large statue of Śākyamuni (the historic Buddha), which the legend claimed to be of Indian origin. I found it to be Nepalese instead. On an altar were the statues of Atīśa and Lodensherab (*bLo ldan śes rab*), the founder; moreover, a small gilt bronze statue of Tārā, undoubtedly of Indian origin, which belonged to Atīśa according to the legend. Even a pair of slippers said to have been Atīśa's were shown to the visitor. That is the most ancient part of the convent. On the walls of the assembly hall and of the porch were painted the main deities of the Yellow sect's secret doctrine: Jigched, Dukor, Demchog and Sangduba. They were good and well-preserved paintings of the 18th century.

On the following day I went back to Magda and resumed the sailing towards Chushul but broke off my journey before reaching it to land a Ushang, some miles W. of Netang, on the Southern bank of the Kyichu, in a pleasant valley

silted up by the river on its edges. At Ushang, King Ral-
pachen built a temple remembered by the chronicles. I
could still find it, but it had been restored. Four rather
modern chortens had been superimposed to the old ones. I
remarked two pillars (*doring*), one away from the temple,
the other in the middle of the open porch, which was as full
of flowers as a garden, but there were no inscriptions on
either of them. The temple was built according to the
ancient pattern and consisted of the porch, the cell and the
circumambulation corridor. Against the main hall of the
cell stood the statues of the Buddhas of the Three Times,
the central one, Śākyamuni, being accompanied by two
disciples. The eight Bodhisattvas, four on each side, looked
on. All statues had been restored after the ancient models.
On the overhanging hill I found traces of walls, possibly of
the royal castles, which should have risen there. Now everything was ruined and deserted. In no country as in Tibet
you could get a first-hand experience of what history
means, of the contrast between the hectic doing and undoing it purports and nature's unruffled majesty; the impassive look of eternity at our passionate, useless hustle and
bustle. I myself would not know anything better to do than
to stare idly at the inert mountains basking in the summer
sun under the indifferent glare of the sky. I would not
exhange any pleasure in the world for one of those hours
and am sorry for myself and my neighbours that we should
drift in a whirlwind of events turning us away from those
quiet hours of idle musing.

On the 5th of August I landed at Chushul, where a few
hours later on the same day Moise and Mele joined me.
They had been long waiting at Yatung for me to get from
the Tibetan Government the permit which had been
formerly denied. As soon as the passport, sent by the shortest way, had reached them, they had dashed on to meet
me. Maraini, who had been denied the permit again, had
left for Italy from Yatung. This time he had not been able to
cross the threshold of Tibet — like one who, headed for

Rome, should stop at Ventimiglia, on the Franco-Italian border. Moise and Mele had made forced marches to make up for the delay, rushing headlong into the forbidden land with the forward thrust of people who had crashed a gate. Thus the expedition, newly equipped and in full efficiency, joined hands again. The photographer I had been forced to engage in Sikkim had done his level best, but owing to his lack of skill and taste, the snapshots he had taken in Lhasa and along the road were a very poor job. Mele's presence was guarantee of a better picture coverage; and Dr Moise, whose fame spread into Tibet, would contribute to get many a door opened by his medical skill and his drugs.

At Chushul we were the guests of Tsarong, a well-known figure in Tibet. He had been the adviser to the late Dalai Lama, and it was he who took him to safety in India at his great personal risk when the Chinese wanted to capture him. During that Dalai Lama's tenure he had been his most influent minister and had always advocated a reasonable though guarded cooperation with Great Britain. He was Finance Minister now, and also in charge of the mint and of public works.

After two days we weighed anchor again, to touch the shore again at Kongkadzong, where we changed boats for Dorjetra. We stopped for the first time on the northern bank, where it skirted a sandy valley bordering on the sunwithered, iron grey screes of mount Semori or Simpori (*Srin-po-ri*) called also Yartö-tra (*Yar stod brag*). On the other side, the Kyichu flowed to join the Tsang-po. Prow-shaped mount Yartö-tra divides the two rivers at their junction. In the village of Sinpori, at its foot, there was a small but renowned temple looking down at the small cluster of houses stubbornly sticking to that desert. According to tradition it had been founded by an Indian master by the name of Vibhūticandra, was dedicated to Demchog and belonged to the Sakyapa sect. It contained a fairly ancient Nepalese statue of Paochig (*dPa' bo gcig*), its protecting deity. I also remarked a stone lamp with a stem as massive as the one of a Romanic holy-water basin, and a small uninscribed pillar in front of the temple.

We went down back to the river and set sail again. We covered an average of twenty to twenty-two miles a day. Letting oneself down the river like that was like resting on Nature's lap, merging into her all-pervading breath and vanishing in it, like human figures in Chinese metaphysical paintings. On both sides the mountain slopes crumbled into the river with heaps of sand. Near Samye the landscape showed African features. The yellow sand dunes looked like herds crouching around reddish, rust-coloured cliffs.

Further south, wide and fertile valleys started furrowing the desert stretch. I could see verdant barley fields studded with villages. There were the feudal holdings of the Lhasa aristocracy and the source of their income.

We put in at Dorjetra, a well-known monastery of the Nyinmapa sect in the heart of the Tra (*sGrags*) district, a name given to the area on the left bank of the river down to Samye. That convent had an incarnate, the tenth of that lineage, a boy of seven or eight, lively and inquisitive, who gravely laid his hands on my head to bless me. The chapels were full of statues and relic shrines holding the mortal remains of the former Rinpoches. Some statues were Nepalese. The Dukang was the temple's oldest room. Its frescoes however went back to the 18th century; at the farther end stood a Buddha surrounded by the eight Bodhisattvas. In Dorjetra village, stooping right down to the edge of the river and reflecting in it the motley bunch of its buildings, there was a printing press where I could buy a copy of a Shitro commentary, a book to be read aloud at death to help the transference of the conscious principle under suitable conditions.

It was hardly possible to reach Samye from Dorjetra in one day's sailing. A storm had started lashing the waters of the river and we had to put in hastily at Tsungkar[37] where we spent the night. As Samye was far inside the valley, away from the river bank, we set out on horseback on the

10th of August, and riding along the road we skirted a notable historical place marked by five white chortens rising on the mountain slope which tumbled down with large boulders towards the river. As the story had it, that was the place where the King of Tibet came to meet half-way the great Indian wonder-worker Padmasambhava, whom he had invited into his country to conquer the evil forces infesting Tibet. Uncertain whether that would befit his dignity, the king held in suspense before kneeling down at the exorcist's feet, but the latter's magic power broke the King's haughtiness, and he fell on his knees. On the rocks near the chortens there were traces of illegible inscriptions.

We made a long halt at Samye, a station of a great historical and religious importance. It was founded by Padmasambhava in the 8th century with King Tisrongdetsen's favour, and was destroyed and reconstructed several times. Its 108 chapels were meant to be a pageant of the Buddhist heaven, a galaxy of divine images like the sparkling of the sun on the sea waves, the unlimited expansion and embodiment of the same shapeless fundamental force. Into the gilt spires of Samye all schools coalesced, forgetting their petty theologic strifes. The Sakyapas, the Yellows and the Reds or at least a few hundred of them lived together in the sacred precincts joining in the worship of Padmasambhava, who was looked upon as an embodiment of Lord Buddha.

Samye cannot quite be termed a temple. In the mind of its founder it was rather a magic reconstruction of the world having the King himself as its ideal centre. By embracing the new religion, the King took possession of a State protected by the new gods, with whom he had himself identified by means of a magic ritual. Around a five-storeyed temple in the middle there are four chapels surrounded by a wall. This central temple is the hub of the world, around which the universe unrolls and revolves. A hidden track leading to the soul's release is laid within its very wall: by walking along it according to prescriptions and consciously taking in the messages conveyed by the rows of deities studding its winding and ascending ways, the visitor receives the key to resolve the manifoldness of the outside world into the unity of primordial consciousness, symbolized in the god Demchog. In each of the temple's storeys the statues of the gods symbolize a different, and further, metaphysical sphere: from the roughest, on the ground floor, the way leads up to the finer, subtler spheres of the uppermost storey. It is like a journey along the spiritual path, a climbing from the world of space and time to the timeless omnipresence of cosmical consciousness. For man, such a process must still be projected into the moulds of time and space that he may receive a pictorial, architectonic view of his supermundane pilgrimage, a stratified display of his spiritual metamorphosis, and grow aware of the inner experiences that will visit him on the way.

On the first floor, Jobo Śākyamuni appeared as a young man wearing a diamond crowned by ten standing Bodhisattvas of Chinese style. The two chokyongs Tamdin and Migyova (*rTa mgrin* and *Mi gyo ba*) watched the door. On the second floor the same cycle was repeated: only the Bodhisattvas and the chokyongs were of Tibetan style. In the middle of the third floor stood Namparnangdze (*rNam par snaṅ mdsad*) viz. Vairocana and around him four statues looking at a different cardinal point each, and standing therefore back against back. It was the Kunrig type of Vairocana, which I often met in Western Tibet.[38] On the fourth and last floor there was Demchog surrounded by the ringa (*rigs lṅa*),[39] the five gods corresponding to the stage of a very first, budding display of the supreme consciousness into a visible, tangible, unfolding and ultimately disintegrating world. Demchog, as the sixth or better first item, stood aloof of display and decay, and meant therefore its very contrary, reintegration, return to that original, undivided light. Thus the temple was like a maṇḍala in itself, built along the same lines. Even outside, the chapels built against the four sides of the main temple stood for the continents into which Buddhist cosmology divides the Uni-

verse, the four temples corresponding to the main continents (*gliṅ bźi*) being placed at the four cardinal points and
the eight representing the minor ones (*gliṅ p'ran rgyad*)
respectively one on the right and one on the left of the
former. At the four sides of the temple in the middle were
four large chortens. Their colours were, beginning SE and
turning clock-wise around the temple, white, red, blue and
green. In the east, nearly covering the NE and SE corners,
there were two small temples dedicated to the moon (*Zla
lha k'aṅ*) and the sun (*Ñi ma lha k'aṅ*). The chapel devoted
to the temple's protector, the dreaded Pe dkar, was on the
north, right of the main temple. Its name was *Pe dkar ąk'or
mdsod lha k'aṅ* and contained the statues of all chokyongs.
But the several devastations had left no trace of anything
ancient. All the statues had been renovated. There was only
an old inscription at the entrance and one bronze bell, both
contemporary with the foundation of the building. The
main chapels were built according to the old pattern of
entrance porch and inner cell surrounded by the circumambulation corridor, and had one main image in the middle
flanked by other standing or squatting figures. An exception was the Jampal (*ąǰam dpal*) chapel on the W, with a
round apse, the only example found by me in Tibet. The
plan of that temple resembled the one of the Sun temple at
Taxila — which is nothing surprising when one thinks of
Padmasambhava's western origin. Moreover, many unusual
things had to be found at Samye, among others several
Sanskrit manuscripts even such a learned master as Atīśa
did not know. According to tradition, he visited that sanctuary, examined its library and acknowledged that many of
the works kept there were unknown in India. The Āryapālo
temple, so often mentioned in the *Padmat'aṅ yig*, was on
the S side.

Samye and its district up to Chimpu and Yamalung were
under the rule of a church dignitary, a *Tsetung*, who received us with great kindness, and helped me to get one
copy of the great guidebook to Samye. In the jealously

guarded treasure there should have been the small magic drum (*ḍāmaru*) used by the Indian master Sāntirakṣita, the one who advised King Tisongdetsen to have Padmasambhava come to Tibet. That drum was said to be finely painted, but it was exhibited only once a year and I could not see it. I could photograph an interesting Indian image instead.[40]

From Samye the road led up for some two thousand yards to the Haspori hill, barring the valley aslant from NE to SW, which was once the royal residence. There was no trace of the palace now, but only a modest temple, restored and devoid of any interest. I vainly scanned the rocks around it in search of inscriptions. On my way back to Samye I visited another temple built after the pattern of the central Samye temple, on whose first floor stood a statue of Jobo Śākyamuni surrounded by standing Bodhisattvas, and on the second the Kunrig cycle. There was moreover an ancient Nepalese statue. Not far from it, I saw another smaller temple, where Padmasambhava stood surrounded by bronze Bodhisattvas. These were perhaps the only really ancient statues extant at Samye, though they did not go back to the age of the convent's foundation: they were Nepalese works of the 14th or 15th century. Not far from there the guide showed us a pond consecrated to a *lu* (*klu*), viz. to one of the subterranean deities ruling over the water of rivers, lakes or pools, in the form of a snake or of a human being. That *lu*, according to tradition, was converted to Buddhism by Padmasambhava, and from that time on became an eager protector of those sacred places.

Back at Samye, we watched a sacred dance. In front of the main building, under a canopy set up for the occasion, sat the abbots on high stools, and on both sides, on lower ones, the players. Their small orchestra consisted of large trumpets, a huge drum resting on a single support, some cymbals and clarions. The music reminded me of the one of the Japanese Nô drama, rather an evocation than a commentary. There was hardly a trace of human gentleness in those sounds. It was a riot of hisses, bellowings and caterwaulings. You might have thought that the whole animal world, frightened by sudden sights, was expressing its fear with its natural voices. At regular intervals the orchestra stopped all at once and the emptiness of a tense expectation set in, in the awe of suspected presences; the choir filled the pauses and commented, by dancing and singing, the sudden and unpredictable assaults of the evil forces from invisible planes. The actors, adjusting their dance to suit the changing moods of the music, from one of frenzied fury to one of soothing stillness, now paced the floor describing gentle, silent circles, now jerked and jumped in a flurry of dizzy whirligigs, as if the demons possessing them had lent their muscles a superhuman strength neutralizing their bodily weight. There were no settings, no stage. The dance was performed on a sacred soil, where mysterious connections paved the way to the descent of the presences. The turquoise blue sky gleamed overhead and lent the yellow hills a transparent sheen. The actors had gone through long, complex rituals before their performance in order to attune their minds to the gods they called upon to impersonate and to second possession. Those rituals had gradually dampened their consciousness, and they had left the temple in a trance-like state, feeling they had been blessed with the presence of the god. During the performance, a choir master stood in the middle and recited the lines underlying the action in a deep-throated voice. The monks wore long, embroidered robes of Chinese silk, which were usually kept in the convent treasure among the most ancient and precious items. The butter and smoke of numberless ceremonies had left black grease stains on them. Diverse hats and diadems, warying according to the beings they represented, were their headwear. Everything was projected into a symbolic world: even the historical events some of these dances evoked were cast into the recurrent pattern of the struggle between good and evil. Some of the scenes had a direct bearing on the onlookers. One of them was the souls' judgment. Loaded with sin and shaken with belated and useless repentance, the dead filed out before the God of the Law, from whom nothing could be hidden, and their good and evil actions were placed and weighed on the unfailing scales. Those present saw materialized before their eyes the destiny awaiting them thereafter, and followed holding their breath the drama of which one day they would be themselves the actors.

Those were strenuous days for the Samye district commissioner. Some of the Sera warrior monks had killed and looted a batch of pilgrims on the Lhasa road. He had mustered all fit to wear arms and had rushed to capture them. In the resulting clash some of the marauders had been shot, and some had died after capture, under the flogging they had been sentenced to. The two or three survivors would be set free again, their hands and feet clamped in heavy wooden shackles and fetters and a chain hanging on them. Thus branded for the rest of their lives, they would shuffle painfully through the markets or in the shadow of temples, relying on the alms of their neighbours. That was the most usual way to punish criminals in Tibet.

Near Samye there were some notable places in the history of Tibetan religion: Tragmar (*Brag dmar*), Yamalung (*gYa' ma luṅ*) and Chimpu (*mC'ims p'u*). The former two are not marked on any map. We reached Tragmar in less than a couple of hours through an increasingly fertile valley. Barrenness receded up the mountain slopes, but even these grew green with bushes as we went on. A small village, fee of the Samye Szong, lay now at Tragmar, which was otherwise only surrounded by ruins and mounds. The modern temple on the hill top is known as Tirongdetsen's palace, whose only ornament were modern and poor statues of Padmasambhaava and Namparnangdse. Way down, I was shown an even smaller chapel marking the place where the king is said to have been born. We turned E into a blossoming valley and walked two hours up to the foot of a wooded mountain where white huts were perched high up on the rocks. That was Yamalung, where Padmasambhava spent some time in meditation. I panted and struggled up the steep hill, as a slight, persistent fever had caught hold of me since a few days, but at last I made it with the help of God. Though Yamalung played a great role in Tibet's religious life and it is often referred to in the literature, I did not find any important religious or artistic documents there. But there might have been some for all I knew, and I was glad to have come so far in order to satisfy myself personally and put my mind at rest; and having gained a first-hand experience of the place was quite different from having read of it in books.

The cradle of Tibet's political power had been in the area between Yarlung and Lhasa. Not for nothing there was a royal palace at Tragmar. Through that green valley a road had run joining Yarlung, the winter capital, with Lhasa, the summer residence. The Tsang-po, very broad between Yarlung and Samye, was easy to ford at the end of winter, when its waters were shallow and sluggish. As the court resided in that province when not engaged in war or hunting elsewhere, it had promoted the building of temples in the neighbourhood, but I could not find much trace of ancient constructions, and was struck by the difference with Western Tibet, where the rage of war and the lapse of centuries could not quite efface the vestiges of the past and wipe off the precious monuments. Possibly what harmed Central Southern Tibet most was the nearness of the capital, which made devastations the more thorough, and strife between sects, involving fatally the monasteries, the harsher. Later the devotion of the wealthy, eager to acquire religious merit, had given devastation the last stroke by restoring and renovating — and there is nothing the art historian can fear more than that kind of devotion, which unconsciously and pitilessly defaces the ancient beauty in order to re-instate the monuments of faith. On this point Tibet had fared no better than Italy, where a few centuries had laid a coat of pompous, rambling baroque on the straight simpleness of Romanesque and the upward lift of Gothic.

In Yamalung's narrow cells I was shown the cave where Padmasambhava withdrew to pray and evoke the gods who endowed him with wonder-working powers. A few yards lower down flowed the miraculous spring whose waters were supposed to prolong human life. As my fever had not left me yet I could not walk up to Chimpu, half-way on the slope of a mountain NE of Samye. I sent Moise there asking him to bring back an accurate description and the printed guidebook of the place. The hermitage was run by nuns and seemed not to contain anything of great historic or artistic value.

On August 15 we set out for Ngari Tratsang.[43] The Tsang po river flows some two and a half miles from Samye. We had to pick our way on the dunes through a dismally barren country: nothing gave us a clue to the right path in the yellow waste. We boarded our boat again with relief. The name Ngari Tratsang means the "Ngari College", namely founded by a Ngari, i.e. Western Tibetan king, a liberal patron of the Yellow sect. The massive building, as redoubtable and inaccessible as a fortress, dominated the valley from the sharp ridge where it stood planted with a warrior's proud bearing. In the cell at the far end of the assembly hall I saw a fine statue of Champa (Maitreya), flanked by the usual eight Bodhisattvas. At the sides of the entrance door stood Tamdin and Dsambhala. These statues were carved with an unusual skill, and a graceful vigour that got the better of the stiffness of formulas. On the walls of the assembly hall were some 17th century frescoes, big statues of the 31 Buddhas and paintings showing the Buddha's "108 deeds". The upper temple yielded many interesting items, among others the main statue (*gtso bo*), representing the Lotsava (learned translator) of Tanag, and a Nepalese chorten of the 15th century containing his mortal remains. What I admired most was a large relic holder shaped like a gilt bronze bell, adorned at the base with a pattern of wavy festoons winding around each other in wide coils, and bearing lofty, dignified figures of Bodhisattvas at

the top. That was an outstanding specimen of the art treasures gathered by the Tibetan kings during the conquest of
Central Asia and the war with China, and donated to those
temples, which must once have garnered precious works of
art. That relic holder was a Chinese piece of the T'ang age
and one of the most remarkable things I saw during my
expedition.

At Ngari Tratsang I pitched my tents[41] and went on
exploring the On country, this being the name of the valley
from the river bank up to Choding. The valley was wide,
fertile, and studded with villages and well-tilled fields. I
paid a short visit to a small temple where Tsonkhapa was
supposed to have spent some time in meditation[42] and made
for Choding (*C'os sdins*), a notable place in the history of the
Yellow sect, as biographers dwell at length on the visions
and revelations Tsonkhapa had there. Another saint, Gyese
(*rGyal sras*), also lived at Choding. His relics were kept in a
large silver chorten studded with gems and semi-precious
stones, where I noticed two Nepalese miniatures overlaid
with pieces of quartz. In the main temple the central statues
represented Jobo between two Buddhas, but the most remarkable piece was a scroll embroidered with figures of
Bodhisattvas, whose names were written in Chinese charac-
ters. It was a piece of Chinese needlework like some of the
tankas Mr Aurel Stein found in Central Asia and, like the
Ngari Tratsang relic holder, it bore witness to the treasures
of Central Asiatic and Chinese art once embellishing the
Tibetan temples, most of which have unfortunately
vanished.

Choding stands in a fine position, overlooking the higher
On valley, a pleasant expanse of land, crossed by the gleaming streak of the river. On the slope W of me I could see
the shimmering white Keru temple, also built by king
Tisrongdetsen. I walked down to it in the hope of some
find, but was disappointed. The layout was certainly
ancient, but the temple had been thoroughly restored. In
the cell on the far side of the Dukang stood a statue of

Śākyamuni surrounded by the eight Bodhisattvas. All I could see worthy of notice was some ancient capital in the porch and two Chinese-style Chokyongs on both sides of the entrance door, dating back to the end of the 16th century. In the adjoining chapel dedicated to Atīśa there was a modern statue of that master and a small white chorten after the model of the Indian classical stupas, opening into another chapel (Kharchung). It was a charming, lonely spot, flowing with water and thick with green. A married couple had come there from Lhasa to spend the summer.

At Ngari Tratsang we had to say farewell to the boats. The river was getting narrower, its current impetuous and sailing was no more possible, I therefore got the caravan in marching order again and set out for Densatil.

12 The Densatil Hermitage and the Maitreya Temple at Dzingji

In the area along the Brahmaputra from Chushul up to Ngari Tratsang and in the On valley we noticed a striking frequency of goitre, most of all at Samye, where huge, double, shapeless goitres could be seen. With it went an obvious tendency towards cretinism and dwarfishness. Many of the monks engaged in the Samye dance had been of a less than normal stature. Goitre was particularly marked in the female sex, probably, as Moise thought, because men were led further away from home by their trade, thus getting an opportunity to change their food and the quality of the water they drank. South of the Brahmaputra goitre, though not thoroughly absent, was less frequent.

In those villages around Samye women wore a particular headgear, a kind of cap with uplifted side brims, replacing the Lhasa *patruk* and the Tsang *pakor*. That kind of hat, however, did not spread much outside that area and was limited to the peasants there.

Densatil[43] is one of the famous places of Tibet, as a noted ascetic, Pagmotru, founded it in the 11th century. The hermitage was for some time a dependency of Digung[44] and later became the sanctuary of the Pagmotru family, which in the 14th century had managed to conquer nearly the whole of Tibet, and whose tombs are at Densatil. The convent is perched high up in a glen, at some 13,000 ft. We reached it by a mountain path winding up the mountain slope and never losing sight of a torrent bounding down the valley from waterfall to waterfall. The path was lined with wild roses, rhododendrons and junipers, which once again went to show that ascetics did not only choose lonely spots, but also lovely ones for their meditation. Saints are often poets, who love God and seek Him in the beauty of creation.

The day we had chosen for our visit happened to be a feast, and the monks were all gathered in the main temple and said their office, now and then breaking the day-long routine with pauses for food, tea and rest.

In the central temple's open porch rose huge chortens holding the remains of the abbots and princes of that lineage, whose two branches held the secular and spiritual throne through many generations. They were huge gilt-bronze monuments carried out by Nepalese craftsmen perhaps with the help of the very skilled local workmen: the Tsetang princes must have gathered the pick of the available architects and sculptors, and their successors did their level best to achieve the same standard. Here could be seen the fixity of an art that went through the centuries without undergoing any sizable change, but for the less accurate finish and the greater harping on minor details of the more recent times. Those chortens were rightly termed "Kumbums", i.e. "the hundred thousand statues", as the architectural lines of those buildings were smothered with a wealth of carvings and reliefs that knew no limits. The whole Olympus of Mahāyāna seemed to have assembled on those monuments. As I cast the light of my torch on the chortens, the several figures sprang into life, glittering with gold outlined and set off by darker hues and deep shadows.

On each of the four sides of the plinth, the shapes of the protectors of the cardinal points were carved, to mark out the sacred area and ward off the evil powers. Their hard, rugged images, like of mail-clad warriors, sharply contrasted with the buoyancy of some female deities gambolling festoon-like around the upper part of some of the oldest chortens. A huge gilt Buddha smiled impassively against the middle of the wall. As I could make out from the inscription on the plinth, the statue was commissioned by King Changchub Gyantsen (*Byaṅ c'ub rgyal mts'an*). The inscription also carried the names of the artists and purported that the statue had been carved according to the models of Nepalese art.[45] On the Buddha's either side were statues of Champa and Chenrezig.

On the several altars facing the chortens were heaped statues of the most different sizes and ages. Some were Indian, but most of them were Nepalese.

The guide then led us into a hut inside the temple, where Drongon Pagmotru (ạGron mgon p'ag mo gru) spent some time in meditation. The whole huge temple developed later on around that lonely hut. An incarnate was now sitting motionlessly and meditating in it. That naked, narrow, dim place breathed mystery and devotion. There you could sit out of reach of wordly distractions, on a small, secluded surface where throughout the centuries pious souls had experienced the ultimate merging in God while still living in this world. I felt unaccountably overpowered by that sense of mystery and it cost me an effort to tear myself away from that cell, as if by entering it I had bodily trodden over the threshold of another world.

In a neighbouring temple I could see two more chortens containing the mortal remains of Drongon Pagmotru.

I spent the rest of the day with the monks. The wife of one Pandetsan, a rich Tibetan merchant at the time on a mission to the U.S., was there too. She was on a pilgrimage and happened just to be visiting the same places as I was. A stout, middle-aged woman, she was suffering from a touch of mountain sickness. Dr. Moise set her on her legs again with the proper drugs.

As we left the Densatil hermitage to rejoin the tent camp we had pitched in the valley, we noticed white ruins of monasteries on the opposite bank of the river. Their names were forgotten and the ruins had been abandoned for good.

On August 20 we reached Zangrikangmar[46] after climbing the mountain which descends by bluff down to the Brahmaputra and forces the river to turn to the north. Ruins of ancient fortresses on the mountain pass bore witness to the powerful defenses once built by the Pagmotru kings in order to slow down the collapse of the state built by Changchub Gyantsen.

Zangrikangmar, a dependency of the Ngari Tratsang monastery, belonged to the Yellow sect and rose in a broad, fertile valley, among luxuriant fields and verdant trees. On the background, against the foot of a hill, stood the white palace of the feudal overlords, the Samdub Potang (*bSam grub p'o bran*). In front a temple devoted to Machiglab watched severely. Machiglab was a notable woman in the history of Tibetan asceticism. From an Indian master by the name of Padampa she learned "shiche" (*ži byed*), that is, the difficult art of checking passions and realizing the unsubstantiality of things. The main temple of Padampa's school was Tingri in Western Tibet, on the road leading to Nepal. Zangrikangmar was entirely restored and only in its Gonkang there were a few ancient statues left. In the main temple I saw some sharply outlined frescoes and paintings representing the Buddha's 108 deeds, of the end of the 18th century.

At Zangrikangmar we also could lay hands on the first fresh fruit for a long time: stinted, sour apples. But after months of tinned fruit even that unripe crop was welcome, as we were badly in need of vitamin-laden food with the taste of the country — and could not enjoy even that for long.

The road wound farther and farther away from the river

as this tore along in narrowing, jagged mountain gorges, and it shrunk to a steep path as it approached the mountain passes. We had to force our way through the rocks, getting our foothold on steps roughly hewn in the red and white stone, shimmering like marble in the sunshine. Left of us was one of the highest mountains of Tibet, the Odegungyal (*'O lde guṅ rgyal*), a name attributed by popular traditions to Tibet's first king. A huge dome of rock, it steadily mounted, each ridge topped by the next one, up to its toothed, abrupt, forbidding crests, glistening with ice and overhanging the snow-blanketed slopes. The Odegungyal was wrapped in an unceasing blizzard. Only in its brief respites did a sudden rend in the clouds and a touch of the fugitive sun allow a glimpse of the mountain in all its glory, and made our desire to look more closely at it keener. We were not to be satisfied, as the weather, rainy and cold at that height of 13,000 ft., was not on our side.

We stayed at that height till we reached Oka (*'Ol dga'*),[47] once a large principality. Only a wing of the old castle was extant at the time, and that was so unsafe that the district commissioner was afraid to live in it. The village consisted of a few houses huddled together against the mountain face to get protection against the ruthless E and N winds. A great sadness weighed over the place. An epidemic had decimated the scanty population and several houses, abandoned by their tenants, were empty shells doomed to collapse soon. Traces of the old fields could still be seen around the village in the valley and on the mountain slopes. Once upon a time Oka must have been a thriving town, surrounded by bumper crops of emerald-green barley in summer. Later, the Mongolian inroads from the north smashed and shattered everything. The place never got another lease of life, and it was further crippled by poverty and disease. The district commissioner met us cheerfully on our arrival. A few hours later Moise and I called on him. We had to force our way through a hedge of cows, sheep and mules herded together in a narrow, dirty yard and to climb up the rickety rungs of a wooden ladder to reach the first floor, where the commissioner gave us a very warm reception and treated us lavishly to tea. There was a regular army of women in that household and I was at a loss to pick out the commissioner's wife — if he had only one — and to make out the relationship between the several girls inquisitively peering at the unusual guests. To get out of the scrape I laid a coral necklace on the tray as a gift in exchange for the ones we had received on our arrival, viz. a leg of mutton and a great deal of eggs, two thirds of which, as it often is the case, were rotten. But, as I remarked before, the quality of a gift in Tibet counts much less than its intention. It was even rated as a discourtesy to send a letter not accompanied by a modest gift. If you had nothing better to give, you could just enclose the dry, thin, silver-filigree-like seeds of a plant thought to bring good luck.

On the next days, the commissioner very kindly took us around to see the sights on horseback. At Oka there was but one temple left where the Buddhas of the Three Times were worshipped, surrounded by ten standing Bodhisattvas. The door was guarded by the usual keepers. Between the statues, I could make out the faint remains of old paintings.

At Dzingji,[48] some 5 miles NE of Oka, there were three main temples. The first, often mentioned in Tsonkapa's biographies, was consecrated to Champa (Maitreya). The seated god's statue was in the innermost chapel, amidst a blaze of gold, and was believed to be one of Tibet's oldest statues, though it had clearly been restored or perhaps even made anew. Anyway it was of no great artistic value. The original had been probably destroyed by the Mongols. But all this meant very little for the devotees when the god mysteriously inhabiting the statue had stayed the same. When mankind has sunk to an even lower level of evil, when hunger, pestilence and wars have filled the world with blood and death, Maitreya is expected to descend from the heaven where he sits in meditation, to give back hope to mankind and to revive love in the withered hearts. According to ancient prophecies, that time should be some four hundred years from now, and they should be four centuries of growing misery. The *Kaliyuga* of the Indian tradition, the age of discord, should be drawing to an end and all but drown mankind in a welter of hatred and destruction. The statue of Champa throned behind the altar, flanked by two minor gods and surrounded by eight Bodhisattvas along the walls. The two door keepers, Tamdin on the left and Chagdor on the right of the door, were modelled according to the Chinese type. A large silver chorten is said to hold the mortal remains of Tāranātha, a well-known Tibetan polygraph, whose convent between Sakya and Tashilhumpo I had visited in 1939. As tradition has it, Tāranātha's relics were thrown into the river and carried by the stream to Katrag, midway between Zangrikangmar and Oka, where they were collected and transported into the Dsingji temple. In a smaller chapel I found quite a few ancient statues, some from Nepal. In the assembly temple the frescoes did not date further back than the 17th century. Nothing noteworthy was in the third temple.

While looking for the monastery chronicles I found out that there was only one copy left, which the monks would not give away. The district commissioner went out of his way to offer to copy the whole book himself, a feat he performed by working around the clock for one day and one night.

We went back from Dzingji to Oka by a roundabout way and stopped at Cholung (*C'os luṅ*), a celebrated spot, where Tsongkhapa had his hermitage built at the foot of the Odegungyal (see above), in the midst of a verdant, shady ravine flowing with water. In that barren wilderness, one of us would hardly find it necessary to climb steep rocks and search the most inaccessible corners of the mountain for further isolation. Yet the hermitages nestled in the remotest ravines, in the shadow of an old juniper tree or in the faint ripple of a mountain spring. They were recesses of deeper loneliness carved out in the vast stillness of those landscapes, already as out of this world as children's dreams. Cholung was a very pleasant retreat from whose very threshold you could have a bird's eye view of the Oka plain, asleep and forsaken, joining the Dzingji valley, by which we had come back, in the NE and widening in the E into a broader valley that ran along the mountains up to Chodegye. Apart from the beauty of the spot I could not find anything of interest at Cholung, where two or three monks were filling the loneliness with the murmur of their prayers. That was like the dwindling voice of asceticism in its struggle to conquer the void of those mountains, for which Tsongkhapa and his disciples had so successfully embattled it. That enthusiasm had spent itself in the course of centuries. The army of ascetics was thinning away and the deadly silent mountains were coming again into their own.

13 In the Yarlung Valley — Tsetang, Chongye and the Tombs of the Kings

A ferry took us from Oka across the river to Ngari Tratsang on the opposite bank. It looked like Noah's ark. As we alighted, the barge set ashore an improbable quantity of pilgrims, merchants, horses and sheep, as if it had been bottomless. Which was not without danger: about one year earlier the overloaded ferry had capsized and all had been drowned in the river. That day was entered as ominous into the calendar: a demon was suspected to have brought about the mishap. To avoid its recurrence the ferry would never ply the river on that day.

The Tsetang monastery rises not far away from the confluence of the Yarlung river with the Tsangpo. Tsetang (*rTse t'aṅ*) was founded in 1390 and grew into a large convent ruled by the Pagmotru abbots, while the princes of the same family sat on the throne of the Netong palace, some ten furlongs further down the river. Though the rulers of the monastery and the palace were nearly always either brothers or close relatives, they were often at daggers drawn, which caused no little trouble in Tibetan history. Netong (*sNe gdoṅ*) has considerably declined whereas Tsetang, on account of its favourable situation near the bank of the river, has grown in importance and population. There was a busy bazaar supplying the provinces S of the Tsangpo, which were known under the general name of Lhokha (South). Like in Lhasa and at Shigatse, some *Kache* families, i.e. naturalized Kashmiri Muslims, lived there too. They did some retail trade and some of them worked as tailors.

The Yarlung valley, beginning there, is for Tibet what the seven hills are for Rome. All legends revolve around that spot. I was camping in a shady garden at the foot of the mountains where Chenrezig, the future protector of the Land of Snows, was embodied in the shape of an ape and mated with a witch. The Tibetan people was born of this match, and he took it under his protection as his own children.[49] A few miles S of them was the ancient palace onto which the first Buddhist book fell from heaven. The king who picked it up did not understand its meaning but worshipped it as something holy and portentous, on the strength of a prophecy to the effect that that book would have marked the beginning of a new religion destined to change the shape of things. In the W, on the top of a steep mountain, in the "crystal cave", the wonder-worker Padmasambhava evoked the beings who could help him to drive away by force of magic and meditation the devils harassing the country. On such holy ground temples and convents have grown as thick as the houses and each sect had its own. At Tsetang, where we stopped a few days to get our bearings before starting the exploration of the valley, muffled memories of Lhasa's social life were revived by a row of official visits. The town had a lay and an ecclesiastic commissioner, and also a "chikyab", a kind of province governor supervising all district commissioners, eighteen in all, residing in the province. The chikyab was a lama. He received us with great loving kindness in his blossomy, flowery estate south of Tsetang. As I was amicably talking to him during lunch, my gaze rested on the garden dozing in the warm, sunny air, and I could have thought I was in the Italian countryside in spring. With such scenery to feast my eyes upon and in the conversation of my kind, educated host, I felt quite at home. I felt I could have settled there as well as anywhere else, perhaps better than elsewhere, as I would enjoy a greater freedom to follow the bidding of my fancy.

The lay commissioner was away on an inspection tour, and we were received by his wife. A Tibetan official must not necessarily stay at his post. Several commissioners were at that time living in Lhasa, engaged in more profitable pursuits, and left their wives and servants to run their office on the spot. My Lhasa recommendation letters were of great help to open all doors. The commissioner's secretary put himself at our disposal as a guide. As he was in charge of justice, people paid him homage when he went around either by taking their hat off or bowing down or, as it is customary in Tibet, by stretching out their tongues. One of his colleagues, a large pock-marked man, provided transportation.

The visit of monasteries took me many days. I went first to the Ganden Chokorling (*dGa' ldan c'os ąk'or glin*), founded by Sonantobgye (*bSods nams stobs rgyas*), a huge convent where hundreds of monks lived under the rule of an abbot from Kham. I went to see him in his small, dark room, where I found him squatting on the floor, reading the sacred texts. A lean, severe, quiet man, he was entirely devoted to his studies and meditations. He was the spiritual centre of the convent, and his aides took care of discipline. While we were talking, inquisitive faces of students peeped through the door and spied at a corner window, eager to overhear what we said. The monastery was a new building where I could find nothing of interest, except a length of painted silk behind a statue, which reminded me of those found by Mr Aurel Stein in Central Asia and certainly had the same origin.

Another big monastery of the Yellow sect was the Ngacho

(*lha c'os*), which was damaged and destroyed in the wars and later reconstructed in such a way as to hold everything which could be saved from destruction. War had often visited that valley, not only in the 18th century, when the Dsungars made their inroads, but still much earlier. After Changchub Gyansen, the last Netong princes had become the "de facto" kings of Tibet, and had to wage war against the rebellious Rinpung lords and Tsang princes. The conflict thus brought about lasted several decades and pitted the two provinces of Tsang and Ü against each other, as these not only defended their interests and independence, but sided respectively for the Sakyapa and Karmapa sect the former, and for the Gelukpas the latter.

In the assembly hall of that temple were the statues of the twelve Bodhisattvas and the Chokyong. Among the ancient statues I noticed two standing Buddhas nearly certainly of Indian origin and a gilt-bronze fragment representing a row of Kandromas (*bKa' ągro ma*) of the golden age of Nepalese art. Those remains and a few extant Nepalese chortens could give an idea of the treasures once gathered in that cradle of Tibetan civilization.

Also in the neighbouring temple known as the *Chokang nyimpa* (the old temple), where the central statues represented, according to the usual pattern, the Buddhas of the Three Times surrounded by the Bodhisattvas, I could find some old pieces.

A fourth temple, the Santamling (*bSam gtan gliñ*) rose on a skull-like, bald hill. In the past, a great Sakya lama, by name Sonamgyantsen (*bSod nams rgyal mts'an*) and other celebrated ascetics of Tibetan esoteric tradition had lived there. Now there was nearly nothing left but a dreary Gonkang, a chorten holding the relics of Sengeygyantsen and a statue of the above mentioned Sakya ascetic. The keeper, who certainly was in a position to meditate on the ups and downs of things human, received us with friendly cheerfulness. Going down by a crooked, bumpy path we skirted the Chinese temple where a large statue of Kuan ti,

the war god, was to be seen. As long as Tibet had been a
Chinese dependency, a strong garrison of imperial soldiers
had stayed at Tsetang. The temple was comparatively recent, as it dated from the end of the 18th century.

On our way back to camp we stopped at Trebuling (*ạBras
bu gliṅ*), a Sakya monastery and one of the most noted
centres of Tibet's religious and political life. All that was
left of its past splendour was a few good paintings on canvas
representing the sect's succession of masters.

But I was still to experience my greatest disappointment.
As we approached Netong, once the capital of Tibet, we
sighted the gnarled ridge crumbling down into the valley
with ravines and screes where Changchub Gyandsen had
built his own palace. All could be seen now was some
insignificant ruin. A Nyingmapa monastery had been built
on the remains of the old foundations. In the vast valley
below there was no trace left of the past glory. Even in the
Tsetsogpa temple, where Tsonkhapa is said to have taken
his vows, I could not detect anything worthy of note.

Some five miles S of Netong I visited the great Tantrup
(*K'ra ạbrug*) temple[50] which, according to tradition, was
built by Srongtsengampo. It was undoubtedly one of
Tibet's oldest temples, but it could not escape the fate of
anything else built in that valley. The layout of the Tsuglakang, flanking the road, reminded me of the Lhasa temple.
The most notable things in it were the bronze standing
Bodhisattvas surrounding a statue of Namparnangtse at the
farther end of the cell, but as they were covered with
drapings and frills I could not make an accurate study of
their style. The Chinese-school door keepers in the chapel
now consecrated to the fifth Dalai Lama also deserved
particular attention. Around a chorten I could read an
inscription still preserving the name of the person to whom
it had been dedicated. A large inscribed bronze bell in the
front porch was the only really ancient document of the
temple extant. On the upper floor the guide conducted us
into a chapel devoted to the eighty-four Siddhas, the mas-

ters of the Indian esoteric schools astride between Buddhism and Hinduism. Those ascetics were portrayed in terracotta statues full of expression in keeping with the tenets of traditional iconography. The protector of the place worshipped in the Gonkang was none less than Tsampachenpo (*Tsaṅs pa c'en po*), i.e. Brahmā.

As I proceeded southward in the Yarlung valley, I thought it worthwhile to branch off E and climb up to Riwocholing (*Riu c'os gliṅ*), a large and pleasant monastery built, or rather re-built by Dalai Lama Kalzengyatso (*sKal bzaṅ rgya mts'o*). In the middle chapel the statue of Jobo was, as usual, surrounded by the eight Bodhisattvas. In another temple a large chorten held the relics of Darmadoday, the son of thaumaturge Marpa (see chapter 3, end), who was the master of Milaraspa. There were some frescoes on the walls, presumably of the 17th century.

The short digression over, I resumed my southerly course along the road and reached Yumbulakang, the palace mentioned at the beginning of this chapter, where the first king of Tibet was living when the first Buddhist revelation fell in book form from heaven. It was a pagoda-like tower daringly rising on top of a short, square structure perched above a jagged mountain spur. Here too tradition had to be taken on trust on the strength of documents, as no outer sign in the entirely re-made building vouched for its truth. In the entire flight of several chapels, all wilted and decayed, only a Nepalese statue of Dolma was worthy of note.

The guidebook recommended Lharumengye (*Lha ru sman brgyad*) to the pilgrims as one of the holiest Yellow-sect temples in the valley. A path in steep descent took us there. The temple had two storeys. On the upper floor I admired a good statue of Kandroma of Nepalese school and a large bronze Buddha. His unusually high ascetical tuft and his subtle features recalled the Siamese statues. A thoughtful and slightly dismal composure showed in his eyes half-closed in meditation, while his gracefully modelled body sat in the yogic posture. He was like a symbol of the peace you can only find by avoiding associate life and embracing loneliness.[51] The lower floor went under the name of Onlakang (*dBon lha k'aṅ*) where *dBon* is equivalent to *rtsis pa,* astrologer. It looked like a Gonkang dominated by terrific gods, and was brimming over with weapons and shields offered to the war-like gods to commemorate battles won through the help of invisible forces.

A few miles further S rose the Potrang, another place of the Tibetan kings. The present building bearing that name was a modest house further down the slope, where no traces of antiquities could be detected. We got a very kind reception and were served lunch in front of a Nepalese-style chorten where Tisrongdetsen's relics were said to be kept. That chorten was certainly not so old as tradition would have it. But that a palace must have risen there of old was borne out by the extensive ruins indenting the hill above the house, running irregularly up the ridge and bristling on the spurs.

There is no doubt tradition is right. Yet, in this breeding ground of Tibet's history and culture you could hardly find any remains dating back to the time of the Kings except at Tragmar, Potrang and Chongye. Personally, I also found less prehistoric remains than I expected. I was especialy keen on what the Tibetans call *tonde* (*t'og rdeu*) viz. "lightening stone", a name covering all stone or bronze objects found underground, like arrow-heads, small statues of gods, buckles, clasps and dressing ornaments; and consistently searched the ground for them in that whole area. They are hard to date, as they do not change appreciably throughout the whole prehistory and the first stages of Tibetan history. They sometimes find their counterpart in the so-called "art of the steppes". Some of those which I found represented the Kyun (*K'yuṅ*) a sacred bird of Bon, the religion which preceded Buddhism. Some others were round or triangular as the ones I had found in great quantity in Western Tibet. There too it was very hard to prevail upon the owners to part with them. The *tondes* were supposed to be good-luck charms, as both the heavens, from where they were thought to have fallen, and the earth, where they had long been buried, had put them in touch with the upper gods and with the *sadag* and *lu*, the spirits of the underground and of the waters, thus loading them with power. People owning nine of them felt quite safe. Nine, in pre-Buddhist tradition — and that was hard to die as all magical beliefs — was, like thirteen, a perfect number.

In order to reach Chongye, the easternmost aim of my journey, I branched off towards Trashichode (*bKra šis c'os sde*), a large Sakya monastery lying at the foot of a hill in a clump of trees kept fresh and lively by the river flowing near by. I stopped in the porch for a talk with the head monks, who were surprised to learn that I was well acquainted with the chief of their sect whose guest I had been at Sakya for two months on a previous expedition, and proceeded to visit the convent. In the assembly hall the walls were covered with murals looking like painted scrolls, depicting the sixteen Arhats, the Buddhas invoked during confession, Demchog, Dukikorlo and the sect's patron: Kyedor. They dated back to the eighteenth century. At the far end of the cell a gilt bronze Buddha had at his sides the usual acolytes, the monks Śāriputra and Maudgalyāyana, two expressive and dignified statues; the three were surrounded by the eight traditional Bodhisattvas, while Tamdin and Chagdor kept watch at the door. I was much engrossed by the chapel devoted to Nantose (*rNam t'os sras* = *Vaiśravaṇa*), the patron of the North and the god of wealth. That god had a very complicated story and bore the unmistakable marks of Eastern and Central Asiatic influences: among others a Chinese armour and cast of features, and a remarkably Persian look. The eight *tadag*, his escorting horsemen, rode menacingly around him. Three other chapels displayed, in bronze or stucco statues, the *lamegyu* (*bla ma'i rgyud*) or the succession of the Sakya masters through whom the doctrine was spread and kept alive on earth. One of the most remarkable things is the entrance of the temple with the four Lokapālas threateningly warding off the forces of evil from the sacred place.

We resumed our way towards Rechungpug (*Ras c'uṅ p'ug* = Rechung's cave). Rechung was the greatest pupil of Milaraspa. He wrote an account of his master's life and mystical songs of his own describing the intoxication of mystical ecstasy and hinting, in deliberate double-talk, at Yoga's subtle doctrine. Above the cave a monastery had been built, dominating the whole irrigated, fertile valley. Large, white villas rose like islands in that sea of crops, a soil which would produce anything within a few months and would be worth its weight in gold if properly culti- vated. The convent rose above the cave, a large hole carved in the live rock, where Rechung had been meditating, and belonged to the Kagyupa sect. Stories of Buddha's lives were frescoed in the assembly hall. In the cell, as usual, rose a statue of the historical Buddha surrounded by the eight Bodhisattvas and two Chokyongs. Stucco statues in other chapels represented the series of the sect's masters.

We left the Yarlung river and went on along the banks of the Chongyechu, a usually sluggish stream frequently slack- ening into backwaters and branching off into a myriad of canals. There the caravan often got bogged down with serious jeopardy to the luggage and the tents, which had usually to be pulled out dripping from such unplanned immersions. Sometimes the waters were, on the contrary, so deep and impetuous that the horses had trouble in stag- gering ashore from the wobbly gravel of the river-beds. All that water got wasted in the end, as it drained away among the barren layers of pebbles and grit, where not a blade of grass grew. The fields snuggled up to the shelter of the mountain ridges in the side valleys, away from the high winds raging there in winter.

Chongye is another landmark. There the fifth Dalai Lama was born, one of the noblest figures of Tibetan his- tory. He was the son of the local feudatories and saw the light in a modest room which was still shown to the visitors in the ruins of the castle, a huge castle straddling the mountain crags, barring the valley with its mighty towers and reaching down to the river with its battlemented ramparts in order to secure water supply during sieges.

On the highest floor of the tower a patched-up chapel, still in a sorry state of disrepair, was devoted to the 16 Arhats. I could hardly detect any traces of ancient art though, as tradition would have it, the tomb of one of Tibet's first kings should lie beneath the tower.

We descended the mountain slope down to the Dzong, which was rebuilt at the time of the eighth Dalai Lama on the pattern of the ancient palace where the Chongye princes had lived. Its finest wing contained the assembly hall, as solemn as the throne room of a barbarian king. There was an opening in the middle of the ceiling and the bright daylight shone through and twinkled among the massive pillars.

We pitched our tents in a camp of poplars and willows on the left bank of the river. There the district commissioner, accompanied by his wife, his brother-in-law and a plump monk, who had come to explain to the inmates of the convent the "Summa Theologica" of Tibetan Buddhism, came to meet us.

But I was eager to trace the tombs of the ancient kings, which according to old documents had been built around there, though the exact location was never mentioned. A few talks with the villagers were enough to put me on the right track. On the opposite river bank, right in front of my tents camp, I was shown the tomb of the founder of the Tibetan dynasty. It was a mound carved by water erosion on the loamy soil, around which a roadlike ledge had been cut, thus making nature's work more regular. On the outer edges of that road traces of walls limiting the sacred surface could be seen. The mound was surmounted by a temple. Other mounds and other temples were outlined on that yellow, wrinkled, moon-like landscape, where man found a graveyard half built already by nature and had only to add a few finishing touches. In each mound a mortuary cell was dug, then the corpse, along with the arms and the servants of the deceased, was laid into it, and a stone slab with an inscription was stuck onto it. The only inscription extant was the one on Tisrongdetsen's tomb. Copying it was a hard job, as the stone slab had been so defaced by time and scribbled over by people that it took us many hours to decipher it. I was helped by a lama in the task, and we must often try to reconstruct a whole sentence from bits of letters. In the rush of discovery we disregarded the rain ceaselessly flowing down on the rough stone and giving cracks and slits the deceptive appearance of letters.

To identify the other tombs I could only have recourse to the literary tradition I had collected in ancient documents. It was on the whole a huge city of the dead, as rough as the chiefs who were buried in it. They had been ruling over a people that flowed like a river from the endless plain and vanished there underground without leaving any lasting trace behind — a people of nomads that went by as swift as a summer storm, to wind up with everything they had, wives and servants, in to the Earth's womb.

Those pillars stuck on top of the graves were not only meant to carry inscriptions. They had a deeper purpose. Elsewhere, for example at Ramagan, we found pillars bearing no inscriptions, but only patterns of dragons and spirals. The like are found in China too, which must not be explained by the imitation of ornamental motives, but by the parallel expression of similar religious ideas. The upright stone slab rising from the grave was the "axis mundi", the pivot of the world, the middle point of a surface which had been magically transformed into the cosmos. When such pillars were driven into the soil and the proper ceremonies performed on them, the dead king was thought to have taken possession of that soil and to have tapped, by means of that key, the supernatural energies living in the deeper layers, the *lus* and *sadags*, which thus fell under his jurisdiction. Those beings were usually represented as dragons in Chinese iconography — an item helping to solve the riddle of those "ornamental" patterns on the Ramagan and Chinese pillars quoted above. By holding sway on those spirits, the dead king could also secure the plentifulness of crops on the fields above. That was also one of the aims of the tombs. From inside them, the spirit of the deceased kings watched over the country.

We know that the inner cell was square and divided into nine compartments. The king's corpse was laid into the middle one, after having been kept somewhere else in seclusion for a certain time. His personal belongings and his arms were then laid into the eight surrounding compartments.

The tombs were placed under the supervision of some officials impersonating the deceased and, as such, they claimed possession of, and laid hands on, any person or animal trespassing into the area reserved to the grave. When funeral ceremonies were performed in the recurrencies, due notice was given that the deceased, viz. his representative, might get out of the way and return later after the ceremony to collect all the offers. One may easily imagine what a mine an archaeologist could tap there. But at the time the Tibetans looked hardly to be prevailed upon to violate the tombs of their own kings, some of whom were held to be embodiments of divine beings. Quite a number, for that matter, were broken open in the 10th century, when the dynasty collapsed and the old religion regained the upper hand. But the plunderers' interests do not tally with those of scholars, and even an excavation of the ravaged tombs might yield remarkable results.

Above the village of Chongye rose the rambling, meandering compound of the Ribodechen (*Ri bo bde c'en*) monastery, a Gelukpa convent built after the model of Ganden. The temples and the chapels were nearly drowned among the houses accommodating the monks. In the Rinchenligme (*Rin c'en gliṅ smad*) building throned the statues of Gigche, Demchog and Dsambhala. The assembly hall was of recent build. In the Champalakang, devoted to

Champa (Maitreya) there was an excellent statue of the god, probably of Indian origin. The Kalzenglakang (*sKal bzaṅ lha k'aṅ*) was consecrated to the Dalai Lama Kalzeng Gyatso (*sKal bzaṅ rgya mts'o*). I stopped a while in a new temple the local artists were building and decorating. They were faithfully and deliberately carrying on along the old lines, and turning out the same seated Buddhas with the Bodhisattvas crowding around. Within a few years the soot of the lamps would darken the colours and it would become hard to tell with certainty the age of the work. Only the fussiness of details and a certain dullness of the motives would enable the connoisseurs to assign the works to the first half of the 20th century.

Near Chongye, in the two valleys branching off the mountain where Srongtsengampo's tomb lies, there are two notable convents. The former is called Tseringjong (*Ts'e riṅ ljoṅs*), and gave birth to a man who detected some of the books hidden by Padmasambhava. Moise went there and had a look around. He found nothing remarkable, but for a chorten with the relics of the founder. The latter, Peri (*dPal ri*), rose on the valley to the south, and was a Nyingmapa convent that had known better days and had been restored of late.

We turned back, heading for Tsetang again. On our left, on the opposite bank of the river lay the large, verdant Shu valley. We went by Sonagthang (*Sol nag t'aṅ*), a large wayside lamasery, with no trace of ancient documents. But its lay-out, the surrounding ruins and the row of chortens along the road bore out that the monastery was one of the oldest in Yarlung. On the opposite bank, the green Shu valley was followed by the parched valley of Shangda, where tradition placed the tomb of another early king of Tibet.

Further along our way back to Tsetang on the left bank of the Yarlung river we stopped briefly at Gungtangbumpa (*Guṅ t'aṅ bum pa*), a large chorten flanked by a temple; and at the Kandenlhakang temple, which we could not visit as the keeper was nowhere to be seen. The Tsechubumpa

(*Ts'e c'u bum pa*) chorten near the latter contained perhaps some documents referring to its foundation. A mountain path branching off there led up to Sheltra (*Śel brag* = the rock crystal crag) where Padmasambhava withdrew in order to conjure up the terrific powers, and where a late disciple of his detected some of the most important books of the Nyingmapa sect. We could see various caves and small gonpas built to protect Padmasambhava's statue.

Having reached Tsetang again, we made a halt in order to have a rest and to reorganize the caravan. We expected to find our mail there, but we were disappointed. We had detailed a servant of the Samye commissioner to call at the Gyantse post office, send our outgoing mail and collect any post lying for us there. Since Lhasa we had lost touch with the rest of the world, and the latest news on the situation in Europe was not reassuring. Unfortunately our envoy, as we learned later, had never reached his destination. He had had a bad fall at Kongkadzong and had developed gangrene at one leg.

I was in possession of a Lhasa warrant empowering me to requisition horses, which each district commissioner in his turn had to place at my disposal at the official fares till I had reached the adjoining district. But the peasants, engaged in farming, went to any lengths to shirk the unpleasant duty, for which they received a mere pittance, as most of the price paid got stuck in the hands of greedy officials on its way. Thus it came about that on the morning of my departure no horses were in sight. Instead of leaving at eight as scheduled I was forced to leave at noon, and with a half of the horses I needed. The luggage was left behind at Tsetang waiting for the rest of the caravan. I learned later that the shirkers had been summoned to court and sentenced to I forget how many lashes each. Feudalism still ruled Tibet. Discipline was harsh, authority respected. Obedience was not only enforced by fear, however, as everybody seemed to have an inborn feeling of awe for those one rung higher on the social ladder.

14 From Yarlung to Gyantse

The road leading from Tsetang to Kongkardzong skirts the southern bank of the Tsangpo, cutting through a sandy, barren terrain which runs as a belt around the network of very fertile valleys wedged into the mountain chain S of the river. We left Yarlung, wended our way around Sheltra and made a halt at Chasa (*Bya sa*), an ancient Sakyapa lamasery. On the lintel of its door, perhaps as old as the temple itself, eleven animals were carved. On both ends the four keepers lurked and sneered threateningly from dark niches. In the middle of the main cell there was a statue of Namparnang-dze with Opame (*'Od dpag med*) on his right and Mitrupa (*Mi ạkrug pa*) on his left. His halo had been restored and repainted at some undefinable time, but was certainly very old. In another chapel the Buddhas of the Three Times were sunk in meditation. Those statues were very probably of the same age as those of Iwang and Nesar. Their attitudes and garb were the same; moreover their wooden or stucco haloes carried pictures of gods, monks and donors bearing a great resemblance to the Iwang pictures. I should have liked to photograph some details, but there was no persuading the old keeper. He showed us everything, was friendly and entertaining — but as to taking snapshots he was irremovable. It took us three days to reach Mindoling from Chasa. It was a long road, winding at first between the river and the hills whose slopes fell abruptly close to one another on a sandy ground full of briars. Not a soul to be seen for miles around. The desert had again swallowed us. But soon the same road led us through the friendly, verdant Mindoling valley, where we had to wade from village to village, splashing in the water which ran everywhere and spilled over the road on its way to the fields. The deepest branches of the river, swollen by the relentless rains, had to be crossed on horseback. The frequent ruins of castles and temples, among which the Dagpola was visible on our left, way up the slope, revealed that the valley must have been even more thickly populated and the houses so crowded as to nearly touch. A constantly rainy sky was unfortunately spreading its gloom on that lovely landscape. Bad weather was persecuting us and our tents were always soaked. That dreary dampness hung over all our nights, and its chill oozed into our beds in spite of the thick blankets. However, we superbly withstood the inclemency of the season and did twenty to twenty-five miles a day, according to circumstances, and on some days even more, with the regularity of habit. I was following a winding itinerary in order to reach all places I intended to visit, on the suggestions of an old Tibetan guide-book of the 18th century I was carrying along. The guidebook,[53] which was written for the pilgrims and was still very popular, was mainly concerned with the holy places — whereas I was especially interested in old monuments. However, the two angles had a way of coinciding, as the oldest monasteries were nearly always the saintliest. The valleys we crossed, like oases astray in the wild desert of mountains, were among the richest in Tibet. The Lhokha province, south of the Tsang po, and the Kongpo district further east were, one could nearly say, Tibet's food reserve, as they abounded in wheat, barley and even some rice in the Lhobrag area. The warmer climate favoured farming, which was still a profitable occupation there, whereas it was losing ground to trade and cattle-breeding elsewhere. Even there, however, the soil was tilled with primitive methods, without the landowners taking an active interest in it. An agriculture minister had just been appointed in Lhasa, an old official who never left the capital and had neither the competence nor the authority necessary to give a new push to the country's flagging farming production. The landed gentry never personally looked after or inspected their estates. These were left in the hands of their attendants, who ran them according to their whims and even administered justice to the peasants. Agriculture's hardest task was to keep in efficiency the irrigation canals, without which the fields would have soon become barren again. The most obvious sign of welfare of those valleys were the large, white, two- or three-storeyed houses. Even those of the peasants were clean. There was no trace of Western Tibet's squalor and poverty there. The estates were in the hands of the lay gentry and also largely of the monasteries, in which case they were run by a church official directly responsible to the monastery concerned. A further sign of well-being were the large, impressive temples, all renovated and recently embellished with gold and washed with garish colours, chiefly a flaming red and a dazzling yellow.

On entering the Mindoling valley we went through a large village by the name of Tsongdutsogpa (*Ts'oṅ ạdus ts'ogs pa*), wrongly marked as Danang on the maps. An ancient Sakyapa monastery rising among the huddled houses there was worth visiting. It contained a large collection of statues a couple of which had some artistic value. In the temple, the eight usual Bodhisattvas were ranged around the central statue. They were dressed in the Indian fashion and wore turbans on their heads — nothing unusual, as I had seen the like elsewhere. Before we reached Mindoling, as the valley slowly rose to a basin-like hollow sheltered all around by the mountains, I was shown a large building watching over the fields. That was Ju, a fief of my friend the Rakasha, or the Tibetan Commander-in-Chief. Further up, in the hollow hugged by the protecting ridges, the Mindoling convent basked in the warm sunshine, straggling fanwise, from the large Kumbum in the middle, with its whitewashed wings along the slopes. The place had been hallowed by celebrated masters, but had unfortunately been restored later and contained no trace of old paintings. It is famous in all Tibet as one of the most venerated monasteries of the Nyinmapa sect. Just on those days a well-known master was imparting the initiation (*dbaṅ luṅ*) on the disciples, that they might draw all the spiritual and ceremonial profit possible from the study of one of the greatest Nyinmapa (and Kagyupa) treatises, the Rinchenterdzo (*Rin c'en gter mdsod*). This work consists of over sixty volumes mainly dealing with ritualistic revolving upon the principal gods of Buddhism. Such treatises fail to make sense unless one is initiated into their meaning by a sacrament imparted by somebody who knows them to the core and has lived through their deepest experiences. Any ritual performed without having received the key to it through initiation would be mere jugglery. Liturgic acts are null and void unless they are enlivened by the inner experience speaking through the master and enabling the magic forces slumbering in the disciple to burst forth and find their proper field of action in the ceremonial. That is why the Nyinmapa monks had gathered there to receive initiation at the hand of a master. The whole affair would last several months.

The master was unfortunately ill and we could not see him. We had a long talk with his brother instead, another incarnate who enjoyed the same fame. He was a serene, solemn man, whose words were as slow as his gestures. Aloof from life, he seemed not to have any interest beyond his own contemplations. He spoke of them at length, insisting on the vanity of any other knowledge. Knowledge, he said, was something outward. When you saw a man, you could describe him, you could report what he looked like, repeat his words, but never claim to know him. Real know-

ledge was not like that, did not find expression in state-
ments or surmises, and had little in common with what you
saw or felt. Knowledge was a mysterious attuning of the
knower to the very being he wanted to know, a merging
into it, into God, or Truth, as you would have it. The more
you spoke of something the farther you were from it. You
had therefore to forget everything else and take the plunge
till you vanished into it. That was the purpose of Yoga, not
of vulgarized fakir tricks. Real Yoga works no miracles —
its only miracle being the taming of our restless mind. We
must shut ourselves in like a frightened turtle till our senses
are blind and deaf to outward stimuli. Then sudden spark-
les will begin to appear to our inner eye. Such masters were
a living contradiction of theology. They seldom lived in
convents, and often withdrew into hermitages, but not to
pore over books: they took to meditation and gave themselves up to those ecstasies where they thought God revealed Himself to them.

We retraced our steps along the Mindoling valley keeping
to the left bank of the Tsang po. We by-passed the village of
Tsongdutsogpa and reached Dranang (*Grva nan*), where a
large monastery rose. It belonged to the Sakyapa sect but
according to tradition had been founded by the Nyingma-
pas. The eight Bodhisattvas, as dignified and as majestic as
kings, stood around the central Buddha statue in the main
cell. Luckily enough, the craze of renovation had not yet
changed the aspect of that temple, which still was one of the
most remarkable and best preserved. The Bodhisattvas
were covered with broad draperies of obviously Persian
pattern, wide robes embroidered with medallions enclosing
lions and birds facing each other.

Many of the frescoes had faded, but those on the wall left
of the Buddha were still visible, and showed Śākyamuni
sitting on the branch of a tree, while the sixteen Arhats were
perched on surrounding branches, and the eight Bodhisattvas encompassed the tree standing on the ground below.
The figures stood out boldly against the background in a

glare of colours time could not dim. Around the abstracted, lofty Buddhas, hosts of saints were ranged, as expressive as portraits, yet set in a hieratic collectedness remindful of Byzantine paintings. There might have been more than a casual coincidence of spiritual attitude to that resemblance. The Hellenistic-Roman painting school drove with slow waves into the heart of Central Asia and left traces of its advance up to the threshold of China. The Dranang frescoes may be the last, indirect echo of that influence, which crossed Asia and tailed off in the Land of Snows.

Unfortunately even those monuments were running the risk of being entirely coated over. At the time the surviving frescoes were fading and beginning to crumble away, and water seeped and leaked everywhere, washing away the colours.

The Gonkang, watched by the statues of Dorjejiche, Gurgon, Pandenlamo and Putraminsin, was a gallery of mighty sculptures influenced by Chinese style, in which the primitive fury of those first beings emerging from initial chaos and touching off the beginning of things found a lucky and adequate expression. The building was after the model of Samye's largest temple. It should have been erected at the same time, but age had told less on it.

A few miles from Dranang rose the Champaling (*aǰam pa gliṅ*) monastery, built around one of Tibet's biggest Kumbums, which was as steep as a fortress and had in its centre a huge chapel containing a giant statue of Champa (Maitreya). The ritual eight Bodhisattvas were painted all around and framed in vertical flourishes and festoons lining the walls: large frescoes, yet well laid out and finished to a nicety. Chinese influence had been at work, but had adapted itself to a different environment. On the whole the Champaling Kumbum reminded me of the one of Gyantse and, though slightly less ancient, was also a monument of the early maturity of Tibetan art. Chapels were to be seen only upstairs, whereas the lower steps led to corridors where a few Chinese-style paintings were to be seen. In the cupola I found some cycles of paintings inspired by the Naljorgyu (*rNal ạbyor rgyud*) Tantras dating back no further than to the 18th century. The Gelukpa convent was not particularly interesting. It happened to be a festal day, and the monks were dining together on the parvis. The abbots and Geshes were sheltered in tents and the disciples seated on the ground in the open. A large bowl lay near every one, into which the cooks poured meat stew and noodles. The valley stretched green as far as the eye could reach on one side, on the other it wedged itself neatly into the notches and dents of the mountain. Far away the Gurutsogpa (*Gu ru ts'ogs pa*) temple rose; farther south, in a gorge I could make out the Targye (*Dar gyas*) monastery.

We resumed our journey towards Kongkadzong and stopped at Kitisho, where we visited the Sakya convent of Dambuchokor, completely restored. The only ancient remains were the plinth of a pillar with carved arabesques and a Chinese inscription of the Kuang-hsü period on the entrance door of a chapel. Industry was flourishing. Kitisho produced the pretty striped woollen aprons, the *pandens* of Tibetan women, made of alternatively red, green, orange and blue material dyed with colours coming from Bhutan.

Our next stop was Ravame (*Ra ba smad*), further W, where all I found was a small Sakya temple with 17th century paintings and some ancient statues. We then proceeded to Kongkachodra (*Koṅ dkar c'os grva*), a large Sakya convent founded by Kunganamgyal,[54] not far from Kongkardzong, the place where we had turned eastward on our way out.

15 New Discoveries

At Kongkar I met an incarnate who was just over twenty.
He had been born in Lhasa and then led to that out-of-the-
way village as soon as his religious education was com-
pleted. He was living in a small community of monks all
older than he, and perhaps longing for the Lhasa society,
his youthful friends and the fun the Holy City offered even
to the incarnates. In Lhasa I had actually met many of his
equals at the parties the noble families exchanged during
the summer. Though they never dropped the modesty and
composure befitting their rank, they did not shrink from
the company of laymen and liked to indulge, even if de-
tachedly and for a short time, in the carefree life of those
who had not renounced the world. That was a pleasant
break in the monotony of convent life. But this poor young
man was shut in a monastery miles away from anywhere,
his heart aburn with the wish, common to all youth, to see
new things, to set foot himself in those foreign countries the
merchants he met were telling him fairy tales about. He was
toying with the idea of going himself to India on pilgrimage,
but the convent was too poor to allow him that. He would
have to wait till some rich devotee covered his travelling
expenses. In the meanwhile, the young incarnate went on

dreaming and had built himself a secret, collected corner in a small garden aglow with flowers and blossoming trees. There he spent the long summer days lost in his musings, busily building his dream world like a poet or a child. The pent-up feelings of the young hermit found their outlet on the flowers, which he fondly tended as the companions of his captivity, as creatures born of his fancies and fed on his need of love.

As soon as he heard of my arrival he rushed to meet me. Something new at long last! He clung to me like to an old friend, invited me to lunch, showed me around the monastery, asked me a thousand questions. He wanted to know what my country looked like, how long it took to reach it, what were a steamer and an airplane, how machines worked. He stared with wide eyes at my answers, like a child listening to the housemaid's tales. He would not leave me, and kept saying he would follow me to India. When however I had to take leave of him he was visibly moved. Such a warm friendship had budded forth from his bitter solitude.

But the young incarnate's friendship was far from fruitless to me. While we were sitting and talking of India's great masters, he drew out of a safe some Indian palm-leaf manuscripts of the 8th or 9th century. They were as fresh as if they had just left the hands of the copyist. My heart abeat, I had a closer look. They were poetical works of two authors unknown till then. One was metrical summary of Buddhist dogmatic and the other a poem on the Buddha's former lives.[55] The history of Indian literature was thus suddenly enriched by two new names and two new works.

During my visit to the monastery I saw the assembly hall, where statues of the Buddhas of the Three Times were surrounded by the eight Bodhisattvas; and the circumambulation corridor with good frescoes of Lord Buddha's life showing a marked Chinese influence. On the walls right and left of the cell were painted the Lamas of the Sakyapa sect and the main events of their lives: dignified but spirited and lively pictures, free from the hieratic stiffness that too often burdens Tibetan art. A statue of Dorjejiche in the Gonkang, the most expressive I ever saw in Tibet, came close of frightening me out of my wits.

From Kongkardzong we set our course on Gyantse by roads new to me. Instead of crossing the Kampala pass we negotiated the Kabrola, a shorter but perhaps more strenuous route which led us by a large, entirely rebuilt Kagyupa convent. From the top of the hill we could see, beyond a mountain barrier in the north, the Kyichu valley and the spires of the Depung monastery aglow in the setting sun. On both sides of the pass there was nothing but a succession of ruins. The traces of formerly cultivated fields could be made out on the slopes. The 17th century war between Ü and Tsang had laid that area waste. Life had not been able to reconquer it since.

We then descended on to the Yamdrog lake, drearily reflecting a leaden sky. Those were safe roads. At Gyantse I had been told to beware of highwaymen on the Kabrola pass. In Lhasa I had been warned of unpleasant encounters on the desert northern banks of the Tsangpo and on the Kongkar roads we were following. This had led me to borrow a rifle and a gun from the Nepalese minister, as I had given away all my arms. But no incident troubled our journey. I found that the danger of bandits in Central Tibet was greatly over-rated. Isolated travellers were certainly attacked by outlaws now and then, but caravans went usually undisturbed.

At Gyantse we came in touch with the world again. For exactly two months we had been in the dark about Europe where, when I left Lhasa, the danger of war had been imminent. The day before reaching Gyantse our apprehensions seemed to take shape and we lived through hours of great excitement. I had sent the Indian photographer ahead to fetch the mail and bring us the latest news. At sunset he was back in a scare. War had broken out in Europe. We spent the evening in great anxiety, talking things over and making plans.

You can easily imagine our relief when we reached Gyantse on the following day to find that our man had been mistaken and all he had heard about was the guerilla in Indonesia. From Gyantse I wired the Tibetan Government applying for permission to get back to India by the Rhe road, an uncharted route only indicated with question marks on maps, which I thought would be interesting as it might lead me up to ancient monasteries. Rhe was not far away from Gyantse, and I thought we could make it in three or four days by crossing two high mountain passes, which were already covered with snow.

I had not to wait long for the Government's answer. I was authorized beyond my hopes, not only to follow that route, but also to go by the roundabout Shigatse road if I liked. That was quite unexpected, as an Englishman who had already been in Central Tibet had been denied that permit in the same year. I could not have received a more sincere proof of the friendliness and the good will of the Tibetan authorities towards me. My companions were happy to be able to visit the second holiest Tibetan city at least. Besides, I was looking forward with pleasure to revisiting a place where I had spent three weeks in 1939, making a lot of friends. But that would lengthen our journey by two weeks.

16 Shigatse and Tashilhumpo

Keeping to the right of the Nyangchu river I covered again the Gyantse-Shigatse road which I had followed on the opposite bank in 1939, when I was going back to Gyantse. At that time I visited the Nesar temple, as important as the one of Iwang, and found my way to the Pokang monastery, which I have described elsewhere.[56] The road led through ruins produced by the long war between Tsang and Ü; at Taktse (*sTag rtse*), which had been a notable fee, there was nothing left but wrecks, and we found more and more of them as we approached Penam. There were ruins of castles on the precipitous rocky ramparts above, and rows of chortens and dismantled temple walls in the valley. Penam, which had once also been a remarkable feudal holding, was now a large village with a massive fort, a great work of military architecture in disrepair, vainly overlooking the quiet field landscape below. The road plunged into heaving barley, and after three hours' walk began rising, leaving behind that luscious, billowing crop. We trudged wearily on the sandy barrenness, and crossed flat, easy passes, having on our right the valley which started running westwards between Nangkartse and Pede Dzong and petered away in a rocky waste where the typically dismal landscape of Western Tibet cropped out. We passed under the Kagyupa monastery of Samdubchoding, perched up on a crag, and at a bend of the road we saw the Shigatse fort shimmering in the distance and towering above the fields surrounding it.

On our arrival at Shigatse we were received by a representative of the governor. The Shigatse governor had much wider powers than the others district commissioners, as the whole of Western Tibet, up to the frontiers with Nepal and Ladakh, was subject to his control. He commanded a large unit of the Dalai Lama's bodyguard, crack troops making up the bulk of the Tibetan army, and entrusted with the defence of the Dalai Lama's sacred person in case of necessity. The governor was a native of Lhasa and the scion of a noble family which claimed descent from the ancient royal dynasty. He was a lordly, but courteous person, well up in religious and historic literature, very devout, but broad-minded. He had been in India and, if I understood him rightly, he would have had nothing against Tibet cautiously opening herself to modern comfort. With his wife and son he was living in the fort overhanging the town, the old, massive, frowning Chinese fortress, which had in its turn been built above the palace of the princes who ruled over the whole of Tibet in the 16th and 17th centuries and hospitably received the first European missionaries to come to Tibet: Cabral and Cacella. Those princes headed the old feudal aristocracy and the ancient religious sects, both opposing the rise of the Yellow sect. But the Yellow sect was irresistibly gaining ground by the prestige of its reforms, and establishing its hold on Tibetan politics, till it carried the day in the end, the Dalai Lamas striking their roots in Lhasa, and Shigatse remained only a large mart under the shadow of the Tashilhumpo abbots. Later, when Tibet succumbed to Chinese domination in 1728, Shigatse became the capital of the Western provinces and the second largest garrison after Lhasa.

The fort was huge and dreary. The governor inhabited a

wing, a few rooms which he had filled with Chinese household furniture, throwing together sacred and profane things as it was usual in Tibetan houses. We made friends at once. He took an immediate interest in my researches and went so far out of his way to help me, that I owe to him some of the most prized items in my collection of Bonpo books.

Bonpos are termed the followers of Tibet's oldest native religion, a kind of Shamanism which was later overpowered and partly absorbed by Buddhism. In the long run the surviving Bonpos had ended by borrowing nearly the whole of Buddhist dogmatics, so that many of their treatises sounded all but adaptations or copies of the latter. A few of the extant typical features still distinguishing the Bonpos from the Buddhists were some special astrologic gods and the worship of the reversed fylfot, an anticlockwise swastika. Also in paying homage to a sacred object or place the Bon used to turn round it like the Buddhists and the Hindus, but unlike them they started turning forward to the right to end on the left side of the object. In many Bonpo books ancient legends can be read shedding light on prehistoric Tibet previous to the advent of Buddhism with its civilizing influence. Through them you can get a glimpse of the bearing remote religions skirting the borders of Tibet, like Manicheism and Nestorianism, had on the spiritual life of that country. At that time the Bonpos were very scarce in Central Tibet, and their main centres were to be found in the Eastern provinces and beyond the Chinese border. If the Buddhists were loath to show their sacred books or part with them, the Bonpos were even more so. That is why we know so little of their traditions and scripture. But that year my efforts were successful. At Gyantse I was lucky enough to get acquainted with the descendant of an old family of Bon masters. Hereditarily, he was a priest, but his frequent business journeys to India had gradually weakened and breached his orthodoxy. So, when I talked to him of my wish to get a thorough acquaintance of the Bon scripture, he was moved, and placed the bulk of his library at my disposal. In the Shigatse district, on the road to Lhasa, rose the largest Bon po monastery of the whole of Central Tibet. Without the Governor's recommendation — which usually worked as an order there — any research of Bon books would have been fruitless. His word opened me every door.

At about one mile from Shigatse were the white walls of Tashilhumpo, the seat of the Tashilama who is the highest religious authority of Tibet along with the Dalai Lama. But even the gods, when incarnated, seem to share our human weaknesses. So it happened that the two pontiffs did not always live in perfect harmony, as the poison of politics troubled their relations. Whereas the Dalai Lama was led by events to get nearer and nearer to Great Britain, and therefore to oppose China's never dropped claims to his own country, the Tashilama stayed faithful to China: hence a violent clash which led the Tashilama to flee the country and seek refuge in China. Some of his relatives were deported. He had died in exile and had been reborn in Inner Mongolia some years back, but it was not at all certain that the boy would be allowed to be reinstated in his monastery, lest the pro-Chinese party he had led would raise its head again. But things earthly are unstable. Events in China could work profound changes in Tibet and either take the wind out of some important parties' sails or give them a new fillip. Meanwhile the Tashilhumpo monastery, where some three thousand monks lived, was run by an abbot, a kind of ecclesiastic governor, a very old man whose authority extended only to the convent, but who had no say in temporal matters.

As it is often the case with much celebrated things, whose sight often deceives the expectation, Tashilhumpo may be a disappointment. With the exception of its largest temple, all chapels had risen, and continued to rise, on the tombs of its lamas. Those chapels were vying with each other in the wealth of their ornaments, in their display of gold, precious and semi-precious stones, in the bulk of their statues. But they lacked the charm of the ancient frescoed temples we had seen elsewhere. Everything was new and garish here. The collected composure of the primitives had been succeeded by baroque pomposity. The abbots' mortal remains were enclosed in huge mausoleums laden with gold and jewels, and overburdened with arabesques and flourishes. As in the Potala, the visitor was dazzled by the glittering display, overwhelmed by the majesty and wealth of the temples, but not innerly moved.

What especially attracted my attention in the Tashilhumpo chapels were some cherubs carved on the plinth of the tomb of the third Tashilama. They were designed and sculpted by Nepalese artists, but their inspiration was obviously Western. A Christian painting brought by one of the first missionaries must have served as a model to the nameless artisans who worked at the tomb of Tashilhumpo's great abbot. Those cherubs, messengers of a far-away world, seemed nearly frightened and lost among the huge, many-headed and many-armed grinning and threatening around. Quite foreign to the surroundings, they simply had to be picked out at once by the visitor's eye.

There are no bells in the monasteries. Time flowed on, unmarked by our clockmade breaks, monotonous and uniform, without people noticing its flow or caring so much as we did about it. Each activity was therefore something arbitrary and unpredictable, which might take place or not, might happen now or God knows when. Watches and clocks bind us to limits and compulsions. The Tibetans, not unlike the Indian peasants, were still very unfamiliar with time-pieces. Time flowed on, and that was all mattered. Their history as known to them, bound to their sixty-year cycles recurring without ordinal numbers unlike our centuries, was subject to confusion and uncertainties. Everything seemed to skid by without landmarks and without strained expectations.

A great festival was held in the first days of summer. On a large wall near the monastery three huge standards bearing the figures of the Buddhas of the Three Times were hung every morning for just over an hour. The faithful climbed up the rocky hill and paid their homage to the images by walking clockwise round them. Thousands of people gathered on the plain down below, knelt and sat down to their food in the open, while troups of wandering actors staged sacred plays in front of them. Strictly speaking there was no direct participation of the people in the religious ceremonies, as the lamas were the exclusive performers and the laymen the audience. There was no such thing as prayers to which the former would lead the latter. There was only a highly complex ritual to whose subtle symbols the priests alone had access. The crowd was content to walk around the sacred objects, to blow low before the statues and to mutter the holy formulas without the mystic intoxication induced by prayer.

A lama of great renown had come from a hermitage far away to preach four or five hours daily in the large Tashilhumpo park. He was reading and explaining a line a day out of a mystical treatise of over two hundred pages. The sermon would last several months. From the top of the convent we could see the monks flocking in small batches into the plain down below to listen to him, their scarlet cassocks trailing against the barren rocky background. There were so many thousands of them that only the first rows had a chance to hear the sermon, but listening was the meritorious work: catching the words or understanding their meaning was another matter. Besides, faith was above anything else; it was the guiding force driving the souls forward towards their release.

Any orderly and closely logical reasoning not supported by appropriate quotations from the scripture would not convince a Tibetan. What mattered for him were the latter, not the former, as if he feared to be committed to his own intelligence alone to face and puzzle out the unknown. The Tibetans seemed not to feel the fascination of discovery, nor to care for the daring adventures of thought. Their mind was rather bent on going over the same ground again and again, and working out new formulations of the old lore, which led to lengthening commentaries and glosses.

Often the lamas would leave their dark Tashilhumpo dens to descend to the great Shigatse bazaar, held a mile away, bask in that motley display of wealth, and hang around to have a look and to strike an occasional bargain.

17 A Miraculous Recovery — Return to India

Shigatse is a large trading centre arisen at the junction of the caravan roads connecting Lhasa to Western Tibet and Nepal. All the wool shorn on the plains north of the Tsangpo was converging and piling up there, providing work to a flourishing community of craftsmen and enriching a host of merchants who monopolized the traffic with India. Shigatse had less inhabitants than Lhasa but they were as varied, with the only difference that then (1948) the Chinese settlement tended to dwindle away. The bazaar was the heart of the town and consisted of a huge rectangular square surrounded on the four sides by shop buildings. In its midst, ranged on parallel lines, there were rows of ramshackle stands, rising side by side and loaded with all sorts of merchandise attracting crowds of curious people and prospective customers. There you could find anything, hats and buttons, aluminium pans from Europe and wooden bowls from Bhutan, Chinese cups from Calcutta's Chinatown, silver altar lamps skilfully wrought out by local goldsmiths, Italian cloth and coral, Gyantse carpets, turquoise, packets of tea and even ladies' rouge and lipstick. All this was not kept apart in the several stands, but rather mixed higgledy-piggledy so that each barrow and each booth and stall was a miniature market in itself. The goods were naturally very expensive as they were carried on horseback all the way from China or India on account of Tibet's unproductiveness, the lack of local industry, the dwindling away of arts and crafts and the growing needs created by the livelier exchanges with India. Had mechanical transport been introduced into Tibet before long, the prices might have sunk, but the prospects of such a revolution in the means of communication with its attending influence on the country's economy seemed very far away. Nor was this due to the roughness of the terrain alone. A few years earlier, the British mission had used a lorry for the mail service between Phari and Gyantse as, in spite of the average height of this road being some 13,000 ft, the track ran comparatively flat on a tableland where, even if jolting and floundering with great wear and tear, a motor vehicle could plough its way. But the Tibetan Government later forbade the use of such conveyances under the pretext that they put out of business the packmen of the towns along the road, thus hurting local economy. Actually not so much the peasants as the officials, the village headmen, the landowners and in one word all those in power risked losing a large part of their income. Church circles also fought tooth and nail everything new out of a supine respect for tradition and a fear of change. To quote an example, the Shigatse-Kampadzong route, though perched among high mountain passes and crossing desert and cold country, would be the only direct connection with India, leading in the shortest time to that country, but for deep, raging river Rhe, which we were compelled to ford two or three times with great danger to our baggage and at the risk of our lives. But all suggestions that a bridge should be built on that river were turned down on the alleged ground that an evil spirit watched over the stream and would sweep away any bridge human hands would try to construct.

As I have often repeated, the Tibetans are prevailingly merchants, but the most important items of trade were in the hands of a few families whose agents resided at Kalimpong and Darjeeling and supplied their country through Indian firms, which of course further contributed to the dearness of the goods. Anyway, Shigatse was a wealthy town: you just had to have a look at the bazaars to meet well-dressed, well-fed, healthy people. But the area of arable ground around the town was cramped up by a surrounding circle of pitilessly barren hills. When reaching Shigatse from Penam you would have thought you were crossing a lunar landscape. Only in the immediate neighbourhood of the town was the barrenness relieved and revived by the usual barley fields and some orchards.

During our stay at Shigatse, Dr Moise saved a monk's life, stunning by his skill the Tibetans, who believed in a miracle of witchcraft. We were having lunch outside our tent when Adu, one of our servants who had served in a hospital in India and worked occasionally as a medical orderly for the doctor, came in to announce coolly that a wounded person was waiting outside the enclosure. Moise, believing it was one of the usual abrasions he had to treat every day, advised him to use iodine. Adu nodded and vanished only to reappear with a sad countenance as soon as our meal was over to remind Moise that the patient was still waiting. At Moise's objection that he should have treated him according to instructions, Adu timidly observed that it was not quite an iodine case.

"Why?" asked Moise. "Because all his inside is out," was the terse answer.

So we rushed out and learned it was a monk who, in a fit of madness, had slit his belly open with a knife. The man lay on the ground in a pool of blood, surrounded by a circle of gaping people and sniffing animals. Without batting a lid, Moise anesthetized him, replaced the bowels and filled the whole cavity with penicilline, instructing Adu to give him four penicilline injections a day. On the fifth day the madman regained his normal appetite without having ever had a touch of fever. As a result, the rumour spread that Moise could even revive the dead, and if we had not luckily departed, all Tashilhumpo would have rushed to our camp to beg for new miraculous healings.

In two days' march from Shigatse we reached Rhe. I could see Narthang in the distance, where I had a long stop in 1939. The road to Rhe went by the village of Nardechen on to a barren, rocky stretch dotted with ruins. We crossed the Ghuling pass and climbed down to the Rhe river which was tearing along in a spate. We forded it once, hoping that the caravan would follow. But dusk was falling and nobody was in sight. On the other hand the stream was swollen and fording would have been dangerous for the caravan at that time of the day. Moise, Mele, a servant and I re-crossed the river where its raging waters were even more vicious and, drenched and chilled, managed to reach a hamlet where we met a very friendly reception. A roaring fire was laid and we crowded around it, our eyes filled with tears in the thick smoke, and tried to get dry. We waited further for the caravan, all gathered in the kitchen, till, late at night, the packmen were heralded by the barking of dogs. The porters were tired and benumbed with cold. The first snow had fallen and wrapped the mountains and the country in a thick blanket. We were at 14,000 ft. We all went peacefully to sleep and, on the next day, forded uneventfully the river and were forcibly held up on the opposite bank by the Rhe Dsongpon, who met us with the usual gifts and the customary friendliness of Tibetan officials and insisted that we should pitch our tents in his garden.

On the next day we faced the steep ascent to the Rhe monastery, a mighty construction which had served as a convent and as a fortress dominating the crossroads which lead fanwise from Kampadzong to Sakya, Shigatse and Gyantse. The fortress was in disrepair, but the walls leading down from it to the river to protect the fort's water supply ran still undemolished on a needle-sharp ridge. It was a

Gelukpa convent and its name had been Rinchentse (*Rin c'en rtse*). There was hardly anything of interest left: the place was militarily too exposed to escape devastation. The keeper showed us the *nangtens* (see page 146) among which I noticed an inlaid stab with a jade hilt made at Jaipur and said to have belonged to Pholane, regent of Tibet from 1728 to 1747; a European mirror painted with figures of ladies and knights of the 15th century; and various objects ascribed by tradition to Remdapa, or Shonnulotro (*gŽon nu blo gros*), Tsongkhapa's master, who had been born in a nearby village.

On the 10th, at half past five a.m., by an intense cold, we set out on our march, crossed the Sangla pass (16,500 ft) and reached by sunset a huge plain, S of which a red blaze was lingering on the tops of the Himalaya range. We were cold and tired and pitched our tents there. An icy wind was blowing from high glaciers resting among precipitous rocks. It was a solemn landscape of a heart-rending sadness. Some miles further up towards Kampadzong, Drokpa camping fires were glimmering. For all my tiredness, the thought that we were at the end of our journey struck me as very painful. In a few days we should wallow in the damp heat of Sikkim. Caravan life would be over; we should first lodge in houses, then in hotels. We should be speedily carried around by motor cars and railways, locked up into those engine-driven boxes which pitilessly subject man to the whims of machinery and contrivances. We should no more file out slowly against the outside world, reviewing with attentive, inquisitive eyes the landscape as if we were wresting it every minute from strenuously conquered distances. A treacherous prodigy would make the landscapes whiz along past our windows, blurring their colours and outlines into a dream-like dimness.

As I unfortunately lived in an allegedly civilized world, I too, when in Europe, was forced to use mechanical conveyances. But I am a nomad at heart, and nomads would either walk or ride, thus staying in close touch with the earth. Nowadays we are skimming over the surface of things. Machines have accustomed us to see things from afar and at the surface, thus contributing to that lack of depth lamented by the wise ones in our modern age.

On the morning of the 11th we were on our toes again at daybreak. We went through Karma and, after twelve hours' march, wrapped in darkness and whipped by a blizzard, we reached Kampadzong, arousing a deafening racket of dog barks. The fortress, which I had visited in 1939 when travelling to Sakya, was dimly outlined in the darkness like an inaccessible Walhalla.

A bright sun was glistening on the Himalaya peaks on the 13th, when we crossed the Sebu la. For the last time I took a farewell glance at the golden mountains on which the first snow falls had drawn white furrows, and felt inexpressibly sad. I was not only longing for a country where life was hard and the landscape fascinatingly beautiful, but also for a friendly people who had received me as a welcome guest for several months.

Remarks on Medicine and the State of Health in Tibet

By Dr. Regolo Moise
Lt. Col. of the Italian Navy Medical Corps

Whereas ancient Indo-Tibetan, or lamaistic, medicine, can well be explored on the escort of the original manuscripts, and there are monographs and essays on the subject, there are no sources at all for an assessment of the state of health and the practice of medicine in present-day Tibet according to the Western scientific point of view. Consequently, we know very little on the matter, as few Western physicians have visited Tibet at all and even fewer stayed long enough to conduct any research. Medical expeditions, inquests or even statistical surveys have never been undertaken, so that it can be assumed that even less is scientifically known about Tibet on that subject than, if possible, on her geology, fauna and flora. On the other hand, we are indebted for extensive information about Tibet's customs, religion and civil institutions to a physician, Major Waddel, I.M.S. Major Waddel, as well as the Italian physician and explorer F. De Filippi, clearly had his eye on the more pleasant and profitable aspects of landscape and folklore rather than slaving at biological research.

Western medicine penetrated first into Tibet with Col. Younghusband's Anglo-Indian expedition to Lhasa in 1904. But it had only a superficial influence and its results can hardly be felt up to date.

The government of British India was well aware how conducive medical help could be to furthering political and social relations with Tibet, but never tried too hard. During the better part of fifty years it only opened two out-patient hospitals: one at Yatung and the other at Gyantse and only in 1937 did it manage to open a dispensary in Lhasa, run by the Political Mission's physician.

Practically, all physicians who have been to Tibet were army doctors, detailed to accompany Expedition Corps or following high officials on mission or posted on duty at the garrisons. The out-patient hospitals had a modest appearance and an obsolete equipment, some beds for occasional in-patients, a rudimentary operation room and a galenic drug-store. They were run by graduated Sikkimese physicians (Subassistant Surgeons), two of whom had been some thirty years in Tibet. That country had, on the whole, only two fully qualified doctors — a British Major of the A.M.S. in Lhasa and an Indian captain at Gyantse.

This nearly absolute lack of facts about health and sanitation over the whole huge territory of Tibet, still so inaccessible to foreigners, led me to record the following impressions, which should be taken only as a mere sketch, as unfortunately I could not carry out any accurate research nor delve deep into the matter. As the whole country is still shrouded in mystery, even these few notes may enable the reader to get a glimpse of Tibet's main hygienic and sanitary problems.

The population, descended of different racial stocks, but showing common distinctive features, is rated at some 3 to 4 millions, perhaps rather less than more, and is spread over an area of about 400,000 square miles. This area can be divided into four main territories: *Northern Tibet* (embracing the Chang-ang desert) and *Western Tibet*, making up about two thirds of the entire area, consisting of high mountains and being generally above 9,000 ft. Their population is scanty and leads a nomadic and primitive life. Then come *Central (and Southern) Tibet* (comprising the Tsang and U provinces) and *Eastern Tibet*, with their great rivers and their lower valleys. The two latter are much more thickly populated and contain the main centres.

In spite of these differences in level, Tibet stays the highest country in the world, as three quarters of her surface are above 9,000 ft, and many valleys and tablelands reach as high as 15,000 ft.

Climate is of course largely dependent upon the characteristics of the single provinces, but on the whole it is cool and dry, with an extraordinarily limpid air. The sun's action is the more intense, and temperature sinks abruptly after sunset. Extremes of heat and cold can therefore be reached in quick succession, the mercury often recording jumps of 87 F. and more. From October to May there is little snow or rain, therefore the snow-line, which slightly oversteps 15,000 ft in Sikkim, reaches 18,000 ft in Tibet. Particularly cold winter winds blow from N. But in the SE and central provinces the Indian monsoon, blowing from July to September, makes itself felt to a larger or a smaller degree and fairly heavy rain can fall, much to the advantage of the fields. The amount of rain can range from roughly 10″ to 40″ a year.

Southern-Central Tibet in a word, the region we visited and I was particularly interested in as a physician, as it holds most of the Tibetan population, often shows notably different features from those described in several books on Tibetan journeys.

In his «Diary», Prof. Tucci often hinted at the food, the housing, the occupations, and the customs of the Tibetans. I shall therefore not dwell any longer on these subjects, and restrict myself to a few remarks on health and sanitation.

The reader should, however, always bear in mind the unique character and the peculiar way of life of this country isolated from her neighbours not only by forbidding deserts and mountain chains, but even more by deep chasms in mental attitude and religious conceptions. Even the physician will not encounter there a primitive, but a highly cultured people, yet one which has not kept in step with our scientific and mechanic progress, but has stayed anchored to century-old customs and beliefs. Thus, while the Tibetans' minds are still wrapped up in medieval religious and philosophical ideas, their bodies are engaged in a constant struggle against the hardships of one of the most rugged and unaccessible regions on earth.

On the other hand, in spite of the essentially religious character of their medicine, held to be a heavenly revelation, and in spite of their so different and sometimes strange curative systems, which often rest on psychological bases looking fairly sound to the Western eye, the Tibetans never seemed to have anything against our medicine. Even those who plied the same trade and could be reasonably expected to fear competition, showed much tolerance. The sick flocked to us driven by curiosity and faith, a faith so strong as to embarrass us sometimes, as it could not always be satisfied. They saw something magical in our medicine too and failed to see the limitations set to it by pathology, surgery, and the time and the means at our disposal.

The sanitary conditions of the country were of course low but not altogether disastrous, nor worse than those of several better known countries, as one might think. Cleanliness was scarce especially on account of the cold climate. Cold, on the other hand, helps the Tibetans in the defence against infective illnesses, by rendering garbage innocuous and making life hard for bacteria and parasites at large. Apart from the wandering shepherds, who live constantly in tents, people live usually in fairly good quarters and are nearly never crammed together — which is on the contrary the case in large monasteries. Indoor air is usually polluted by the smell of the stables below and made sometimes un-breathable by yak-dung smoke, which is used for fuel. Acute or chronical irritation of the mucoses of the breathing channels and of the conjunctiva are the usual result. Outdoor winter temperatures, in the highest and most exposed areas, can be fairly low, particularly during blizzards driven by N winds. Readings as low as −22 F were recorded.

Clothing and foot-wear are of course adequate to such low temperatures, and wool and pelts are liberally used. However, I could notice that some old beggars bore the marks of frost on their limbs and had lost some knuckles.

In order to obtain protection from the biting cold and the burning sun of the high mountains, Tibetan women usually keep their faces coated with dark ointments, mainly consisting of mustard oil. Several people wear dark goggles while travelling in order to avoid the effects of the glare of sun and snow (snow and sun ophthalmia), or muffle their faces wholly up with shawls and Balaclava helmets. Erythemas and serious burnings would otherwise be the regular result.

The level of feeding is generally fairly good, though food is, for the bulk of the population, rather monotonous, as it mainly consists of Tibetan tea and roasted barley meal. Tea is drunk by the dozen of cups and contains a fair amount of butter. But when circumstances allow, Tibetans have recourse to vegetables, beans, roots, potatoes, fresh or dried yak meat or mutton, soups and fruit. Fishing is not practiced as religion forbids it, though lakes and seas are full of fish of every kind and size. The same applies to hunting. With the upper classes, food is extremely varied and even too plentiful, according to Chinese customs.

I never could observe any obvious case of scurvy from lack of vitamines, though fresh food is very scarce in winter. But seasonal troubles, probably due to scurvy, were described to me. Vitamines soluble in fat seem on the contrary to cover the needs, as milk and butter are available in plenty.

There is no dearth of water in Tibet, as sources, brooks,

torrents, rivers and lakes are well distributed over the whole area and winter brings plenty of snow and ice. The water is usually soft and clear, though at some places, as at Phari, it can be hard and muddy. The water of the Tsang-po is always yellowish owing to the great quantity of sand and clay floating in it. But Tibetans usually drink little unboiled water and stick to the healthier habit of drinking tea.

Alcoholism exists, though it is not very wide-spread. The favourite liquors are chan (barley beer) or arak (distilled from the former).

Tobacco is in use, and cigarettes and snuff are imported. The Tibetans smoke no opium, except in some Lhasa and Eastern Tibet pubs, which is obviously due to Chinese influence.

The population seems to grow steadily less. The reasons are manifold. First of all, the low birth-rate, connected perhaps with the altitude and the climate; then the high rate of child mortality, polyandry and monkhood (about a half of the males live in monasteries). Other reasons are small-pox epidemics, venereal diseases and, in some areas, endemic goitre.

The following notes are partly the fruit of my personal researches and partly drawn from facts supplied by local physicians, like Rai Sahib Bo Tsering of Gyantse and Rai Sahib Tonyot Tsering of Yatung, both of whom had been on duty in Tibet for some decades. More detailed data I obtained from Major J. Guthrie, I.M.S., whom I met at Gyantse as he was leaving Tibet after having stayed many years in Lhasa. I could have a look at hospital books and statistical records (very scanty for that matter) and compare their facts with the results of my experience with the patients who flocked to me everywhere ... In order to meet the needs of the local population I had taken with me a fair supply of drugs (particularly novarsenobenzol drugs, sulphonamides, intestinal antiseptics, antirheumatic remedies, vitamines, penicilline, sera and vaccines) and some nursing equipment. I had also carried a portable microscope, some clinical implements, surgical instruments and the strictly necessary technical tools. We covered much ground and came in touch with large sections of the population. The people were willing to let themselves be examined everywhere. But when it came to striking the balance of the country's health condition I could not help feeling rather disappointed, chiefly as regards epidemiology. Infective and parasitical diseases were conspicuous for their absence at least in their endemic form. On the other hand, one wide-spread epidemic illness held the field.

That was *small-pox,* an illness known in Tibet since time immemorial and apt to sweep across her again and again, with serious epidemics, one of which struck in 1900 and claimed over 6000 casualties only in Lhasa, the Dalai Lama himself being affected. Pock-marked people are very frequently seen. In Lhasa's market place there is a stone inscription in Tibetan and Chinese with quarantine instructions in case of a small-pox epidemic, issued by the Emperor of China probably about the end of the 18th century, and mentioning the setting up of lazarets and the like. Even today, vaccinations amount to a few hundreds or thousands, and are restricted to the few localities where Western medical assistance can be obtained.

In spite of my repeated enquiries I could gather no facts as to *plague,* even from the historical point of view, as literature on Tibet and Tibetan texts do not mention it, whereas medical treatises still claim that Tibet is one of its main endemic hotbeds. I heard of a few cases of *exanthematic typhoid* (agglutination: Proteus X19) and of *recurrent fever* (spirochaeta recurrens), which had recently been recorded in Lhasa and confirmed by the Tropical School of Calcutta. Infestions, obviously carried by lice, were said to have spread epidemically in the large monasteries near the capital, but I could not gather any facts on the spot

No traces of *common exanthemas, diphtheria* or *whooping cough* occurred to me. Throughout years the cases of *influenza* were few and far between. Some cases of *cerebro-*

spinal meningitis in grown-ups were described to me, but no bacteriological tests had been carried out.

Pneumonia was rather rare. At Yatung only two cases were recorded during a whole year. At Gyantse, out of 12,000 patients treated by the local physicians, only about forty carried a diagnosis involving pneumonia at all. It was even harder to gather data on *pulmonary tuberculosis* which, according to those physicians, does not occur at all in Tibet and is never mentioned in any statistical record. My observations were too few to draw any conclusions on this very serious subject. Anyway, the low number of lung patients calling at the medical inspection rooms in contrast with the high incidence of serious or mild affections of the other organs seems noteworthy.

Comparatively frequent were instead the cases of obviously tuberculose and often fistulous affections of the bones and articulations (coxitis, Pott, *spina ventosa*, many of which, when healed, left behind remarkable deformities. They were observed especially among the monks, and were certainly to be traced back to the poor sanitary conditions in monasteries. I never found any mention of *carbuncle* in spite of the large number of cattle, especially sheep, whose wool is the country's staple export and main wealth. In Lhasa I head about a few cases of *rabies*. I am certainly not in a position to doubt those reports. But strangely enough the Yatung and Gyantse doctors never recorded any case of rabies, whereas more or less serious bitings by dogs were treated in large numbers. Stray dogs were swarming all over Tibet.

The fact that there was so much greater variety of illnesses in Lhasa than elsewhere should not seem too strange, as a greater scientific exactitude could certainly be expected from the capital's better qualified physicians, and Lhasa was the meeting point of nomads and pilgrims from the remotest territories and Central Asia, besides being Tibet's largest and most populated centre.

I noted in that town, especially in summer, also some

cases of *typhoid* and *paratyphoid fever* and *bacillary dysentery*, though not in a markedly epidemic form. The existence of an indigenous breed of *leprosy* was confirmed in Tibet. The lepers could be often seen begging at the doors of the largest temples.

At Gyantse I could diagnose a case of *amoebic dysentery* on microscopical examination of a woman who had always been residing there. But the books of that infirmary carried only the record of a few dysentery-like affections without any further specification.

As to *intestinal worms,* tapeworm (Taenia saginata) and ascaris affections were very widespread. Microscopical examination of the stools often revealed eggs of thricocephalus. I could also diagnose a large *echinococcus* cyst in the liver of a Yatung packman, who had carried it without excessive trouble till then. Such a disease, of course, was not among the recorded affections.

Among the skin diseases I shall mention *scabies*, quite a frequent ailment in all its widest and most chronical aspects.

There were several cases of external and middle *otitis*, of acute and chronical *rhinitis* and of *sinusitis*. Particularly worthy of note were the *eye disease,* as conjuctivitis and blepharitis, as the outcome of panophthalmitis and of luetic affections at large. Trachoma is met everywhere, with its most serious after-effects, like trichiasis etc., though they are not always diagnosed as such. Physicians devote much more time to the treatment of cataract, which is very frequent in Tibet and, according to the records and to what I was told myself, is mostly successfully operated. Such lucky results of Western medicine earn everybody's admiration and thankfulness and contribute further to spread around it that aura of miracle and witchcraft to which I have hinted above.

The high church and lay officials make a large use of spectacles. That is why oculistic, together with surgery, could at that time constitute of the main instruments of sanitary penetration into Tibet, and it was also widely resorted to by practitioners in India.

The large incidence of cataract and of eyelid conjunctivitis is certainly connected with the action of ultra-violet rays.

I treated ordinary cases of *traumatic lesions*, wounds and local infections, did some general nursing and performed some minor operations. Tibetans usually reacted very well to my treatments. Sores and wounds, even if neglected, tended to heal, and broken bones to join again.

I did not observe any cases of *rickets*.

I had often to treat cases of *dental decay*, alveolar periostitis and dysodontiasis, but I do not think that such affections can be looked on as particulary frequent.

Malignant tumours are certainly present in Tibet, even if the above mentioned physicians seldom diagnose them. I was confronted with two such ailments in their final stages: one stomach cancer with metastasis and one cancer of the liver, which I could not further identify, accompanied by jaundice and ascitis.

Before dealing with the only illnesses of real epidemiological interest in Tibet, I want to stress the frequency of *rheumatic affections* in that country, ranging from acute articular rheumatism, often coupled with endocarditis, to chronical arthritis, to myositis and neuritis (especially of the hip). Cold and humidity certainly lie at the root of all this.

As I was saying above, *venereal illnesses* are of the utmost importance in Tibetan pathology. They are remarkably widespread and are mentioned by all travellers. Things may have been overstressed and all diagnoses may not have been correct, but the fact cannot be doubted and my observations can but confirm it. Pox and blennorrhoea were probably imported from China and their spreading is due to an absolute ignorance and lack of preventive measures and as well as to an unrestrained sexual intercourse.

I shall quote some figures. Out of 12,000 reported sick at Gyantse within two years, there were 608 cases of syphilis and 374 of blennorrhoea. In one year at Yatung the figures were 165 and 68. Findings by the physician of a mission, embracing only a few months in 1935, recorded 506 cases of syphilis and 139 of blennorrhoea on a total of 1720 patients. The "semo" kind of syphilis is well known to all Tibetans and appears in all its stages and most various aspects, from initial "syphilomas" through the secondary skin and mucose eruptions up to the tertiary stage. Neither neurosyphilitic forms like tabes and progressive paralysis nor the attending phenomena and visceral localizations have ever been observed.

Very frequent were the cases of periostitis of the nasal bones. The "trang-shi" brand of blennorrhoea presented itself with the usual retinue of acute and chronical complications: orchiepididymitis, prostatitis, cystitis, bartolinitis, salpingitis, arthritis and conjunctivitis.

The venereal ulcer's presence was also confirmed. It was often accompanied by inguinal adenitis. Such illnesses, though feared, practically received no efficient treatment by the local physicians, which made the help of an occasionally visiting doctor the more appreciated.

Goitre can be met all over Tibet. It is unknown in Sikkim, but it exists in Bhutan as well. People suffering from goitre can already be seen in great numbers in the Himalayan valleys S of Yatung. The cases grow less on the mountain passes and dwindle to nothing on the tableland. At Gyantse, an important town at some 12,000 ft on the sea level, goitre was very rare, whereas more cases could be observed in Lhasa. Where goitre got the upper hand of all other ailments was along the valleys of the Tsangpo and its tributaries, especially in the villages of the left bank (Samye, Ngari-Tratsang, Oka).

All forms of struma can be observed there, together with numerous cases of cretinism, dwarfishness and myxoedema. These illnesses prevail among the women, the grownups and the poor. Goitre and cretinism in their endemic form hold sway in those regions and have a great influence on the people's health and social conditions. The stunted growth, both bodily and mental, of these populations, is apt to catch the traveller's eye at once. Goitre may have largely been responsible for those valleys having been deserted and so many fields, once tilled, lying fallow.

As to the *neuro-psychical* affections, the monasteries would, I thought, supply a good deal of mental cases, as I saw in the conditions prevailing there hotbeds of mental derangement. However, I could only observe fairly frequent cases of psycho-neurosis, epilepsy and hysteria, but I could never lay hands on a real psychosis. On the other hand I had twice to cure very serious wounds of people who had tried to commit suicide. They were both monks. One had slit his belly open and the other had cut his own throat. Isolated cases of monks who had run amuck and attacked other monks were also reported.

The above-mentioned troubles can be traced back to alcoholism, which was certainly also responsible for the cases of polyneuritis I observed in drunkards.

Notes on Medical Zoology

The following notes are to be considered in close relation to the geographical position, the climate and the altitude of the areas they concern.

In the Himalayan State of Sikkim, where the traveller gradually crosses from the tropical jungle to the mountain forest, and where water is found in plenty, the carriers of the main tropical diseases malaria, kala-azar and filariasis are present, anchylostome infection is intense, poisonous snakes, like colubridae and viperoid serpents, as well as large spiders, centipedes and scorpions abound. Mountain forests between 4700 and 8000 ft. of altitude teem with ticks and very aggressive leeches (Hirudo Silvestris, Blanchard-Assam, Darjeeling, Sikkim, Burma). Such land leeches are much smaller than the officinal species known in Europe; they creep on the soil, attack the animals and even the human beings by swarming into the shoes and the clothes. When they are bloated and sated they simply drop of, and a small bleeding wound marks the suction spot. To get rid of them people simply strewed tobacco or kitchen salt on them.

In Tibet the conditions necessary to the life and the spread of such animals are lacking. As the traveller climbs the valleys and crosses the mountain ranges they grow less and less and end by vanishing altogether. I am reporting here below the results of some medical entomology researches I carried out at Yatung where I stayed longer than anywhere else and could more leisurely attend to such work, stretching from May to July.

As to my findings, there may be some interest in the fact that a few *arthropodae* have been detected in the Land of Snows, but this does not mean that they matter or that their number constitutes a menace.

Yatung is a small village at a height of about 19,000 ft., in a narrow Himalayan gorge where the torrent Chumbi tears along. The Indian monsoon still reaches it and pours down a yearly amount of rain ranging from 32″ to 40″. Its latitude, 28 N, corresponds to the one of Lower Egypt. I set up there, by whatever means I could lay hands on, a small station for the capture, the breeding and the study of larvae and winged insects.

Anopheles — In the second half of May I could capture in my room two kinds of winged insects and identify them as varieties of the species Anopheles Lindsayi (Giles) and Anopheles Gigas (Swell & Rodenwaldt). Both were large enough to stand Himalayan altitudes. I made a close study of their breeding grounds, where the water stagnated along the banks of the torrent and the irrigation canals, which were all exposed to the sun and constantly dredged. The larvae developed rather slowly and lasted from two and a half to three weeks and even longer. On account of the air temperature in Tibet malaria cannot spread locally, though the gametes can be found in the blood of the packmen, who usually contract the illness in India. The average maximum and minimum temperatures of the warmest months at Yatung were as follows: May, 62 and 41; June, 66 and 45; July, 68 and 48; August, 67 and 49. The temperature of the water in the sun topped the one of the air by some degrees in the day time and did not sink remarkably at night.

I found breeding nests of larvae of anopheles up to a height of nearly 10,000 ft., on the Lingmatang tableland, along on the road leading to Gautsa and Phari. Ponds and brooks are frequent there, the yaks graze in the meadows and the monks of the neighbouring Trummo Gompa camp there in the summer. However, the area where I carried out my researches, though ethnically and politically belonging to Tibet, is not really part of Tibet from a geographical point of view and could be well defined "Himalayan Tibet". In every other area of Tibet I visited I never succeeded in detecting more specimens of the anopheles genus, neither as full-fledged insect nor as larvae, though I still engaged in persistent and accurate researches. We stayed constantly above the 10,000 ft. level. As far as I could gather, anophelism, as well as malaria, is widespread in only one region of Tibet, viz. in the south-eastern provinces bordering on Chinese Yunnan, a low-lying, rice growing country.

Culex — During the same period I noticed several winged insects of the culex species flying into the houses. Their breeding grounds were everywhere, as for instance in the puddles immediately surrounding the houses and in the backwaters along the streams. That water was often dirty and contained rotting substances. I captured specimens of the culex, aedes and mansonia genus but could not yet classify them.

I often captured phlebotomes and simulides indoors, viz., among the brachiceres, some species of tabanides; among the cyclorrhaphes, the genera musca, stomoxys, lucilia, sarcophaga etc.; among the reduvides, a triatoma entering the houses, which I have not classified yet (probably Triatoma rubrofasciata). Among the thrombididae, I detected an itch-mite of the genus thrombicula, red, small and velvety, perhaps a thrombicula deliensis. Of the Syphonacterides the genus pulex was detected as well.

In the rest of Tibet I never came across any mosquito-like

insects at Phari and Dochen in spite of the lake, nor in the watery Gyantse valley. The researches I carried out along the banks of the Yamdrok-Tso, at Chushul on the Kyi-Chu and elsewhere, never achieved any result. In the area along the Tsang po and the Oka district I found very few. At the same time I was told that such insects were to be seen in Lhasa in the summer, but never any anopheles or phleboto-mae. No mosquitoes had ever been seen around Gyantse, I was told. Swarms of flies, on the contrary, fell upon the Tsang po valley fields, and clouds of non-bloodsucking diptera (cheironomidae, tipulidae, corethrinae etc.) ho-vered over the caravan and frightened the horse sometimes.

I never noticed either snakes or poisonous arthropodae. It goes without saying that lice (capitis et vestimenti) as well as bugs are widespread everywhere in Tibet.

As the last item I may mention a fact which may be of some interest. On the Karo-La pass between Gyantse and Lhasa, at a height of some 16,000 ft. I found, in the puddles at the edge of the glacier, some breeding grounds of aedes, larvae and pupae (2nd Aug., 1948).

The Sanitary Conditions of the Members of the Expedition

In such a far flung expedition across territories where there was absolutely no relying on local resources, the physical efficiency of the members was a matter largely dependent on an accurate and sufficient equipment of foodstuffs, clothing and medicines. This last point concerned especially the surgeon in charge who therefore, beyond supplying himself in advance with everything the local population might need, had also to foresee all needs arising from a possible emergency among the members of the expedition itself. Surgical first-aid instruments, apparatuses and equipment, the symptomatic and specific drugs needed in each case had therefore to be taken along as well. The whole material placed at our disposal by the Italian Navy Medical Corps had to be carefully selected and packed in such a way as to take up the least possible room and to stand the wear and tear of the journey. Liquid drugs had therefore to be avoided or to be canned and, when possible, replaced by vials and tablets. Ointments had to be preserved in tubes or aluminium cans. Bandages and gauze were packed in waterproof rolls. The food was chosen with a view to securing

230

adequate and balanced daily rations sufficient for four. Special stress was laid on the energy-producing quality, having regard to Tibet's climate and to the strains we were looking forward to. The difficulties arising from the lower boiling point (between 175 and 195 F) at great altitudes had to be considered as well.

Keeping all this in mind, the problem of food was successfully solved in Italy. Whenever possible, local purchases of poultry eggs, vegetables, potatoes and, less often, fruit, like small apples and apricots, supplemented our diet. In order to prevent lack of vitamines from the excessive intake of canned food, multivitaminic drugs were dispensed to the members daily for many weeks on end. As to the clothing, it had to cover all kinds of weather, but also to be especially designed to protect from cold and water. Woollens, furs and water-proof wind jackets were chosen. The tents and their special features have been described by Prof. Tucci.

The expedition spent in Tibet the six months from April 21 to October 19, the most favourable part of the year as far as the temperature is concerned, as the extremes of cold were avoided, whereas the monsoon rains fell in plenty, and the sky was often overcast and the air damp. The daily temperature jumps were sometimes considerable. At the beginning and at the end of the journey, in the neighbourhood of Shigatse, the caravan met constantly snow and frost, as greater heights had to be climbed before and after the summer proper. All six months were spent above 9000 ft. and a couple of months above 12,000 ft. at a pressure of 453 mm. Passes above 15,000 ft., at a pressure of 395 mm., were crossed. Some 1200 miles were covered either on foot or on horseback. The daily stages amounted to between 20 and 25 miles, but reached sometimes even 31, and took from 6 to 10 hrs to cover, according to the nature of the ground and the roughness of the going. Apart from the long stops at Yatung and, obviously, at the other large centres, the marches were continuous.

The state of health of the members of the expedition was

232 To Lhasa and Beyond

throughout good from every point of view. No serious incident or trouble ever struck any of us and the small occasional indispositions were soon overcome. Exceptional performances exacting a particular sturdiness or a special preparation were never required. A normal balance of strain and rest, a good constitution and an average physical and nervous resistance were enough to stand the hardships and the unavoidable restrictions of caravan life and to reach the ultimate goal.

Regolo Moise
Lt.-Col. of the Italian Navy Med. Corps.

Notes

1. *La* means "mountain pass" in Tibetan. The writing of geographical names is taken from the Survey. The others are transcribed according to the rule "consonants as in English, vowels as in Italian".

2. Or *Šar šiṅ*. See Tucci, *Tibetan Folksongs*, p. 62. A local tradition traces the word back to *ša ba* = stag.

3. *Bar c'ad bsèl ba*. The ceremony performed by the Yatung lama was founded on the ritual expounded in the *Kloṅ c'en sñin t'ig*, one of the rÑiṅ ma pa's fundamental works, about which see G. Tucci, *Tibetan Painted Scrolls* (from now on abbreviated *TPS*), p. 109.

4. *Studi di Metapsichica*, I, 1946, p. 7: A. Tanagras, *La teoria della psicobolia* (= The Theory of Psychoboly).

5. About this see *TPS*, p. 177.

6. The origins and the meaning of this drum, which is common to many Asiatic peoples, have been illustrated by Przyluski, *Les Unipèdes*, in *Mélanges chinois et Bouddhiques*, II, pp. 307-332.

7. *Cronaca della Missione scientifica Tucci nel Tibet occidentale*, Roma, 1934, p. 105.

8. G. Tucci, *Indo-Tibetica*, vol. IV, parts 1-3: The Gyantse Temples.

9. *rim* = degree; *bži* = four.

10. The title of this drama is: *Draṅ sroṅ gi bu mo bram ze gzugs gyi ñi mai rnam t'ar.*

11. His biography can be read in *Indo-Tibetica*, vol. 4, part I, p. 79 and foll., or in *TPS, p. 665.*

12. *gži* = soil; *bdag* = lord.

13. This book has been translated by Evans Wentz, *The Tibetan Book of the Dead*, Oxford, 1927, and by G. Tucci, *Il libro tibetano dei morti*, Milano, 1949.

14. For example in one of the chapters of Naropa's "Six Laws", a practical handbook of *haṭhayoga* meditation popular with the Kagyupa sect.

15. See *La vie de Marpa*, translated by J. Bacot, Paris, 1937, p. 50 and foll.

16. Though it could be simply a place name, cfr. rGya ras pa = "the ascetic of rGya", one of the greatest ascetics of gTsaṅ belonging to the bKa' rgyud pa sect.

17. Gu ru c'os dbaṅ was born in 1222; see *TPS*, p. 259.

18. According to tradition, *Ra lung* is said to have been so called because a wonder-working goat (*ra ma*), which had gone astray, was found again there by the shepherd while she was spurting milk on a stone. When the heat dried the milk, the three syllables *Om ā hūm* were found impressed on the stone, viz. the syllables symbolizing the three planes, the physical, verbal and spiritual one. When Gliṅ ras pa heard of it, he took it to be an omen (*luṅ bstan*), named the place Raluṅ (the goat's omen) and withdrew into a cave to meditate. See also Padma dkar po's *gNas c'en po ra luṅ gi k'yad àpags pa cuṅ zad brjod pa ṅo mts'ar gyi gter*. The same story is told in the *Myaṅ c'uṅ*, the guidebook of gTsaṅ.

19. *gser skyems;* it is *chang* mixed with wheat.

20. See *TPS*, p. 80. His biography is found in a book by Prof. L. Petech, to be published soon.

21. On the Survey map marked as Samden.

22. About this lama see *TPS*, p. 704, n. 848.

23. *lcags* = iron and *zam* or *zam pa* = bridge.

24. See *TPS*, p. 163, 550.
25. On Atīśa see S. Ch. Das, *Indian Pandits in the Land of Snow*, Calcutta 1893, and *TPS*, p. 390.
26. See *TPS*, p. 660.
27. On the *Ts'a ts'a* see *Indo-Tibetica*, vol. I.
28. About the cycle of the 16 Arhats and Dharmatala see *TPS*, p. 555.
29. On the Na rag see *Indo-Tibetica*, vol. III, part I, p. 123 and foll.
30. The sanskrit original of *Yan lang brgyad* is Vāg-bhaṭa's *Aṣṭāṅgahṛdaya*. The original of *brGyud bži* is the *Amṛtahṛdayāṣṭāṅgaguhyopadeśatantra*, which was lost in the 8th century.
31. Pictures of *mdo* are to be found in A. H. Francke's *Tibetische Hochzeitslieder*, Hagen i. W., 1923, fig. 14; and in S. H. Ribbach's, *Drog pa Namgyal*, München, 1940, fig. against p. 161. On *mdo* see also *TPS*, p. 725.
32. On the four great monasteries of the Yellow sect: Ganden, Depung, Sera and Tashilhumpo, see *Grva c'en po bži daṅ rgyud bstod smad c'ags ts'ul pad dkar ạp'ren ba*, a treatise written by Nag dbaṅbyams pa at P'ur by lcog in the year Wood-Mouse 1744 by order of P'o lha nas bSod nams stobs rgyas. Reference could be made also to the *Vai dū rya ser po*. On the Survey map the name is wrong.
33. On the *Kālacakra, Guhyasamāja, Śaṃvara* and *rDo rje ạj'igs byed* see Grünwedel, *Mythologie des Buddhismus in Tibet und Mongolei;* see. *Indo-Tibetica* passim, and *TPS*, p. 209 and foll. While the four great monasteries had been built to lead the monks on the way of Gnosis by teaching them the Prajñāpāramitā as it was handed down by the Indian masters from Maitreya, Asaṅga and Haribhadra, the two main groups of Tantras, the "father Tantras" (*Guhyasamāja*) and the "mother Tantras" (*Cakrasaṃvara, Śaṃvara* etc.), were taught in two special groups of seminaries: Upper Tantras (*rgyud stod*) and Lower Tantras (*rgyud smad*). They were founded by Sherab senge (Šes rab seṅ ge).

34. Mar ston is perhaps the same as Mar pa.

35. This is how the Tibetan paintings usually hung on the walls and the columns of temples are named.

36. The road skirts a crag on which are the ruins of the Nen rdsoṅ, a feudal holding of the Tsetang princes.

37. Zur mk'ar; the five chortens are known as the "five families".

38. *Indo-Tibetica* vol. 3, part. I, p. 35 and foll.

39. On the *rigs lṅa* see again *Indo-Tibetica* and *TPS*, p. 233.

40. This represents Padmapāṇi and is said to have belonged to Padmavajra, who hid it till it was discovered again by Ñaṅ rin po c'e.

41. The map is very inaccurate here and there: the area between Samye and the Tsang po is not wooded, but a barren row of dunes. The Gerba Ferry Camp is on the right, not on the left.

42. On the map Tashedotokh, bKra šis rdo ka.

43. gDan sa t'il originally depended on ạBri guṅ.

44. ạBri guṅ was very important in the 13th and 14th centuries.

45. This inscription will soon be published.

46. Zaṅs ri mk'ar dmar. On Ma gcig lab sgron ma: see *TPS*, p. 92.

47. The spelling wavers between 'Ol k'a and 'Od k'a. The name of the castle is 'Ol k'a stag rtse.

48. rDsiṅ p'yi was founded by Gar mi ston yon tan gyu ruṅ, a pupil of dGoṅs pa rab gsal, the same as founded the Bya sa convent. The title of the ạDsiṅ p'yi guidebook is *'Od dga' rdsiṅ p'yi dga' ldan gliṅ yi gnas yig dpag bsam sñe ma.*

49. The mountain is named Zo daṅ gaṅs po ri.

50. *K'ra ạbrug* and the probable date of its foundation are discussed in *Tombs of the Tibetan Kings* published in the "Serie Orientale Roma" of the Italian Institute for the Middle and Far East.

51. Near *Lha ru sman rgyad* there is a great chorten called *rTa spyan bum pa* where the eye of the Prajñāpāramitā's *rTag tu ṅu ba* Bodhisattva is said to be preserved.

52. See *Artibus Asiae*, vol. V, 1935, p. 105.

53. About this guidebook see *Indo-Tibetica*, vol. IV, part. I, p. 45.

54. His biography, written by Byań c'ub dbań rgyal and printed at rDo rje gdan mi ạgyno bde ba c'en po, is extant and bears the following title: *C'os rje t'ams cad mk'ye rdo rje ạc'ań po kun dga' rnam rgyal dpal bzań po rnam par t'ar ńo mts'ar rin po c'ei gter mdsod.*

55. *Abhidharmasamuccayakārikā* by Sańghatrāta and *Mańicūḍajātaka* by Sarvarakṣita.

56. See *TPS*, p. 205.